ABOUT THIS PUBLICATION

FOR SERVICE ASSISTANCE

Customer Service
1.704.898.0770

North Carolina General Statues is published by The Muliti-Media Group of Greater Charlotte in Charlotte, North Carolina. Copyright 2015 by the Multi-Media Group of Greater Charlotte. This book or parts thereof may not be reproduced in any form, stored in a retrieval system, or transmitted in any form by any means—electronic, mechanical, photocopy, recording or otherwise—without prior written permission of the publisher, except as provided by United States of America copyright law.

The records required by U.S. Code 2257(a) through (c) and the pertinent regulations 28 C.F.R. Cli. 1, Part 75 with respect to this publication and all materials associated with such records are maintained by The Multi-Media Group of Greater Charlotte, Publisher and available for review by Attorney General.

www.visionbooks.org

Copyright © 2015 by MMGGC
All rights reserved!

TID: 5064434
ISBN (10) digit: 150293437X
ISBN (13) digit: 978-1502934376

123-4-56789-01239-Paperback
123-4-56789-01239-Hardback

First Edition

090520140547

Printed in the United States of America

2015 EDITION

# North Carolina Criminal Law And Procedure-Pamphlet # 59

# Printed In conjunction with the Administration of the Courts

North Carolina Criminal Law and Procedure
Pamphlet Reference Guide

| Chapters | Pamphlet |
|---|---|
| Chapter 1 Civil Procedure | 1 |
| Chapter 1 Civil Procedure (Continue) | 2 |
| Chapter 1A Rules of Civil Procedure | 2 |
| Chapter 1B Contribution. | 2 |
| Chapter 1C Enforcement of Judgments. | 2 |
| Chapter 1D Punitive Damages. | 2 |
| Chapter 1E Eastern Band of Cherokee Indians. | 2 |
| Chapter 1F North Carolina Uniform Interstate Depositions and Discovery Act. | 2 |
| Chapter 2 - Clerk of Superior Court [Repealed and Transferred.] | 3 |
| Chapter 3 - Commissioners of Affidavits and Deeds [Repealed.] | 3 |
| Chapter 4 - Common Law | 3 |
| Chapter 5 - Contempt [Repealed.] | 3 |
| Chapter 5A - Contempt | 3 |
| Chapter 6 - Liability for Court Costs | 3 |
| Chapter 7 - Courts [Repealed and Transferred.] | 3 |
| Chapter 7A – Judicial Department | 3 |
| Chapter 7A – Continuation (Judicial Department) | 4 |
| Chapter 7A – Continuation (Judicial Department) | 5 |
| Chapter 7B - Juvenile Code | 5 |
| Chapter 8 - Evidence | 6 |
| Chapter 8A - Interpreters for Deaf Persons [Recodified.] | 6 |
| Chapter 8B - Interpreters for Deaf Persons | 6 |
| Chapter 8C - Evidence Code | 6 |
| Chapter 9 - Jurors | 6 |
| Chapter 10 - Notaries [Repealed.] | 6 |
| Chapter 10A - Notaries [Recodified.] | 6 |
| Chapter 10B - Notaries | 6 |
| Chapter 11 - Oaths | 6 |
| Chapter 12 - Statutory Construction | 6 |
| Chapter 13 - Citizenship Restored | 6 |
| Chapter 14 - Criminal Law | 7 |
| Chapter 14 –Criminal Law (Continuation) | 8 |
| Chapter 15 - Criminal Procedure | 9 |
| Chapter 15A - Criminal Procedure Act (Continuation) | 10 |
| Chapter 15A - Criminal Procedure Act (Continuation) | 11 |
| Chapter 15B - Victims Compensation | 11 |
| Chapter 15C - Address Confidentiality Program | 11 |
| Chapter 16 - Gaming Contracts and Futures | 11 |
| Chapter 17 - Habeas Corpus | 11 |

| | |
|---|---|
| Chapter 17A - Law-Enforcement Officers [Recodified.] | 11 |
| Chapter 17B - North Carolina Criminal Justice Education and Training System [Recodified.]  Chapter 17C - North Carolina Criminal Justice Education and Training Standards Commission | 11 |
| Chapter 17D - North Carolina Justice Academy | 11 |
| Chapter 17E - North Carolina Sheriffs' Education and Training Standards Commission | 11 |
| Chapter 18 - Regulation of Intoxicating Liquors [Repealed.] | 12 |
| Chapter 18A - Regulation of Intoxicating Liquors [Repealed.] | 12 |
| Chapter 18B - Regulation of Alcoholic Beverages | 12 |
| Chapter 18C - North Carolina State Lottery | 12 |
| Chapter 19 - Offenses against Public Morals | 12 |
| Chapter 19A - Protection of Animals | 12 |
| Chapter 20 - Motor Vehicles | 13 |
| Chapter 20 - Motor Vehicles (Continuation) | 14 |
| Chapter 20 - Motor Vehicles (Continuation) | 15 |
| Chapter 20 - Motor Vehicles (Continuation) | 16 |
| Chapter 21 - Bills of Lading | 17 |
| Chapter 22 - Contracts Requiring Writing | 17 |
| Chapter 22A - Signatures | 17 |
| Chapter 22B - Contracts Against Public Policy | 17 |
| Chapter 22C - Payments to Subcontractors | 17 |
| Chapter 23 - Debtor and Creditor | 17 |
| Chapter 24 – Interest | 17 |
| Chapter 25 – Uniform Commercial Code | 18 |
| Chapter 25 – Uniform Commercial Code (Continuation) | 19 |
| Chapter 25A – Retail Installment Sales Act | 20 |
| Chapter 25B - Credit | 20 |
| Chapter 25C - Sales of Artwork | 20 |
| Chapter 26 - Suretyship | 20 |
| Chapter 27 - Warehouse Receipts [Repealed.] | 20 |
| Chapter 28 - Administration [Repealed.] | 20 |
| Chapter 28A - Administration of Decedents' Estates | 20 |
| Chapter 28B - Estates of Absentees in Military Service | 20 |
| Chapter 28C - Estates of Missing Persons | 20 |
| Chapter 29 - Intestate Succession | 21 |
| Chapter 30 - Surviving Spouses | 21 |
| Chapter 31 - Wills | 21 |
| Chapter 31A - Acts Barring Property Rights | 21 |
| Chapter 31B - Renunciation of Property and Renunciation of Fiduciary Powers Act | 21 |
| Chapter 31C - Uniform Disposition of Community Property Rights at Death Act | 21 |
| Chapter 32 - Fiduciaries | 21 |
| Chapter 32A - Powers of Attorney | 21 |
| Chapter 33 - Guardian and Ward [Repealed and Recodified.] | 21 |

| | |
|---|---|
| Chapter 33A - North Carolina Uniform Transfers to Minors Act | 21 |
| Chapter 33B - North Carolina Uniform Custodial Trust Act | 21 |
| Chapter 34 - Veterans' Guardianship Act | 22 |
| Chapter 35 - Sterilization Procedures | 22 |
| Chapter 35A - Incompetency and Guardianship | 22 |
| Chapter 36 - Trusts and Trustees [Repealed.] | 22 |
| Chapter 36A - Trusts and Trustees | 22 |
| Chapter 36B - Uniform Management of Institutional Funds Act [Repealed.] | 22 |
| Chapter 36C - North Carolina Uniform Trust Code | 22 |
| Chapter 36D - North Carolina Community Third Party Trusts, Pooled Trusts | 23 |
| Chapter 36E - Uniform Prudent Management of Institutional Funds Act | 23 |
| Chapter 37 - Allocation of Principal and Income [Repealed.] | 23 |
| Chapter 37A - Uniform Principal and Income Act | 23 |
| Chapter 38 - Boundaries | 23 |
| Chapter 38A - Landowner Liability | 23 |
| Chapter 39 - Conveyances | 23 |
| Chapter 39A - Transfer Fee Covenants Prohibited | 23 |
| Chapter 40 - Eminent Domain [Repealed.] | 23 |
| Chapter 40A - Eminent Domain | 23 |
| Chapter 41 - Estates | 23 |
| Chapter 41A - State Fair Housing Act | 23 |
| Chapter 42 - Landlord and Tenant | 23 |
| Chapter 42A - Vacation Rental Act | 23 |
| Chapter 43 - Land Registration | 23 |
| Chapter 44 - Liens | 24 |
| Chapter 44A - Statutory Liens and Charges | 24 |
| Chapter 45 - Mortgages and Deeds of Trust | 24 |
| Chapter 45A - Good Funds Settlement Act | 24 |
| Chapter 46 - Partition | 24 |
| Chapter 47 - Probate and Registration | 25 |
| Chapter 47A - Unit Ownership | 25 |
| Chapter 47B - Real Property Marketable Title Act | 25 |
| Chapter 47C - North Carolina Condominium Act | 25 |
| Chapter 47D - Notice of Settlement Act [Expired.] | 25 |
| Chapter 47E - Residential Property Disclosure Act | 25 |
| Chapter 47F - North Carolina Planned Community Act | 25 |
| Chapter 47G - Option to Purchase Contracts | 25 |
| Chapter 47H - Contracts for Deed | 25 |
| Chapter 48 - Adoptions + | 26 |
| Chapter 48A - Minors | 26 |
| Chapter 49 - Bastardy | 26 |
| Chapter 49A - Rights of Children | 26 |
| Chapter 50 - Divorce and Alimony | 26 |
| Chapter 50A - Uniform Child-Custody Jurisdiction and | |

| | |
|---|---|
| Enforcement Act | 26 |
| Chapter 50B - Domestic Violence | 26 |
| Chapter 50C - Civil No-Contact Orders | 26 |
| Chapter 51 - Marriage | 26 |
| Chapter 52 - Powers and Liabilities of Married Persons | 27 |
| Chapter 52A - Uniform Reciprocal Enforcement of Support Act [Repealed.] | 27 |
| Chapter 52B - Uniform Premarital Agreement Act | 27 |
| Chapter 52C - Uniform Interstate Family Support Act | 27 |
| Chapter 53 - Banks | 27 |
| Chapter 53A - Business Development Corporations and North Carolina Capital Resource Corporations | 28 |
| Chapter 53B - Financial Privacy Act | 28 |
| Chapter 54 - Cooperative Organizations | 28 |
| Chapter 54A - Capital Stock Savings and Loan Associations [Repealed.] | 28 |
| Chapter 54B - Savings and Loan Associations | 29 |
| Chapter 54C - Savings Banks | 29 |
| Chapter 55 - North Carolina Business Corporation Act | 30 |
| Chapter 55A - North Carolina Nonprofit Corporation Act | 31 |
| Chapter 55B - Professional Corporation Act | 31 |
| Chapter 55C - Foreign Trade Zones | 31 |
| Chapter 55D - Filings, Names, and Registered Agents for Corporations, Nonprofit Corporations, and Partnerships | 31 |
| Chapter 56 - Electric, Telegraph and Power Companies [Repealed.] | 31 |
| Chapter 57 - Hospital, Medical and Dental Service Corporations [Recodified.] | 31 |
| Chapter 57A - Health Maintenance Organization Act [Recodified.] | 31 |
| Chapter 57B - Health Maintenance Organization Act [Recodified.] | 31 |
| Chapter 57C - North Carolina Limited Liability Company Act. | 31 |
| Chapter 58 - Insurance. | 32 |
| Chapter 58 - Insurance (Continuation) | 33 |
| Chapter 58 - Insurance (Continuation) | 34 |
| Chapter 58 - Insurance (Continuation) | 35 |
| Chapter 58 - Insurance (Continuation) | 36 |
| Chapter 58 - Insurance (Continuation) | 37 |
| Chapter 58 - Insurance (Continuation) | 38 |
| Chapter 58A - North Carolina Health Insurance Trust Commission [Recodified.] | 38 |
| Chapter 59 - Partnership. | 39 |
| Chapter 59B - Uniform Unincorporated Nonprofit Association Act. | 39 |
| Chapter 60 - Railroads and Other Carriers [Repealed and Transferred.] | 39 |
| Chapter 61 - Religious Societies | 39 |
| Chapter 62 - Public Utilities | 39 |

| | |
|---|---|
| Chapter 62 - Public Utilities (Continuation) | 40 |
| Chapter 62A - Public Safety Telephone Service And Wireless Telephone Service | 40 |
| Chapter 63 - Aeronautics | 40 |
| Chapter 63A - North Carolina Global TransPark Authority | 40 |
| Chapter 64 - Aliens | 40 |
| Chapter 65 – Cemeteries | 40 |
| Chapter 66 - Commerce and Business | 41 |
| Chapter 67 - Dogs | 41 |
| Chapter 68 - Fences and Stock Law | 41 |
| Chapter 69 - Fire Protection | 41 |
| Chapter 70 - Indian Antiquities, Archaeological Resources and Unmarked Human Skeletal Remains Protection | 42 |
| Chapter 71 - Indians [Repealed.] | 42 |
| Chapter 71A - Indians | 42 |
| Chapter 72 - Inns, Hotels and Restaurants | 42 |
| Chapter 73 - Mills | 42 |
| Chapter 74 - Mines and Quarries | 42 |
| Chapter 74A - Company Police [Repealed.] | 42 |
| Chapter 74B - Private Protective Services Act [Repealed.] | 42 |
| Chapter 74C - Private Protective Services | 42 |
| Chapter 74D - Alarm Systems | 42 |
| Chapter 74E - Company Police Act | 42 |
| Chapter 74F - Locksmith Licensing Act | 42 |
| Chapter 74G - Campus Police Act | 42 |
| Chapter 75 - Monopolies, Trusts and Consumer Protection | 42 |
| Chapter 75A - Boating and Water Safety | 43 |
| Chapter 75B - Discrimination in Business | 43 |
| Chapter 75C - Motion Picture Fair Competition Act | 43 |
| Chapter 75D - Racketeer Influenced and Corrupt Organizations | 43 |
| Chapter 75E - Unlawful Activities in Connection With Certain Corporate Transactions | 43 |
| Chapter 76 - Navigation | 43 |
| Chapter 76A - Navigation and Pilotage Commissions | 43 |
| Chapter 77 - Rivers, Creeks, and Coastal Waters | 43 |
| Chapter 78 - Securities Law [Repealed.] | 43 |
| Chapter 78A - North Carolina Securities Act | 43 |
| Chapter 78B - Tender Offer Disclosure Act [Repealed.] | 43 |
| Chapter 78C - Investment Advisers | 43 |
| Chapter 78D - Commodities Act | 43 |
| Chapter 79 - Strays [Repealed.] | 43 |
| Chapter 80 - Trademarks, Brands, etc. | 44 |
| Chapter 81 - Weights and Measures [Recodified.] | 44 |
| Chapter 81A - Weights and Measures Act of 1975. | 44 |
| Chapter 82 - Wrecks [Repealed.] | 44 |
| Chapter 83 - Architects [Recodified.] | 44 |

| | |
|---|---|
| Chapter 83A - Architects | 44 |
| Chapter 84 - Attorneys-at-Law | 44 |
| Chapter 84A - Foreign Legal Consultants | 44 |
| Chapter 85 - Auctions and Auctioneers [Repealed.] | 44 |
| Chapter 85A - Bail Bondsmen and Runners [Recodified.] | 44 |
| Chapter 85B - Auctions and Auctioneers | 44 |
| Chapter 85C - Bail Bondsmen and Runners [Recodified.] | 44 |
| Chapter 86 - Barbers [Recodified.] | 44 |
| Chapter 86A - Barbers | 44 |
| Chapter 87 - Contractors | 44 |
| Chapter 88 - Cosmetic Art [Repealed.] | 44 |
| Chapter 88A - Electrolysis Practice Act | 44 |
| Chapter 88B - Cosmetic Art | 45 |
| Chapter 89 - Engineering and Land Surveying [Recodified.] | 45 |
| Chapter 89A - Landscape Architects | 45 |
| Chapter 89B - Foresters | 45 |
| Chapter 89C - Engineering and Land Surveying | 45 |
| Chapter 89D - Landscape Contractors | 45 |
| Chapter 89E - Geologists Licensing Act | 45 |
| Chapter 89F - North Carolina Soil Scientist Licensing Act | 45 |
| Chapter 89G - Irrigation Contractors | 45 |
| Chapter 90 - Medicine and Allied Occupations | 45 |
| Chapter 90 - Medicine and Allied Occupations (Continuation) | 46 |
| Chapter 90 - Medicine and Allied Occupations (Continuation) | 47 |
| Chapter 90 - Medicine and Allied Occupations (Continuation) | 48 |
| Chapter 90A - Sanitarians and Water and Wastewater Treatment Facility Operators | 48 |
| Chapter 90B - Social Worker Certification and Licensure Act | 48 |
| Chapter 90C - North Carolina Recreational Therapy Licensure Act | 48 |
| Chapter 90D - Interpreters and Transliterators | 48 |
| Chapter 91 - Pawnbrokers [Repealed.] | 48 |
| Chapter 91A - Pawnbrokers Modernization Act of 1989 | 48 |
| Chapter 92 - Photographers [Deleted.] | 48 |
| Chapter 93 - Certified Public Accountants | 48 |
| Chapter 93A - Real Estate License Law | 49 |
| Chapter 93B - Occupational Licensing Boards | 49 |
| Chapter 93C - Watchmakers [Repealed.] | 49 |
| Chapter 93D - North Carolina State Hearing Aid Dealers and Fitters Board. | 49 |
| Chapter 93E - North Carolina Appraisers Act | 49 |
| Chapter 94 - Apprenticeship | 49 |
| Chapter 95 - Department of Labor and Labor Regulations | 49 |
| Chapter 95 - Department of Labor and Labor Regulations (Continuation) | 50 |
| Chapter 96 - Employment Security | 50 |
| Chapter 97 - Workers' Compensation Act | 50 |
| Chapter 97 - Workers' Compensation Act (Continuation) | 51 |

| | |
|---|---|
| Chapter 98 - Burnt and Lost Records | 51 |
| Chapter 99 - Libel and Slander | 51 |
| Chapter 99A - Civil Remedies for Criminal Actions | 51 |
| Chapter 99B - Products Liability | 51 |
| Chapter 99C - Actions Relating to Winter Sports Safety and Accidents | 51 |
| Chapter 99D - Civil Rights | 51 |
| Chapter 99E - Special Liability Provisions | 51 |
| Chapter 100 - Monuments, Memorials and Parks | 51 |
| Chapter 101 - Names of Persons | 51 |
| Chapter 102 - Official Survey Base | 51 |
| Chapter 103 - Sundays, Holidays and Special Days | 51 |
| Chapter 104 - United States Lands | 51 |
| Chapter 104A - Degrees of Kinship | 51 |
| Chapter 104B - Hurricanes or Other Acts of Nature | 51 |
| Chapter 104C - Atomic Energy, Radioactivity and Ionizing Radiation [Repealed and Recodified.] | 51 |
| Chapter 104D - Southern States Energy Compact | 51 |
| Chapter 104E - North Carolina Radiation Protection Act | 51 |
| Chapter 104F - Southeast Interstate Low-Level Radioactive Waste Management Compact [Repealed] | 51 |
| Chapter 104G - North Carolina Low-Level Radioactive Waste Management Authority Act of 1987 [Repealed] | 51 |
| Chapter 105 - Taxation | 51 |
| Chapter 105 - Taxation (Continuation) | 52 |
| Chapter 105 - Taxation (Continuation) | 53 |
| Chapter 105 - Taxation (Continuation) | 54 |
| Chapter 105A - Setoff Debt Collection Act | 55 |
| Chapter 105B - Defaulted Student Loan Recovery Act | 55 |
| Chapter 106 - Agriculture | 55 |
| Chapter 106 - Agriculture (Continue) | 56 |
| Chapter 106 - Agriculture (Continue) | 57 |
| Chapter 107 - Agricultural Development Districts [Repealed.] | 57 |
| Chapter 108 - Social Services [Repealed and Recodified.] | 57 |
| Chapter 108A - Social Services | 57 |
| Chapter 108B - Community Action Programs | 58 |
| Chapter 108C Medicaid and Health Choice Provider Requirements. | 58 |
| Chapter 108D Medicaid Managed Care for Behavioral Health Services. | 58 |
| Chapter 109 - Bonds [Recodified.] | 58 |
| Chapter 110 - Child Welfare | 58 |
| Chapter 111 - Aid to the Blind | 58 |
| Chapter 112 - Confederate Homes and Pensions [Repealed.] | 58 |
| Chapter 113 - Conservation and Development | 58 |
| Chapter 113 - Conservation and Development (Continuation) | 59 |

| | |
|---|---|
| Chapter 113A - Pollution Control and Environment | 59 |
| Chapter 113A - Pollution Control and Environment (Continuation) | 60 |
| Chapter 113B - North Carolina Energy Policy Act of 1975 | 60 |
| Chapter 114 - Department of Justice | 60 |
| Chapter 115 - Elementary and Secondary Education [Repealed.] | 60 |
| Chapter 115A - Community Colleges, Technical Institutes, and Industrial Education Centers [Repealed.] | 60 |
| Chapter 115B - Tuition and Fee Waivers | 60 |
| Chapter 115C - Elementary and Secondary Education | 60 |
| Chapter 115C - Elementary and Secondary Education (Continuation) | 61 |
| Chapter 115C - Elementary and Secondary Education (Continuation) | 62 |
| Chapter 115C - Elementary and Secondary Education (Continuation) | 63 |
| Chapter 115D - Community Colleges | 63 |
| Chapter 115E - Private Educational Facilities Finance Act [Recodified] | 63 |
| Chapter 116 - Higher Education | 63 |
| Chapter 116 - Higher Education (Continuation) | 63 |
| Chapter 116A - Escheats and Abandoned Property [Repealed.] | 64 |
| Chapter 116B - Escheats and Abandoned Property | 64 |
| Chapter 116C - Continuum of Education Programs | 64 |
| Chapter 116D - Higher Education Bonds | 64 |
| Chapter 117 - Electrification | 64 |
| Chapter 118 - Firemen's and Rescue Squad Workers' Relief and Pension Funds [Recodified.] | 64 |
| Chapter 118A - Firemen's Death Benefit Act [Repealed.] | 64 |
| Chapter 118B - Members of a Rescue Squad Death Benefit Act [Repealed.] | 64 |
| Chapter 119 - Gasoline and Oil Inspection and Regulation | 64 |
| Chapter 120 - General Assembly | 65 |
| Chapter 120 - General Assembly (Continuation) | 66 |
| Chapter 120 - General Assembly (Continuation) | 67 |
| Chapter 120C - Lobbying | 67 |
| Chapter 121 - Archives and History | 67 |
| Chapter 122 - Hospitals for the Mentally Disordered [Repealed.] | 67 |
| Chapter 122A - North Carolina Housing Finance Agency | 67 |
| Chapter 122B - North Carolina Agricultural Facilities Finance Act [Repealed.] | 67 |
| Chapter 122C - Mental Health, Developmental Disabilities, and Substance Abuse Act of 1985 | 67 |
| Chapter 122C - Mental Health, Developmental Disabilities, and Substance Abuse Act of 1985 (Continuation) | 68 |
| Chapter 122D - North Carolina Agricultural Finance Act | 68 |

| | |
|---|---|
| Chapter 122E - North Carolina Housing Trust and Oil Overcharge Act | 68 |
| Chapter 123 - Impeachment | 69 |
| Chapter 123A - Industrial Development [Repealed.] | 69 |
| Chapter 124 - Internal Improvements | 69 |
| Chapter 125 - Libraries | 69 |
| Chapter 126 - State Personnel System | 69 |
| Chapter 127 - Militia [Repealed.] | 69 |
| Chapter 127A - Militia | 69 |
| Chapter 127B - Military Affairs | 69 |
| Chapter 127C - Advisory Commission on Military Affairs | 69 |
| Chapter 128 - Offices and Public Officers | 69 |
| Chapter 128 - Offices and Public Officers (Continuation) | 70 |
| Chapter 129 - Public Buildings and Grounds | 70 |
| Chapter 130 - Public Health [Repealed.] | 70 |
| Chapter 130A - Public Health | 70 |
| Chapter 130A - Public Health (Continuation) | 71 |
| Chapter 130A - Public Health (Continuation) | 72 |
| Chapter 130B - Hazardous Waste Management Commission [Repealed.] | 72 |
| Chapter 131 - Public Hospitals [Repealed.] | 72 |
| Chapter 131A - Health Care Facilities Finance Act | 72 |
| Chapter 131B - Licensing of Ambulatory Surgical Facilities [Repealed.] | 72 |
| Chapter 131C - Charitable Solicitation Licensure Act [Repealed.] | 72 |
| Chapter 131D - Inspection and Licensing of Facilities | 72 |
| Chapter 131E - Health Care Facilities and Services | 72 |
| Chapter 131E - Health Care Facilities and Services (Continuation) | 73 |
| Chapter 131F - Solicitation of Contributions | 73 |
| Chapter 132 - Public Records | 73 |
| Chapter 133 - Public Works | 74 |
| Chapter 134 - Youth Development [Recodified.] | 74 |
| Chapter 134A - Youth Services [Repealed.] | 74 |
| Chapter 135 - Retirement System for Teachers and State Employees; Social Security; Health Insurance Program for Children | 74 |
| Chapter 135 - Retirement System for Teachers and State Employees; Social Security; Health Insurance Program for Children | 75 |
| Chapter 136 - Transportation | 75 |
| Chapter 136 - Transportation (Continuation) | 76 |
| Chapter 137 - Rural Rehabilitation [Repealed.] | 76 |
| Chapter 138 - Salaries, Fees and Allowances | 76 |
| Chapter 138A - State Government Ethics Act | 76 |
| Chapter 139 - Soil and Water Conservation Districts | 76 |

| | |
|---|---|
| Chapter 140 - State Art Museum; Symphony and Art Societies | 76 |
| Chapter 140A - State Awards System | 76 |
| Chapter 141 - State Boundaries | 76 |
| Chapter 142 - State Debt | 76 |
| Chapter 143 - State Departments, Institutions, and Commissions | 77 |
| Chapter 143 - State Departments, Institutions, and Commissions (Continuation) | 78 |
| Chapter 143 - State Departments, Institutions, and Commissions (Continuation) | 79 |
| Chapter 143 - State Departments, Institutions, and Commissions (Continuation) | 80 |
| Chapter 143A - State Government Reorganization | 80 |
| Chapter 143B - Executive Organization Act of 1973 | 80 |
| Chapter 143B - Executive Organization Act of 1973 (Continuation) | 81 |
| Chapter 143B - Executive Organization Act of 1973 (Continuation) | 82 |
| Chapter 143C - State Budget Act | 83 |
| Chapter 143D - The State Governmental Accountability and Internal Control Act | 83 |
| Chapter 144 - State Flag, Official Governmental Flags, Motto, and Colors | 83 |
| Chapter 145 - State Symbols and Other Official Adoptions. | 83 |
| Chapter 146 - State Lands | 83 |
| Chapter 147 - State Officers | 83 |
| Chapter 148 - State Prison System | 84 |
| Chapter 149 - State Song and Toast | 84 |
| Chapter 150 - Uniform Revocation of Licenses [Repealed.] | 84 |
| Chapter 150A - Administrative Procedure Act [Recodified.] | 84 |
| Chapter 150B - Administrative Procedure Act | 84 |
| Chapter 151 - Constables [Repealed.] | 84 |
| Chapter 152 - Coroners | 84 |
| Chapter 152A - County Medical Examiner [Repealed.] | 84 |
| Chapter 152A - County Medical Examiner [Repealed.] (Continuation) | 85 |
| Chapter 153 - Counties and County Commissioners [Repealed.] | 85 |
| Chapter 153A - Counties | 85 |
| Chapter 153B - Mountain Resources Planning Act | 85 |
| Chapter 153C - Uwharrie Regional Resources Act | 85 |
| Chapter 154 - County Surveyor [Repealed.] | 85 |
| Chapter 155 - County Treasurer [Repealed.] | 85 |
| Chapter 156 - Drainage | 85 |
| Chapter 156 – Drainage (Continuation) | 86 |

| | |
|---|---|
| Chapter 157 - Housing Authorities and Projects | 86 |
| Chapter 157A - Historic Properties Commissions [Transferred.] | 86 |
| Chapter 158 - Local Development | 86 |
| Chapter 159 - Local Government Finance | 86 |
| Chapter 159 - Local Government Finance (Continuation) | 87 |
| Chapter 159A - Pollution Abatement and Industrial Facilities Financing Act [Unconstitutional.] | 87 |
| Chapter 159B - Joint Municipal Electric Power and Energy Act | 87 |
| Chapter 159C - Industrial and Pollution Control Facilities Financing Act | 87 |
| Chapter 159D - The North Carolina Capital Facilities Financing Act | 87 |
| Chapter 159E - Registered Public Obligations Act | 87 |
| Chapter 159F - North Carolina Energy Development Authority [Repealed.] | 87 |
| Chapter 159G - Water Infrastructure | 87 |
| Chapter 159H - [Reserved.] | 87 |
| Chapter 159I - Solid Waste Management Loan Program and Local Government Special Obligation Bonds | 87 |
| Chapter 160 - Municipal Corporations [Repealed And Transferred.] | 87 |
| Chapter 160A - Cities and Towns | 88 |
| Chapter 160A - Cities and Towns (Continuation) | 89 |
| Chapter 160B - Consolidated City-County Act | 89 |
| Chapter 160C - Baseball Park Districts [Repealed.] | 90 |
| Chapter 161 - Register of Deeds | 90 |
| Chapter 162 - Sheriff | 90 |
| Chapter 162A - Water and Sewer Systems | 90 |
| Chapter 162B Continuity of Local Government in Emergency. | 90 |
| Chapter 163 Elections and Election Laws. | 90 |
| Chapter 163 Elections and Election Laws. (Continuation) | 91 |
| Chapter 164 Concerning the General Statutes of North Carolina. | 92 |
| Chapter 165 Veterans. | 92 |
| Chapter 166 Civil Preparedness Agencies [Repealed.] | 92 |
| Chapter 166A North Carolina Emergency Management Act. | 92 |
| Chapter 167 State Civil Air Patrol [Repealed.] | 92 |
| Chapter 168 Persons with Disabilities. | 92 |
| Chapter 168A Persons With Disabilities Protection Act. | 92 |

§ 113-208. Protection of private shellfish rights.

(a) It is unlawful for any person, other than the holder of private shellfish rights, to take or attempt to take shellfish from any privately leased, franchised, or deeded shellfish bottom area without written authorization of the holder and with actual knowledge it is a private shellfish bottom area. Actual knowledge will be presumed when the shellfish are taken or attempted to be taken:

(1) From within the confines of posted boundaries of the area as identified by signs, whether the whole or any part of the area is posted, or

(2) When the area has been regularly posted and identified and the person knew the area to be the subject of private shellfish rights.

A violation of this section shall constitute a Class A1 misdemeanor, which may include a fine of not more than five thousand dollars ($5,000). The written authorization shall include the lease number or deed reference, name and address of authorized person, date of issuance, and date of expiration, and it must be signed by the holder of the private shellfish right. Identification signs shall include the lease number or deed reference and the name of the holder.

(b) The prosecutor shall dismiss any case brought for a violation of this section if the defendant produces a notarized written authorization in conformance with subsection (a) which states that the defendant had permission to take oysters or clams from the leased area at the time of the alleged violation; except the prosecutor may refuse to dismiss the case if he has reason to believe that the written authorization is fraudulent. (1979, c. 537; 1987, c. 463; 1989, c. 281, s. 2; 1993, c. 539, s. 842; 1994, Ex. Sess., c. 24, s. 14(c); 1998-225, s. 3.7.)

§ 113-209. Taking polluted shellfish at night or with prior conviction forbidden; penalty.

(a) It is unlawful for any person between sunset and sunrise to willfully take or attempt to take shellfish from areas closed to harvest by statute, rule, or proclamation because of suspected pollution.

(b)     It is unlawful for any person to willfully possess, sell or offer for sale shellfish taken between sunset and sunrise from areas closed to harvest by statute, rule, or proclamation because of suspected pollution.

(c)     It is unlawful for any person who has been convicted of an offense under this Chapter within the preceding two years involving shellfish taken from areas closed because of suspected pollution to willfully take, attempt to take, possess, sell or offer for sale shellfish from areas closed to harvest by statute, rule, or proclamation because of suspected pollution.

(d)     Any person violating any provisions of this section shall be guilty of a Class I felony which may include a fine no less than two thousand five hundred dollars ($2,500). Upon conviction of any person for a violation of this section, the court shall order the confiscation of all weapons, equipment, vessels, vehicles, conveyances, fish, and other evidence, fruit, and instrumentalities of the offense. The confiscated property shall be disposed of in accordance with G.S. 113-137. (1989, c. 275, s. 1; 1993, c. 539, s. 1301; 1994, Ex. Sess., c. 24, s. 14(c).)


§ 113-210. Under Dock Oyster Culture.

(a)     Under Dock Oyster Culture Permit. - An Under Dock Oyster Culture Permit authorizes the holder of the permit to attach up to 90 square feet of oyster cultivation containers to a dock or pier owned by the permit holder.

(b)     Application. - The owner of a dock or pier who wishes to obtain an Under Dock Oyster Culture Permit shall apply to the Director of the Division of Marine Fisheries.

(c)     Issuance. - The Director of the Division of Marine Fisheries shall issue an Under Dock Oyster Culture Permit only if the Director determines all of the following:

(1)     That the dock or pier is not located in an area that the State Health Director has recommended be closed to shellfish harvest due to pollution or that has been closed to harvest by statute, rule, or proclamation due to suspected pollution.

(2) That the owner of the dock or pier has satisfied the training requirements established by the Marine Fisheries Commission pursuant to subsection (j) of this section.

(3) That the attachment of the oyster cultivation containers to the dock or pier will be compatible with all lawful uses by the public of other marine and estuarine resources. Other lawful public uses include, but are not limited to, navigation, fishing, and recreation.

(d) Duration. - An Under Dock Oyster Culture Permit is valid for a one-year period from the date of issuance.

(e) Renewal. - The Director of the Division of Marine Fisheries shall renew an Under Dock Oyster Culture Permit only if the Director determines the requirements of subsection (c) of this section continue to be satisfied and the holder of the permit is attempting to utilize the permit to cultivate oysters on a continuing basis.

(f) Reporting Requirements. - The holder of an Under Dock Oyster Culture Permit shall comply with the biological data sampling and survey programs of the Marine Fisheries Commission and the Division of Marine Fisheries.

(g) Posting of Signs. - The holder of an Under Dock Oyster Culture Permit shall post signs that indicate the presence of the oyster cultivation containers and that the oyster cultivation containers and their contents are private property.

(h) Sale of Oysters Prohibited. - It is unlawful for the holder of an Under Dock Oyster Culture Permit to sell oysters cultivated pursuant to the permit.

(i) Assignment and Transfer Prohibited. - An Under Dock Oyster Culture Permit is not assignable or transferable.

(j) Oyster Cultivation Training Requirements. - The Marine Fisheries Commission, in consultation with the Sea Grant College Program at The University of North Carolina, shall develop and adopt rules for the training of individuals who cultivate oysters pursuant to this section.

(k) Revocation of Permit. - If the Director of the Division of Marine Fisheries determines that the holder of an Under Dock Oyster Culture Permit has failed to comply with any provision of this section, the Director shall revoke the Permit.

The owner of the dock or pier shall remove the oyster cultivation containers that were authorized by the revoked permit within 15 days of revocation.

(l) Fees. - Under Dock Oyster Culture Permit shall be issued annually upon payment of a fee of one hundred dollars ($100.00).

(m) Advance Sale of Permits; Permit Revenue. - To ensure an orderly transition from one permit year to the next, the Division may issue a permit prior to July 1 of the permit year for which the permit is valid. Revenue that the Division receives for the issuance of a permit prior to the beginning of a permit year shall not revert at the end of the fiscal year in which the revenue is received and shall be credited and available to the Division for the permit year in which the permit is valid. (2004-124, s. 12.7B; 2013-360, s. 14.8(t).)

§§ 113-211 through 113-220: Reserved for future codification purposes.

Article 17.

Administrative Provisions; Regulatory Authority of Marine Fisheries Commission and Department.

§ 113-221. Rules.

(a) Chapter 150B of the General Statutes governs the adoption of rules under this Article.

(b) Upon purchasing a license, each licensee shall be given a copy of the rules concerning the activities authorized by the license.

(c) The Fisheries Director shall notify licensees of a new rule or change to a rule by sending each licensee either a newsletter containing the text of the rule or change or an updated codification of the rules of the Marine Fisheries Commission that contains the new rule or change.

(d) Unless there are overriding policy considerations involved, any rule of the Marine Fisheries Commission that will result in severe curtailment of the usefulness or value of equipment in which fishermen have any substantial investment shall be given a future effective date so as to minimize undue potential economic loss to fishermen. Whether or not any rule will result in severe curtailment of the usefulness or value of equipment in which fishermen have any substantial investment and whether or not a future effective date should be set is a matter within the sole discretion of the Marine Fisheries Commission. This subsection does not require the Marine Fisheries Commission to establish an effective date that is more than two years later than the date on which the rule is adopted.

(e) Repealed by Session Laws 2003-154, s. 1, effective July 1, 2003.

(e1) Repealed by Session Laws 2003-154, s. 1, effective July 1, 2003.

(f) All persons who may be affected by rules adopted by the Marine Fisheries Commission are under a duty to keep themselves informed of the current rules. It is no defense in any criminal prosecution for the defendant to show that the defendant in fact received no notice of a particular rule. In any prosecution for violation of a rule, or in which proof of matter contained in a rule is involved, the Department is deemed to have complied with publication procedures and the burden is on the defendant to show by the greater weight of the evidence substantial failure of compliance by the Department with the required publication procedures.

(g) Every court shall take judicial notice of any codification of rules issued by the Fisheries Director within two years preceding the date of the offense charged or transaction in issue. In the absence of any indication to the contrary, the codifications are to be deemed accurate and current statements of the text of the rules in question and it is incumbent upon any person asserting that a relevant portion of the codified text is inaccurate, or has been amended or deleted, to satisfy the court as to the text of the rules that is in fact properly applicable.

(h) Repealed by Session Laws 1983, c. 221, s. 1. (1915, c. 84, s. 21; 1917, c. 290, s. 7; C.S., s. 1878; 1925, c. 168, s. 2; 1935, c. 35; 1945, c. 776; 1953, cc. 774, 1134, 1251; 1963, c. 1097, s. 1; 1965, c. 957, s. 2; 1973, c. 1262, ss. 28, 86; c. 1331, s. 3; 1975, 2nd Sess., c. 983, s. 70; 1979, c. 388, s. 6; 1983, cc. 221, 619, 620; 1987, c. 641, ss. 7, 19; c. 827, s. 7; 1997-400, s. 4.3; 1998-225, s. 3.8; 2000-189, s. 9; 2003-154, s. 1.)

§ 113-221.1. Proclamations; emergency review.

(a) Chapter 150B of the General Statutes does not apply to proclamations issued under this Article.

(b) The Marine Fisheries Commission may delegate to the Fisheries Director the authority to issue proclamations suspending or implementing, in whole or in part, particular rules of the Commission that may be affected by variable conditions. These proclamations shall be issued by the Fisheries Director or by a person designated by the Fisheries Director. Except as provided in this subsection, all proclamations shall state the hour and date upon which they become effective and shall be issued at least 48 hours in advance of the effective date and time. A proclamation that prohibits the taking of certain fisheries resources for reasons of public health or that governs a quota-managed fishery may be made effective immediately upon issuance. A proclamation to reopen the taking of certain fisheries resources closed for reasons of public health shall be issued at least 12 hours in advance of the effective date and time of the reopening. A person who violates a proclamation that is made effective immediately upon issuance shall not be charged with a criminal offense for the violation if the violation occurred between the time of issuance and 48 hours after the issuance and the person did not have actual notice of the issuance of the proclamation. Fisheries resources taken or possessed by any person in violation of any proclamation may be seized regardless of whether the person had actual notice of the proclamation. A permanent file of the text of all proclamations shall be maintained in the office of the Fisheries Director. Certified copies of proclamations are entitled to judicial notice in any civil or criminal proceeding. The Fisheries Director shall make every reasonable effort to give actual notice of the terms of any proclamation to persons who may be affected by the proclamation. Reasonable effort includes a press release to communications media, posting of a notice at docks and other places where persons affected may gather, personal communication by inspectors and other agents of the Fisheries Director, and other measures designed to reach the persons who may be affected. It is a defense to an enforcement action for a violation of a proclamation that a person was prevented from receiving notice of the proclamation due to a natural disaster or other act of God occasioned exclusively by violence of nature without interference of any human agency and that could not have been prevented or avoided by the exercise of due care or foresight.

(c) All persons who may be affected by proclamations issued by the Fisheries Director are under a duty to keep themselves informed of current proclamations. It is no defense in any criminal prosecution for the defendant to show that the defendant in fact received no notice of a particular proclamation. In any prosecution for violation of a proclamation, or in which proof of matter contained in a proclamation is involved, the Department is deemed to have complied with publication procedures; and the burden is on the defendant to show, by the greater weight of the evidence, substantial failure of compliance by the Department with the required publication procedures.

(d) Pursuant to the request of five or more members of the Marine Fisheries Commission, the Chair of the Marine Fisheries Commission may call an emergency meeting of the Commission to review an issuance or proposed issuance of proclamations under the authority delegated to the Fisheries Director pursuant to subsection (b) of this section or to review the desirability of directing the Fisheries Director to issue a proclamation to prohibit or allow the taking of certain fisheries resources. At least 48 hours prior to any emergency meeting called pursuant to this subsection, a public announcement of the meeting shall be issued that describes the action requested by the members of the Marine Fisheries Commission. The Department shall make every reasonable effort to give actual notice of the meeting to persons who may be affected. After its review is complete, the Marine Fisheries Commission, consistent with its duty to protect, preserve, and enhance the commercial and sports fisheries resources of the State, may approve, cancel, or modify the previously issued or proposed proclamation under review or may direct the Fisheries Director to issue a proclamation that prohibits or allows the taking of certain fisheries resources. An emergency meeting called pursuant to this subsection and any resulting orders issued by the Marine Fisheries Commission are exempt from the provisions of Article 2A of Chapter 150B of the General Statutes. The decisions of the Marine Fisheries Commission shall be the final decision of the State and shall not be set aside on judicial review unless found to be arbitrary and capricious. (1915, c. 84, s. 21; 1917, c. 290, s. 7; C.S., s. 1878; 1925, c. 168, s. 2; 1935, c. 35; 1945, c. 776; 1953, cc. 774, 1134, 1251; 1963, c. 1097, s. 1; 1965, c. 957, s. 2; 1973, c. 1262, ss. 28, 86; c. 1331, s. 3; 1975, 2nd Sess., c. 983, s. 70; 1979, c. 388, s. 6; 1983, cc. 221, 619, 620; 1987, c. 641, ss. 7, 19; c. 827, s. 7; 1997-400, s. 4.3; 1998-225, s. 3.8; 2000-189, s. 9; 2003-154, s. 2.)

§ 113-221.2. Additional rules to establish sanitation requirements for scallops, shellfish, and crustacea; permits and permit fees authorized.

(a) Authority to Adopt Certain Rules and Establish Permits. - For the protection of the public health, the Marine Fisheries Commission shall adopt rules establishing sanitation requirements for the harvesting, processing and handling of scallops, shellfish, and crustacea of in-State origin. The rules of the Marine Fisheries Commission may also regulate scallops, shellfish, and crustacea shipped into North Carolina. The Department is authorized to enforce the rules and may issue and revoke permits according to the rules. The Department is authorized to establish a fee for each permit not to exceed one hundred dollars ($100.00).

(b) Advance Sale of Permits; Permit Revenue. - To ensure an orderly transition from one permit year to the next, the Division may issue a permit prior to July 1 of the permit year for which the permit is valid. Revenue that the Division receives for the issuance of a permit prior to the beginning of a permit year shall not revert at the end of the fiscal year in which the revenue is received and shall be credited and available to the Division for the permit year in which the permit is valid. (1965, c. 783, s. 1; 1967, c. 1005, s. 1; 1973, c. 476, s. 128; 1983, c. 891, s. 2; 2011-145, s. 13.3(ppp), (qqq); 2013-360, s. 14.8(u).)


§ 113-221.3. Monitoring program for State coastal fishing and recreation waters; removal or destruction of warning signs.

(a) For the protection of the public health of swimmers and others who use the State's coastal fishing waters for recreational activities, the Department shall develop and implement a program to monitor the State's coastal fishing waters for contaminants. The monitoring program shall cover all coastal fishing waters up to the point where those waters are classified as inland fishing waters.

(b) The Marine Fisheries Commission shall adopt rules to provide for a water quality monitoring program for the coastal recreation waters of the State and to allow the Department to implement the federal Beaches Environmental Assessment and Coastal Health Act of 2000 (Pub. L. No. 106-284; 114 Stat. 870, 875; 33 U.S.C. §§ 1313, 1362). The rules shall address, but are not limited to, definitions, surveys, sampling, action standards, and posting of information on the water quality of coastal recreation waters.

(c) No person shall remove, destroy, damage, deface, mutilate, or otherwise interfere with any sign posted by the Department pursuant to subsection (b) of this section. No person, without just cause or excuse, shall have in his or her possession any sign posted by the Department pursuant to subsection (b) of this section. Any person who violates this section is guilty of a Class 2 misdemeanor.

(d)     As used in this section, coastal recreation waters has the same meaning as in 33 U.S.C. § 1362. (1997-443, s. 15.17(a); 2003-149, s. 1; 2011-145, s. 13.3(rrr), (sss).)


§ 113-221.4. Embargo.

(a)     If the Secretary of Environment and Natural Resources or a local health director has probable cause to believe that any scallops, shellfish, or crustacea is adulterated or misbranded, the Secretary of Environment and Natural Resources or a local health director may detain or embargo the article by affixing a tag to it and warning all persons not to remove or dispose of the article until permission for removal or disposal is given by the official by whom it was detained or embargoed or by the court. It shall be unlawful for any person to remove or dispose of the detained or embargoed article without that permission.

(b)     The official by whom the scallops, shellfish, or crustacea was detained or embargoed shall petition a judge of the district or superior court in whose jurisdiction the article is detained or embargoed for an order for condemnation of the article. If the court finds that the article is adulterated or misbranded, that article shall be destroyed under the supervision of the petitioner. All court costs and fees, storage and other expense shall be taxed against the claimant of the article. If, the article, by proper labelling can be properly branded, the court, after the payment of all costs, fees, expenses, and an adequate bond, may order that the article be delivered to the claimant for proper labelling under the supervision of the petitioner. The bond shall be returned to the claimant after the petitioner represents to the court that the article is no longer mislabelled and that the expenses of supervision have been paid. (1983, c. 891, s. 2; 1997-261, s. 109; 1997-443, s. 11A.63A; 2006-80, s. 1; 2007-7, s. 1; 2011-145, s. 13.3(ttt), (uuu).)


§ 113-222. Arrest, service of process and witness fees of inspectors.

All arrest fees and other fees that may be charged in any bill of costs for service of process by inspectors must be paid to the county in which the trial is held. No witness fee may be taxed in any bill of costs by virtue of the appearance of an inspector as a witness in a criminal case within his enforcement jurisdiction. Acceptance by any inspector of any arrest fee, witness fee, or any other fee to which he is not entitled is a Class 1 misdemeanor. (1965, c. 957, s. 2; 1993, c. 539, s. 843; 1994, Ex. Sess., c. 24, s. 14(c).)


§ 113-223. Reciprocal agreements by Department generally.

Subject to the specific provisions of G.S. 113-169.5 and G.S. 113-170.1 relating to reciprocal provisions as to landing and selling catch and as to licenses, the Department is empowered to make reciprocal agreements with other jurisdictions respecting any of the matters governed in this Subchapter. Pursuant to such agreements the Department may modify provisions of this Subchapter in order to effectuate the purposes of such agreements, in the overall best interests of the conservation of marine and estuarine resources. (1915, c. 84, s. 5; 1917, c. 290, s. 10; C.S., s. 1883; 1953, c. 1086; 1965, c. 957, s. 2; 1973, c. 1262, s. 28; 1977, c. 771, s. 4; 1989, c. 727, s. 104; 1998-225, s. 4.22.)


§ 113-224. Cooperative agreements by Department.

The Department is empowered to enter into cooperative agreements with public and private agencies and individuals respecting the matters governed in this Subchapter. Pursuant to such agreements the Department may expend funds, assign employees to additional duties within or without the State, assume additional responsibilities, and take other actions that may be required by virtue of such agreements, in the overall best interests of the conservation of marine and estuarine resources. (1965, c. 957, s. 2; 1973, c. 1262, s. 28; 1977, c. 771, s. 4; 1989, c. 727, s. 105.)


§ 113-225. Inspectors not to have financial interest in fisheries.

Except as provided in this Subchapter respecting operations of demonstration and research projects by employees of the Department as part of their employment, no inspector may be financially interested in any fishing industry in the State of North Carolina. (1965, c. 957, s. 2.)


§ 113-226. Administrative authority of Department; administration of funds; delegation of powers.

(a) In the overall best interests of the conservation of marine and estuarine resources, the Department may lease or purchase lands, equipment, and other property; accept gifts and grants on behalf of the State; establish boating and fishing access areas; establish fisheries, fishery processing or storage plants, planted seafood beds, fish farms, and other enterprises related to the conservation of marine and estuarine resources as research or demonstration projects either alone or in cooperation with some individual or agency; sell the catch or processed fish or other marine and estuarine resources resulting from research fishing operations or demonstration projects; provide matching funds for entering into projects with some other governmental agency or with some scientific, educational, or charitable foundation or institution; condemn lands in accordance with the provisions of Chapter 40A of the General Statutes and other governing provisions of law; and sell, lease, or give away property acquired by it. Provided, that any private person selected to receive gifts or benefits by the Department be selected:

(1) With regard to the overall public interest that may result, and

(2) From a defined class upon such a rational basis open to all within the class as to prevent constitutional infirmity with respect to requirements of equal protection of the laws or prohibitions against granting exclusive privileges or emoluments.

(b) All money credited to, held by, or to be received by the Department in respect of the conservation of marine and estuarine resources must be deposited with the Department. In administering such funds and recommending expenditures, the Department must give attention to the sources of the revenues received so as to encourage disbursements to be made on an equitable basis; nevertheless, except as provided in this section, separate funds may not be established and particular projects and programs deemed to be of sufficient importance in the conservation of marine and estuarine resources may receive proportional shares of Department expenditures that are greater than the proportional shares of license and other revenues produced by such projects or programs for the Department.

(c) If as a precondition of receiving funds under any cooperative program there must be a separation of license revenues received from certain classes of licensees and utilization of such revenues for limited purposes, the Department is directed to make such arrangements for separate accounting or for separate funding as may be necessary to insure the use of the revenues for the required purposes and eligibility for the cooperative funds. In such instance, if required, such revenues may be retained by the Department until expended upon the limited purposes in question. This subsection applies whether the cooperative program is with a public or private agency and whether the Department acts alone on behalf of the State or in conjunction with the Wildlife Resources Commission or some other State agency.

(d) Repealed by Session Laws 1973, c. 1262, s. 28. (1965, c. 957, s. 2; 1973, c. 1262, s. 28; 1987, c. 827, s. 103; 1989, c. 727, s. 106.)


§ 113-227. Repealed by Session Laws 1973, c. 1262, s. 28.


§ 113-228. Adoption of federal regulations.

To the extent that the Department is granted authority in this Subchapter over subject matter as to which there is concurrent federal jurisdiction, the Marine Fisheries Commission in its discretion may by reference in its rules adopt relevant provisions of federal laws and regulations as State rules. To prevent confusion or conflict of jurisdiction in enforcement, the Marine Fisheries Commission is exempt from any conflicting limitations in G.S. 150B-21.6 so that it may provide for automatic incorporation by reference into its rules of future changes within any particular set of federal laws or regulations relating to some subject clearly within the jurisdiction of the Department. (1965, c. 957, s. 2; 1973, c. 1262, s. 28; 1987, c. 641, s. 11; c. 827, s. 104; 1991 (Reg. Sess., 1992), c. 890, s. 7.)

§ 113-229. Permits to dredge or fill in or about estuarine waters or State-owned lakes.

(a) Except as hereinafter provided before any excavation or filling project is begun in any estuarine waters, tidelands, marshlands, or State-owned lakes, the party or parties desiring to do such shall first obtain a permit from the Department. Granting of the State permit shall not relieve any party from the necessity of obtaining a permit from the United States Army Corps of Engineers for work in navigable waters, if the same is required. The Department shall continue to coordinate projects pertaining to navigation with the United States Army Corps of Engineers.

(b) All applications for such permits shall include a plat of the areas in which the proposed work will take place, indicating the location, width, depth and length of any proposed channel, the disposal area, and a copy of the deed or other instrument under which the applicant claims title to the property adjoining the waters in question, (or any land covered by waters), tidelands, or marshlands, or if the applicant is not the owner, then a copy of the deed or other instrument under which the owner claims title plus written permission from the owner to carry out the project on his land.

(c) In lieu of a deed or other instrument referred to in subsection (b) of this section, the agency authorized to issue such permits may accept some other reasonable evidence of ownership of the property in question or other lawful authority to make use of the property.

(c1) The Coastal Resources Commission may, by rule, designate certain classes of major and minor development for which a general or blanket permit may be issued. In developing these rules, the Commission shall consider all of the following:

(1) The size of the development.

(2) The impact of the development on areas of environmental concern.

(3) How often the class of development is carried out.

(4) The need for on-site oversight of the development.

(5) The need for public review and comment on individual development projects.

(c2) General permits may be issued by the Commission as rules under the provisions of G.S. 113A-118.1. Individual development carried out under the provisions of general permits shall not be subject to the mandatory notice provisions of this section. The Commission may impose reasonable notice provisions and other appropriate conditions and safeguards on any general permit it issues. The variance, appeals, and enforcement provisions of this Article shall apply to any individual development projects undertaken under a general permit.

(d) An applicant for a permit, other than an emergency permit, shall notify the owner of each tract of riparian property that adjoins that of the applicant. An applicant may satisfy the required notification of adjoining riparian property owners by either (i) obtaining from each adjoining riparian property owner a signed statement that the adjoining riparian property owner has no objection to the proposed project or (ii) providing a copy of the applicant's permit application to each adjoining riparian property owner by certified mail. If the owner's address is unknown and cannot be ascertained with due diligence or if a diligent but unsuccessful effort has been made to serve the copy by certified mail, publication in accordance with the rules of the Commission shall serve to satisfy the notification requirement. An owner may file written objections to the permit with the Department for 30 days after the owner is served with a copy of the application by certified mail. In the case of a special emergency dredge or fill permit the applicant must certify that the applicant took all reasonable steps to notify adjacent riparian owners of the application for a special emergency dredge and fill permit prior to submission of the application. Upon receipt of this certification, the Secretary shall issue or deny the permit within the time period specified in subsection (e) of this section, upon the express understanding from the applicant that the applicant will be entirely liable and hold the State harmless for all damage to adjacent riparian landowners directly and proximately caused by the dredging or filling for which approval may be given.

(e) Applications for permits except special emergency permit applications shall be circulated by the Department among all State agencies and, in the discretion of the Secretary, appropriate federal agencies having jurisdiction over the subject matter which might be affected by the project so that such agencies will have an opportunity to raise any objections they might have. The Department may deny an application for a dredge or fill permit upon finding: (1) that there will be significant adverse effect of the proposed dredging and filling on the use of the water by the public; or (2) that there will be significant adverse effect on the value and enjoyment of the property of any riparian owners; or (3) that there will be significant adverse effect on public health, safety, and welfare; or (4) that there will be significant adverse effect on the conservation of public and private water supplies; or (5) that there will be significant adverse effect on wildlife or fresh water, estuarine or marine fisheries. In the absence of such findings, a permit shall be granted. Such permit may be conditioned upon the applicant amending his proposal to take whatever measures are reasonably necessary to protect the public interest with respect to the factors enumerated in this subsection. Permits may allow for projects granted a permit the right to maintain such project for a period of up to 10 years. The right to maintain such project shall be granted subject to such conditions as may be reasonably necessary to protect the public interest. The Coastal Resources Commission shall coordinate the issuance of permits under this section and G.S. 113A-118 and the granting of variances under this section and G.S. 113A-120.1 to avoid duplication and to create a single, expedited permitting process. The Coastal Resources Commission may adopt rules interpreting and applying the provisions of this section and rules specifying the procedures for obtaining a permit under this section. Maintenance work as defined in this subsection shall be limited to such activities as are required to maintain the project dimensions as found in the permit granted. The Department shall act on an application for permit within 75 days after the completed application is filed, provided the Department may extend such deadline by not more than an additional 75 days if necessary properly to consider the application, except for applications for a special emergency permit, in which case the Department shall act within two working days after an application is filed, and failure to so act shall automatically approve the application.

(e1) The Secretary is empowered to issue special emergency dredge or fill permits upon application. Emergency permits may be issued only when life or structural property is in imminent danger as a result of rapid recent erosion or sudden failure of a man-made structure. The Coastal Resources Commission may elaborate by rule upon what conditions the Secretary may issue a special emergency dredge or fill permit. The Secretary may condition the emergency permit upon any reasonable conditions, consistent with the emergency situation, he feels are necessary to reasonably protect the public interest. Where an application for a special emergency permit includes work beyond which the Secretary, in his discretion, feels necessary to reduce imminent dangers to life or property he shall issue the emergency permit only for that part of the proposed work necessary to reasonably reduce the imminent danger. All further work must be applied for by application for an ordinary dredge or fill permit. The Secretary shall deny an application for a special dredge or fill permit upon a finding that the detriment to the public which would occur on issuance of the permit measured by the five factors in G.S. 113-229(e) clearly outweighs the detriment to the applicant if such permit application should be denied.

(f) A permit applicant who is dissatisfied with a decision on his application may file a petition for a contested case hearing under G.S. 150B-23 within 20 days after the decision is made. Any other person who is dissatisfied with a decision to deny or grant a permit may file a petition for a contested case hearing only if the Coastal Resources Commission determines, in accordance with G.S. 113A-121.1(c), that a hearing is appropriate. A permit is suspended from the time a person seeks administrative review of the decision concerning the permit until the Commission determines that the person seeking the review cannot commence a contested case or the issuance of a final decision in a contested case, as appropriate, and no action may be taken during that time that would be unlawful in the absence of the permit.

(g) G.S. 113A-122 applies to an appeal of a permit decision under subsection (f).

(h) Repealed by Session Laws 1987, c. 827, s. 105.

(h1) Except as provided in subsection (h2) of this section, all construction and maintenance dredgings of beach-quality sand may be placed on the affected downdrift ocean beaches or, if placed elsewhere, an equivalent quality and quantity of sand from another location shall be placed on the downdrift ocean beaches.

(h2) Clean, beach quality material dredged from navigational channels within the active nearshore, beach or inlet shoal systems shall not be removed permanently from the active nearshore, beach or inlet shoal system. This dredged material shall be disposed of on the ocean beach or shallow active nearshore area where it is environmentally acceptable and compatible with other uses of the beach.

(i) Subject to subsections (h1) and (h2) of this section, all materials excavated pursuant to such permit, regardless of where placed, shall be encased or entrapped in such a manner as to minimize their moving back into the affected water.

(j) None of the provisions of this section shall relieve any riparian owner of the requirements imposed by the applicable laws and regulations of the United States.

(k) Any person, firm, or corporation violating the provisions of this section shall be guilty of a Class 2 misdemeanor. Each day's continued operation after notice by the Department to cease shall constitute a separate offense. A notice to cease shall be served personally or by certified mail.

(l) The Secretary may, either before or after the institution of proceedings under subsection (k) of this section, institute a civil action in the superior court in the name of the State upon the relation of the Secretary, for damages, and injunctive relief, and for such other and further relief in the premises as said court may deem proper, to prevent or recover for any damage to any lands or property which the State holds in the public trust, and to restrain any violation of this section or of any provision of a dredging or filling permit issued under this section. Neither the institution of the action nor any of the proceedings thereon shall relieve any party to such proceedings from the penalty prescribed by this section for any violation of the same.

(m) This section shall apply to all persons, firms, or corporations, their employees, agents, or contractors proposing excavation or filling work in the estuarine waters, tidelands, marshlands and State-owned lakes within the State, and the work to be performed by the State government or local governments. Provided, however, the provisions of this section shall not apply to the activities and functions of the Department and local health departments that are engaged in mosquito control for the protection of the health and welfare of the people of the coastal area of North Carolina as provided under G.S. 130A-346 through G.S. 130A-349. Provided, further, this section shall not impair the riparian right of ingress and egress to navigable waters.

(n) Within the meaning of this section:

(1) "State-owned lakes" include man-made as well as natural lakes.

(2) "Estuarine waters" means all the waters of the Atlantic Ocean within the boundary of North Carolina and all the waters of the bays, sounds, rivers, and tributaries thereto seaward of the dividing line between coastal fishing waters and inland fishing waters agreed upon by the Department and the Wildlife Resources Commission, within the meaning of G.S. 113-129.

(3) "Marshland" means any salt marsh or other marsh subject to regular or occasional flooding by tides, including wind tides (whether or not the tidewaters reach the marshland areas through natural or artificial watercourses), provided

this shall not include hurricane or tropical storm tides. Salt marshland or other marsh shall be those areas upon which grow some, but not necessarily all, of the following salt marsh and marsh plant species: Smooth or salt water Cordgrass (Spartina alterniflora), Black Needlerush (Juncus roemerianus), Glasswort (Salicornia spp.), Salt Grass (Distichlis spicata), Sea Lavender (Limonium spp.), Bulrush (Scirpus spp.), Saw Grass (Cladium jamaicense), Cattail (Typha spp.), Salt-Meadow Grass (Spartina patens), and Salt Reed-Grass (Spartina cynosuroides). (1969, c. 791, s. 1; 1971, c. 1159, s. 6; 1973, c. 476, s. 128; c. 1262, ss. 28, 86; c. 1331, s. 3; 1975, c. 456, ss. 1-7; 1977, c. 771, s. 4; 1979, c. 253, ss. 1, 2; 1983, c. 258, ss. 1-3; c. 442, s. 2; 1987, c. 827, s. 105; 1989, c. 727, s. 107; 1993, c. 539, s. 844; 1994, Ex. Sess., c. 24, s. 14(c); 1993 (Reg. Sess., 1994), c. 777, s. 6(a), (b); 1995, c. 509, s. 55.1(a)-(c); 2000-172, ss. 3.1, 3.2; 2002-126, ss. 29.2(h)-(j); 2011-398, s. 36; 2013-413, s. 55.)

§ 113-230. Orders to control activities in coastal wetlands.

(a) The Secretary, with the approval of the Coastal Resources Commission, may from time to time, for the purpose of promoting the public safety, health, and welfare, and protecting public and private property, wildlife and marine fisheries, adopt, amend, modify, or repeal orders regulating, restricting, or prohibiting dredging, filling, removing or otherwise altering coastal wetlands. In this section, the term "coastal wetlands" shall mean any marsh as defined in G.S. 113-229(n)(3), as amended, and such contiguous land as the Secretary reasonably deems necessary to affect by any such order in carrying out the purposes of this section.

(b) The Secretary shall, before adopting, amending, modifying or repealing any such order, hold a public hearing thereon in the county in which the coastal wetlands to be affected are located, giving notice thereof to interested State agencies and each owner or claimed owner of such wetlands by certified or registered mail at least 21 days prior thereto.

(c) Upon adoption of any such order or any order amending, modifying or repealing the same, the Secretary shall cause a copy thereof, together with a plan of the lands affected and a list of the owners or claimed owners of such lands, to be recorded in the register of deeds office in the county where the land is located, and shall mail a copy of such order and plan to each owner or claimed owner of such lands affected thereby.

(d) Any person, firm or corporation that violates any order issued under the provisions of this section shall be guilty of a Class 2 misdemeanor.

(e) The superior court shall have jurisdiction in equity to restrain violations of such orders.

(f) Any person having a recorded interest in or registered claim to land affected by any such order may, within 90 days after receiving notice thereof, petition the superior court to determine whether the petitioner is the owner of the land in question, and in case he is adjudged the owner of the subject land, whether such order so restricts the use of his property as to deprive him of the practical uses thereof and is therefore an unreasonable exercise of the police power because the order constitutes the equivalent of a taking without compensation. If the court finds the order to be an unreasonable exercise of the police power, as aforesaid, the court shall enter a finding that such order shall not apply to the land of the petitioner; provided, however, that such finding shall not affect any other land than that of the petitioner. The Secretary shall cause a copy of such finding to be recorded forthwith in the register of deeds office in the county where the land is located. The method provided in this subsection for the determination of the issue of whether any such order constitutes a taking without compensation shall be exclusive, and such issue shall not be determined in any other proceeding.

(g) After a finding has been entered that such order shall not apply to certain land as provided in the preceding subsection, the Department of Administration, upon the request of the Coastal Resources Commission, shall take the fee or any lesser interest in such land in the name of the State by eminent domain under the provisions of Chapter 146 of the General Statutes and hold the same for the purposes set forth in this section.

(h) This section shall not repeal the powers, duties and responsibilities of the Department under the provisions of G.S. 113-229. (1971, c. 1159, s. 7; 1973, c. 1262, ss. 28, 86; 1977, c. 771, s. 4; 1979, c. 253, s. 4; 1989, c. 727, s. 108; 1993, c. 539, s. 845; 1994, Ex. Sess., c. 24, s. 14(c).)

§§ 113-231 through 113-240. Reserved for future codification purposes.

Article 18.

Commercial and Sports Fisheries Advisory Board.

§§ 113-241 through 113-250. Repealed by Session Laws 1973, c. 1262, ss. 28, 72.

Article 19.

Atlantic States Marine Fisheries Compact and Commission.

§ 113-251. Definition of terms.

As used in this Article:

(1)     "Commission" means the Atlantic States Marine Fisheries Commission.

(2)     "Commissioner" means a member of the Atlantic States Marine Fisheries Commission.

(3)     "Compact" means the Atlantic States Marine Fisheries Compact.

(4)     "Fisheries Director" means the Director of the Division of Marine Fisheries of the Department of Environment and Natural Resources. (1965, c. 957, s. 2; 1973, c. 1262, s. 28; 1977, c. 771, s. 4; 1989, c. 727, s. 109; 2003-92, s. 2.)

§ 113-252. Atlantic States Marine Fisheries Compact and Commission.

The Governor of this State is hereby authorized and directed to execute a compact on behalf of the State of North Carolina with any one or more of the states of Maine, New Hampshire, Massachusetts, Connecticut, Rhode Island, New York, New Jersey, Delaware, Maryland, Virginia, South Carolina, Georgia, and Florida and with such other states as may enter into the compact, legally joining therein in the form substantially as follows:

## ATLANTIC STATES MARINE FISHERIES COMPACT

The contracting states solemnly agree:

Article I

The purpose of this Compact is to promote the better utilization of the fisheries, marine, shell and anadromous, of the Atlantic seaboard by the development of a joint program for the promotion and protection of such fisheries, and by the prevention of the physical waste of the fisheries from any cause. It is not the purpose of this Compact to authorize the states joining herein to limit the production of fish or fish products for the purpose of establishing or fixing the price thereof, or creating and perpetuating monopoly.

Article II

This agreement shall become operative immediately as to those states executing it whenever any two or more of the states of Maine, New Hampshire, Massachusetts, Rhode Island, Connecticut, New York, New Jersey, Delaware, Maryland, Virginia, South Carolina, North Carolina, Georgia and Florida have executed it in the form that is in accordance with the laws of the executing state and the Congress has given its consent. Any state contiguous with any of the aforementioned states and riparian upon waters frequented by anadromous fish, flowing into waters under the jurisdiction of any of the aforementioned states, may become a party hereto as hereinafter provided.

Article III

Each state joining herein shall appoint three representatives to a commission hereby constituted and designated as the Atlantic States Marine Fisheries Commission. One shall be the executive officer of the administrative agency of the state charged with the conservation of the fisheries resources to which this compact pertains. The second shall be a member of the legislature appointed by the Governor. The third shall be a citizen who has knowledge of and interest in marine fisheries issues, appointed by the Governor. This Commission shall be a body corporate, with the powers and duties set forth herein.

Article IV

The duty of the said Commission shall be to make inquiry and ascertain from time to time such methods, practices, circumstances and conditions as may be disclosed for bringing about the conservation and the prevention of the depletion and physical waste of the fisheries, marine, shell and anadromous, of the Atlantic seaboard. The Commission shall have power to recommend the coordination of the exercise of the police powers of the several states within their respective jurisdictions to promote the preservation of those fisheries and their protection against overfishing, waste, depletion or any abuse whatsoever and to assure a continuing yield from the fisheries resources of the aforementioned states.

To that end the Commission shall draft and, after consultation with the advisory committee hereinafter authorized, recommend to the governors and legislatures of the various signatory states legislation dealing with the conservation of the marine, shell and anadromous fisheries of the Atlantic seaboard. The Commission shall more than one month prior to any regular meeting of the legislature in any signatory state, present to the governor of the state its recommendations relating to enactments to be made by the legislature of that state in furthering the intents and purposes of this Compact.

The Commission shall consult with and advise the pertinent administrative agencies in the states party hereto with regard to problems connected with the fisheries and recommend the adoption of such regulations as it deems advisable.

The Commission shall have power to recommend to the states party hereto the stocking of the waters of such states with fish and fish eggs, or joint stocking by some or all of the states party hereto, and when two or more of the states shall jointly stock waters the Commission shall act as the coordinating agency for such stocking.

Article V

The Commission shall elect from its number a chairman and a vice-chairman and shall appoint and at its pleasure remove or discharge such officers and employees as may be required to carry the provisions of this Compact into effect, and shall fix and determine their duties, qualifications and compensation. Said Commission shall adopt rules and regulations for the conduct of its business. It may establish and maintain one or more offices for the transaction of its business and may meet at any time or place but must meet at least once a year.

Article VI

No action shall be taken by the Commission in regard to its general affairs except by the affirmative vote of a majority of the whole number of compacting states present at any meeting. No recommendation shall be made by the Commission in regard to any species of fish except by the affirmative vote of a majority of the compacting states which have an interest in such species. The Commission shall define what shall be an interest.

Article VII

The Fish and Wildlife Service of the Department of the Interior of the government of the United States shall act as the primary research agency of the Atlantic States Marine Fisheries Commission, cooperating with the research agencies in each state for that purpose. Representatives of the said Fish and Wildlife Service shall attend the meetings of the Commission.

An advisory committee to be representative of the commercial fishermen and the saltwater anglers and such other interests of each state as the Commission deems advisable shall be established by the Commission as soon as practicable for the purpose of advising the Commission upon such recommendations as it may desire to make.

Article VIII

When any state other than those named specifically in Article II of this Compact shall become a party thereto for the purpose of conserving its anadromous fish in accordance with the provisions of Article II the participation of such state in the action of the Commission shall be limited to such species of anadromous fish.

Article IX

Nothing in this Compact shall be construed to limit the powers of any signatory state or to repeal or prevent the enactment of any legislation or the enforcement of any requirement by any signatory state imposing additional conditions and restrictions to conserve its fisheries.

Article X

Continued absence of representation or of any representative on the Commission from any state party hereto shall be brought to the attention of the governor thereof.

Article XI

The states party hereto agree to make annual appropriations to the support of the Commission in proportion to the primary market value of the products of their fisheries, exclusive of cod and haddock, as recorded in the most recently published reports of the Fish and Wildlife Service of the United States Department of the Interior, provided no state shall contribute less than two hundred dollars ($200.00) per annum and the annual contribution of each state above the minimum shall be figured to the nearest one hundred dollars ($100.00).

The compacting states agree to appropriate initially the annual amounts scheduled below, which amounts are calculated in the manner set forth herein, on the basis of the catch record of 1938. Subsequent budgets shall be recommended by a majority of the Commission and the cost thereof allocated equitably among the states in accordance with their respective interests and submitted to the compacting states.

Schedule of Initial Annual State Contributions

Maine $ 700

New Hampshire ................................................................................................ 200

Massachusetts ................................................................................................ 2300

Rhode Island .................................................................................................
300

Connecticut .................................................................................................
400

New York .................................................................................................
1300

New Jersey .................................................................................................
800

Delaware .................................................................................................
200

Maryland .................................................................................................
700

Virginia .................................................................................................
1300

North Carolina .................................................................................................
600

South Carolina .................................................................................................
200

Georgia .................................................................................................
200

Florida .................................................................................................
1500

Article XII

This Compact shall continue in force and remain binding upon each compacting state until renounced by it. Renunciation of this Compact must be preceded by sending six months' notice in writing of intention to withdraw from the Compact to the other states party hereto. (1949, c. 1086, s. 1; 1965, c. 957, s. 18; 2003-92, s. 3.)


§ 113-253. Amendment to Compact to establish joint regulation of specific fisheries.

The Governor is authorized to execute on behalf of the State of North Carolina an amendment to the Compact set out in G.S. 113-252 with any one or more of the states of Maine, New Hampshire, Massachusetts, Rhode Island, Connecticut, New York, New Jersey, Pennsylvania, Delaware, Maryland, Virginia, South Carolina, Georgia, and Florida or such other states as may become party to that Compact for the purpose of permitting the states that ratify this amendment to establish joint regulation of specific fisheries common to those states through the Atlantic States Marine Fisheries Commission and their representatives on that body. Notice of intention to withdraw from this amendment shall be executed and transmitted by the Governor and shall be in accordance with Article XII of the Atlantic States Marine Fisheries Compact and shall be effective as to this State with those states which similarly ratify this amendment. This amendment shall take effect as to this State with respect to such other of the aforesaid states as take similar action.


Amendment No. 1 of the Atlantic States Marine Fisheries Compact


The states consenting to this amendment agree that any two or more of them may designate the Atlantic States Marine Fisheries Commission as a joint regulatory agency with such powers as they may jointly confer from time to time for the regulation of the fishing operations of the citizens and vessels of such designating states with respect to specific fisheries in which such states have a common interest. The representatives of such states on the Atlantic States Marine Fisheries Commission shall constitute a separate section of such Commission for the exercise of the additional powers so granted, provided that the states so acting shall appropriate additional funds for this purpose. The creation of such section as a joint regulatory agency shall not deprive the states participating therein of any of their privileges or powers or responsibilities in the

Atlantic States Marine Fisheries Commission under the general compact. (1949, c. 1086, s. 2; 1965, c. 957, s. 18.)

§ 113-254. North Carolina members of Commission.

(a) In pursuance of Article III of the Compact, there shall be three commissioners from North Carolina. The first commissioner shall be the Fisheries Director, ex officio. The term of this commissioner shall terminate at the time the commissioner ceases to hold office as the Fisheries Director. The successor to this commissioner shall be the commissioner's successor as Fisheries Director. The second commissioner shall be a legislator appointed by the Governor. The term of this commissioner shall terminate at the time the commissioner ceases to hold legislative office. This commissioner's successor shall be appointed by the Governor. The third commissioner from the State of North Carolina shall be a citizen of the State with knowledge of and interest in marine fisheries issues appointed by the Governor. The term of this commissioner shall be three years. This commissioner may be reappointed for successive terms and shall hold office until the commissioner's successor is appointed and qualified. A vacancy occurring in the office of this commissioner for any reason or cause shall be filled by appointment by the Governor for the unexpired term.

(b) The Fisheries Director may delegate to any deputy or other subordinate of the Fisheries Director the power to be present, participate, and vote as the Fisheries Director's representative or substitute at any meeting, hearing, or other proceeding of the Commission.

(c) Any commissioner may be removed from office by the Governor upon charges and after a hearing. (1949, c. 1086, s. 3; 1965, c. 957, s. 18; 1973, c. 1262, ss. 28, 86; 1977, c. 771, s. 4; 1987, c. 641, s. 9; 1989, c. 727, s. 110; 2003-92, s. 4.)

§ 113-255. Powers of Commission and commissioners.

There is hereby granted to the Commission and the commissioners thereof all the powers provided for in the said Compact and all the powers necessary or incidental to the carrying out of said Compact in every particular. All officers of the State of North Carolina are hereby authorized and directed to do all things falling within their respective provinces and jurisdiction necessary or incidental to the carrying out of said Compact in every particular; it being hereby declared to be the policy of the State of North Carolina to perform and carry out the said Compact and to accomplish the purposes thereof. All officers, bureaus, departments and persons of and in the State government or administration of the State of North Carolina are hereby authorized and directed at convenient times and upon request of the said Commission to furnish the said Commission with information and data possessed by them or any of them and to aid said Commission by loan of personnel or other means lying within their legal rights respectively. (1949, c. 1086, s. 4; 1965, c. 957, s. 18.)


§ 113-256. Powers herein granted to Commission are supplemental.

Any powers herein granted to the Commission shall be regarded as in aid of and supplemental to and in no case a limitation upon any of the powers vested in said Commission by other laws of the State of North Carolina or by the laws of the states of Maine, New Hampshire, Massachusetts, Connecticut, Rhode Island, New York, New Jersey, Delaware, Maryland, Virginia, South Carolina, Georgia and Florida or by the Congress or the terms of said Compact. (1949, c. 1086, s. 5; 1965, c. 957, s. 18.)


§ 113-257. Report of Commission to Governor and legislature; recommendations for legislative action; examination of accounts and books by Auditor.

The Commission shall keep accurate accounts of all receipts and disbursements and shall report to the Governor and the legislature of the State of North Carolina on or before the tenth day of December in each year, setting forth in detail the transactions conducted by it during the 12 months preceding December 1 of that year and shall make recommendations for any legislative action deemed by it advisable, including amendments to the statutes of the State of North Carolina which may be necessary to carry out the intent and purposes of the compact between the signatory states.

The Auditor of the State of North Carolina is hereby authorized and empowered from time to time to examine the accounts and books of the Commission, including its receipts, disbursements and such other items referring to its financial standing as such Auditor may deem proper and to report the results of such examination to the Governor of such State. (1949, c. 1086, s. 6; 1955, c. 236, s. 2; 1965, c. 957, s. 18.)

§ 113-258. Commission subject to provisions of State Budget Act.

The Atlantic States Marine Fisheries Commission of the State of North Carolina shall be subject to all the terms and provisions of the State Budget Act, Chapter 143C of the General Statutes of North Carolina.(1949, c. 1086, s. 7; 1955, c. 236, s. 1; 1965, c. 957, s. 18; 2006-203, s. 27.)

Article 19A.

Fishery Management Councils.

§ 113-259. North Carolina members of the South Atlantic Fishery Management Council.

(a)     In pursuance of Section 302 of the Magnuson-Stevens Fishery Conservation and Management Act, 16 U.S.C. § 1801, et seq., there shall be at least two members of the South Atlantic Fishery Management Council from the State of North Carolina.

(b)     The first Council member shall be the principal State official with marine fishery management responsibility and expertise in the State, which official is the Director of the Division of Marine Fisheries of the Department or his designee.

(c)     Pursuant to the enabling legislation, other members from the state of North Carolina are selected by the United States Secretary of Commerce from a list of qualified individuals submitted by the Governor of the State. The list of nominees shall be compiled by the Marine Fisheries Commission and must be comprised of individuals who are knowledgeable and experienced with regard to the management, conservation, or commercial or recreational harvest of the fishery resources in the Atlantic Ocean seaward of the states of North Carolina, South Carolina, Georgia, and Florida. Prior to submission of the list of nominees, the Governor may consult with the Commission regarding additions to the list of nominees to be submitted. Should it be necessary for the Governor to submit additional nominees, the list of nominees shall be compiled by the Marine Fisheries Commission. (1987, c. 641, s. 18; 1989, c. 727, s. 111; 1998-225, s. 4.23.)

§ 113-260. North Carolina members of the Mid-Atlantic Fishery Management Council.

(a)  In pursuance of Section 302 of the Magnuson-Stevens Fishery Conservation and Management Act, 16 U.S.C. § 1801, et seq., there shall be at least two members of the Mid-Atlantic Fishery Management Council from the State of North Carolina.

(b)  The first Council member shall be the principal State official with marine fishery management responsibility and expertise in the State, which official is the Director of the Division of Marine Fisheries of the Department or his designee.

(c)  Pursuant to the enabling legislation, other members from the State of North Carolina are selected by the United States Secretary of Commerce from a list of qualified individuals submitted by the Governor of the State. The list of nominees shall be compiled by the Marine Fisheries Commission and must be comprised of individuals who are knowledgeable and experienced with regard to the management, conservation, or commercial or recreational harvest of the fishery resources in the Atlantic Ocean seaward of the states of New York, New Jersey, Delaware, Pennsylvania, Maryland, Virginia, and North Carolina. Prior to submission of the list of nominees, the Governor may consult with the Commission regarding additions to the list of nominees to be submitted. Should it be necessary for the Governor to submit additional nominees, the list of nominees shall be compiled by the Marine Fisheries Commission. (1998-225, s. 4.23.)

§§ 113-260.1 through 113-260.5. Reserved for future codification purposes.

Article 20.

Miscellaneous Regulatory Provisions.

§ 113-261. Taking fish and wildlife for scientific purposes; permits to take in normally unauthorized manner; cultural and scientific operations.

(a) The Department, the Wildlife Resources Commission, and agencies of the United States with jurisdiction over fish and wildlife are hereby granted the right to take marine, estuarine, and wildlife resources within the State, to conduct fish cultural operations and scientific investigations in the several waters of North Carolina, to survey fish and wildlife populations in the State, to conduct investigations to determine the status and requirements for survival of resident species of fish and wildlife, to propagate animals, birds, and fish, and to erect fish hatcheries and fish propagating plants without regard to any licensing or permit requirements of this Subchapter.

(b) The Department with respect to fish in coastal fishing waters and the Wildlife Resources Commission with respect to wildlife may provide for the issuance of permits, on such terms as they deem just and in the best interest of conservation, authorizing persons to take such fish or wildlife through the use of drugs, poisons, explosives, electricity, or any other generally prohibited manner. Such permits need not be restricted solely to victims of depredations or to scientific or educational institutions, but should be issued only for good cause. No permit to take wildlife other than fish by means of poison may be issued, however, unless the provisions of Article 22A are met.

(c) The Department, the Wildlife Resources Commission, and agencies of the United States with jurisdiction over fish and wildlife may, as necessary in their legitimate operations, take fish and wildlife in a manner generally prohibited by this Subchapter or by rules made under the authority of this Subchapter. (1915, c. 84, s. 7; C.S., s. 1886; 1965, c. 957, s. 2; 1973, c. 1262, s. 18; 1979, c. 830, s. 1; 1987, c. 827, s. 98.)


§ 113-262. Taking fish or wildlife by poisons, drugs, explosives or electricity prohibited; exceptions; possession of illegally killed fish or wildlife prohibited.

(a) Except as otherwise provided in this Subchapter, or in rules permitting use of electricity to take certain fish, it is a Class 2 misdemeanor to take any fish or wildlife through the use of poisons, drugs, explosives, or electricity. This subsection does not apply to any person lawfully using any poison or pesticide under the Structural Pest Control Act of North Carolina of 1955, as amended, or the North Carolina Pesticide Law of 1971, as amended.

(b)     Except under a valid permit it is unlawful to possess any fish or wildlife:

(1)     Bearing evidence of having been taken in violation of subsection (a); or

(2)     With knowledge or reason to believe that the fish or wildlife was taken in violation of subsection (a). (1883, c. 290; Code, s. 1094; Rev., s. 3417; C.S., ss. 1968, 2124; 1927, c. 107; 1935, c. 486, ss. 18-20; 1939, c. 235, s. 1; 1949, c. 1205, ss. 2, 3; 1953, c. 1134; 1955, c. 104; c. 1053, ss. 1, 3, 4; 1957, c. 1056; 1959, c. 207; c. 500; 1961, c. 1182; 1963, c. 381; c. 697, ss. 1, 3 1/2; 1965, c. 904, s. 1; c. 957, s. 2; 1967, c. 728, s. 1; c. 858, s. 1; c. 1149, s. 1.5; 1969, c. 75; c. 140; 1971, c. 439, ss. 1-3; c. 449, s. 1; c. 461; c. 648, s. 1; c. 899, s. 1; 1973, c. 1096; c. 1210, ss. 1-3, 5; c. 1262, s. 18; 1975, c. 669; c. 728; 1977, c. 493; c. 794, s. 4; 1979, c. 830, s. 1; 1987, c. 827, s. 98; 1993, c. 539, s. 846; 1994, Ex. Sess., c. 24, s. 14(c).)


§ 113-263. Inspecting plans and specifications of dams.

The Department and the Wildlife Resources Commission, in addition to other agencies primarily responsible, may inspect the plans and specifications of all dams proposed to be built, in North Carolina or elsewhere within the United States, the design or proposed mode of construction of which may have an adverse effect upon fish within the State. The Department or the Wildlife Resources Commission, as the case may be, may be heard before the appropriate agency charged with approving said plans and specifications, and due consideration shall be given to said Department or Wildlife Resources Commission in the approval or disapproval of the plans and specifications of proposed dams by the agencies so charged with said duty. (1965, c. 957, s. 2; 1973, c. 1262, s. 18.)


§ 113-264. Regulatory power over property of agency; public hunting grounds; scheduling of managed big game hunts.

(a) The Department and the Wildlife Resources Commission are granted the power by rule to license, regulate, prohibit, or restrict the public as to use and enjoyment of, or harm to, any property of the Department or the Wildlife Resources Commission, and may charge the public reasonable fees for access to or use of such property. "Property" as the word is used in this section is intended to be broadly interpreted and includes lands, buildings, vessels, vehicles, equipment, markers, stakes, buoys, posted signs and other notices, trees and shrubs and artificial constructions in boating and fishing access areas, game lands, wildlife refuges, public waters, public mountain trout waters, and all other real and personal property owned, leased, controlled, or cooperatively managed by either the Department or the Wildlife Resources Commission.

(a1) Every wildlife protector and every law enforcement officer of this State and its subdivisions shall have the authority within his or her established jurisdiction to enforce the rules promulgated pursuant to the power granted by this section regarding the willful removal of, damage to, or destruction of any property of the Department or the Wildlife Resources Commission.

(a2) To the extent that subsection (a1) of this section conflicts with any provision of any local act, subsection (a1) of this section prevails.

(b) Unless a different level of punishment is elsewhere set out, willful removal of, damage to, or destruction of any property of the Department or the Wildlife Resources Commission is a Class 1 misdemeanor.

(c) The Wildlife Resources Commission may cooperate with private landowners in the establishment of public hunting grounds. It may provide for the posting of these areas and of restricted zones within them, require that authorized hunters obtain written permission from the owner to hunt, enforce general laws concerning trespass by hunters and concerning damage or injurious activities by hunters and by others carrying weapons on or discharging weapons across public hunting grounds or restricted zones.

(d) The Wildlife Resources Commission may schedule managed hunts for any species of wildlife to be held on game lands. Participants in such hunts shall be selected at random by computer. The Wildlife Resources Commission may require by rule that an applicant 16 years of age or older have the required hunting license before the drawing for the hunt, and that an applicant less than 16 years of age apply as a member of a party that includes a properly licensed adult if the young applicant does not have the proper hunting license. When licenses are required prior to the drawing, all applications shall be screened for compliance. A nonrefundable fee of five dollars ($5.00) will be required of each applicant to defray the cost of processing the applications.

(e) A wildlife protector or law enforcement officer of this State or its subdivisions may have a vehicle towed at a Commission-owned or operated public boating access area if the vehicle:

(1) Is parked in an area other than one designated for parking; or

(2) Is left by an individual for a purpose other than launching, operating, or retrieving a vessel. (1965, c. 957, s. 2; 1973, c. 1262, ss. 18, 28; 1977, c. 771, s. 4; 1979, c. 830, s. 1; 1983, c. 403; 1985 (Reg. Sess., 1986), c. 996, s. 2; 1987, c. 827, s. 98; 1989, c. 221; c. 642, s. 1; 1993, c. 539, s. 847; 1994, Ex. Sess., c. 24, s. 14(c); 2005-82, s. 1; 2005-164, s. 2.)


§ 113-265. Obstructing or polluting flow of water into hatchery; throwing fish offal into waters.

(a) No person may obstruct, pollute, or diminish the natural flow of water into or through any fish hatchery in violation of the requirements of the Environmental Management Commission.

(b) It is unlawful for any person to throw or cause to be thrown into the channel of any navigable waters fish offal in any quantity likely to hinder or prevent the passage of fish along such channel. The Marine Fisheries Commission and the Wildlife Resources Commission may by rule impose further restrictions upon the throwing of fish offal in any coastal fishing waters or inland fishing waters respectively.

(c) to (e) Repealed by Session Laws 1987, c. 636, s. 2. (1883, c. 137, s. 5; Code, ss. 3385, 3386, 3389, 3407, 3418; Rev., ss. 2444, 2465, 2478; C.S., ss. 1969, 1971, 1972; 1959, c. 405; 1965, c. 957, s. 2; 1971, c. 690, s. 4; 1973, c. 1262, ss. 18, 28; 1985 (Reg. Sess., 1986), c. 996, s. 3; 1987, c. 636, s. 2; c. 827, s. 98.)


§ 113-266. Interference with artificial reef marking devices.

It shall be a Class 1 misdemeanor for any person to destroy, injure, relocate, or remove any navigational aids, buoys, markers, or other devices lawfully set out by the Division of Marine Fisheries in connection with the marking of any artificial reef in the coastal waters of the State and in the Atlantic Ocean to the seaward extent of the State's jurisdiction as now or hereafter defined. (1985 (Reg. Sess., 1986), c. 996, s. 1; 1993, c. 539, s. 848; 1994, Ex. Sess., c. 24, s. 14(c).)

§ 113-267. Replacement costs of marine, estuarine, and wildlife resources; rules authorized; prima facie evidence.

To provide information to the courts and other officials taking action under G.S. 15A-1343(b1)(5), under G.S. 143-215.3(a)(7), or under any other pertinent authority of law, the Marine Fisheries Commission and the Wildlife Resources Commission are authorized to adopt rules setting forth the factors that should be considered in determining the replacement costs of fish and wildlife and other marine, estuarine, and wildlife resources that have been taken, injured, removed, harmfully altered, damaged, or destroyed. The Marine Fisheries Commission and the Wildlife Resources Commission may make similar rules respecting costs of investigations required by G.S. 143-215.3(a)(7) or which are made pursuant to a court order. For common offenses resulting in the destruction of marine, estuarine, and wildlife resources the Marine Fisheries Commission and the Wildlife Resources Commission may adopt schedules of costs which reasonably state the likely replacement costs and necessary investigative costs when appropriate. Rules of the Marine Fisheries Commission and the Wildlife Resources Commission stating scheduled costs or cost factors must be treated as prima facie evidence of the actual costs, but do not prevent a court or jury from examining the reasonableness of the rules or from assessing the special factors in a case which may make the true costs either higher or lower than the amount stated in the rules. The term "replacement costs" must be broadly construed to include indirect costs of replacement through habitat improvement or restoration, establishment of sanctuaries, and other recognized conservation techniques when direct stocking or replacement is not feasible. (1979, c. 830, s. 1; 1985, c. 509, s. 7; 1987, c. 827, s. 98.)

§ 113-268. Injuring, destroying, stealing, or stealing from nets, seines, buoys, pots, etc.

(a) It is unlawful for any person without the authority of the owner of the equipment to take fish from nets, traps, pots, and other devices to catch fish which have been lawfully placed in the open waters of the State.

(b) It is unlawful for any master or other person having the management or control of a vessel in the navigable waters of the State to willfully, wantonly, and unnecessarily do injury to any seine, net or pot which may lawfully be hauled, set, or fixed in such waters for the purpose of taking fish except that a net set across a channel may be temporarily moved to accommodate persons engaged in drift netting, provided that no fish are removed and no damage is done to the net moved.

(c) It is unlawful for any person to willfully steal, destroy, or injure any buoys, markers, stakes, nets, pots, or other devices on property lawfully set out in the open waters of the State in connection with any fishing or fishery.

(d) Violation of subsections (a), (b), or (c) is a Class A1 misdemeanor.

(e) The Department may, either before or after the institution of any other action or proceeding authorized by this section, institute a civil action for injunctive relief to restrain a violation or threatened violation of subsections (a), (b), or (c) of this section pursuant to G.S. 113-131. The action shall be brought in the superior court of the county in which the violation or threatened violation is occurring or about to occur and shall be in the name of the State upon the relation of the Secretary. The court, in issuing any final order in any action brought pursuant to this subsection may, in its discretion, award costs of litigation including reasonable attorney and expert-witness fees to any party. (1987, c. 636, s. 1; 1989, c. 727, s. 112; 1993, c. 539, s. 849; 1994, Ex. Sess., c. 24, s. 14(c); 1998-225, s. 3.9.)


§ 113-269. Robbing or injuring hatcheries and other aquaculture operations.

(a) The definitions established in G.S. 106-758 are incorporated by reference into this section. For the purposes of this section, a shellfish lease issued pursuant to G.S. 113-202 is defined as an aquaculture facility only when it has been amended pursuant to G.S. 113-202.1 to authorize use of the water column and when it is or has been regularly posted and identified in accordance with the rules of the Marine Fisheries Commission.

(b) It is unlawful for any person without the authority of the owner of an aquaculture facility to take fish or aquatic species being cultivated or reared by the owner from an aquaculture facility.

(c) It is unlawful for any person to receive or possess fish or aquatic species stolen from an aquaculture facility while knowing or having reasonable grounds to believe that the fish or aquatic species are stolen.

(d) It is unlawful for any person to willfully destroy or injure an aquaculture facility or aquatic species being reared in an aquaculture facility.

(e) Violation of subsections (b) or (c) for fish or aquatic species valued at more than four hundred dollars ($400.00) is punishable under G.S. 14-72. Violation of subsections (b) or (c) for fish or aquatic species valued at four hundred dollars ($400.00) or less is a Class 1 misdemeanor.

(f) Violation of subsection (d) is a Class 1 misdemeanor.

(g) In deciding to impose any sentence other than an active prison sentence, the sentencing judge shall consider and may require, in accordance with G.S. 15A-1343, restitution to the victim for the amount of damage to the aquaculture facility or aquatic species or for the value of the stolen fish or aquatic species.

(h) The district attorney shall dismiss any case brought pursuant to subsections (b) and (c) if defendant produces a notarized written authorization for taking fish or aquatic species from the aquaculture facility or if the fish or aquatic species taken from a shellfish lease aquaculture facility was not a shellfish authorized for cultivation on the lease. (1989, c. 281, s. 1; 1993, c. 539, ss. 850, 851; 1994, Ex. Sess., c. 24, s. 14(c).)

§ 113-270. Reserved for future codification purposes.

Article 21.

Licenses and Permits Issued by the Wildlife Resources Commission.

§ 113-270.1. License agents.

(a)     The Wildlife Resources Commission may by rule provide for the appointment of persons as license agents to sell licenses and permits that the Commission is authorized to issue by this Subchapter or by any other provisions of law. To facilitate the convenience of the public, the efficiency of administration, the need to keep statistics and records affecting the conservation of wildlife resources, boating, water safety, and other matters within the jurisdiction of the Wildlife Resources Commission, and the need to issue licenses and permits containing special restrictions, the Wildlife Resources Commission may issue licenses and permits in any particular category through:

(1)     License agents.

(2)     The Wildlife Resources Commission's headquarters.

(3)     Employees of the Wildlife Resources Commission.

(4)     Two or more such sources simultaneously.

(a1)    When there are substantial reasons for differing treatment, the Wildlife Resources Commission may issue a type of license or permit by one method in one locality and by another method in another locality.

(b)     License agents may charge a fee of two dollars ($2.00) per transaction for licenses or permits issued.

(b1)    When licenses or permits are to be issued by license agents as provided by subsection (a) of this section, the Wildlife Resources Commission may adopt rules to provide for any of the following:

(1)     Qualifications of the license agents.

(2)     Duties of the license agents.

(3)     Methods and procedures to ensure accountability and security for proceeds and unissued licenses and permits.

(4) Types and amounts of evidence that a license agent must submit to relieve the agent of responsibility for losses due to occurrences beyond the control of the agent.

(5) Any other reasonable requirement or condition that the Wildlife Resources Commission deems necessary to expedite and control the issuance of licenses and permits by license agents.

(b2) The Wildlife Resources Commission may adopt rules to authorize the Executive Director to take any of the following actions related to license agents:

(1) Select and appoint license agents in areas most convenient for the sale of licenses and permits.

(2) Limit the number of license agents in an area if necessary for efficiency of operation.

(3) Require prompt and accurate reporting and remittance of public funds or documents by license agents.

(4) Conduct periodic and special audits of accounts.

(5) Suspend or terminate the authorization of any license agent found to be noncompliant with rules adopted by the Wildlife Resources Commission or when State funds or property are reasonably believed to be in jeopardy.

(6) Require the immediate surrender of all equipment, forms, licenses, permits, records, and State funds and property, issued by or belonging to the Wildlife Resources Commission, in the event of the termination of a license agent.

(b3) The Wildlife Resources Commission is exempt from the contested case provisions of Chapter 150B of the General Statutes with respect to determinations of whether to authorize or terminate the authority of a person to sell licenses and permits as a license agent of the Wildlife Resources Commission.

(b4) If any check or bank account draft of any license agent for the issuance of licenses or permits shall be returned by the banking facility upon which the same is drawn for lack of funds, the license agent shall be liable to the Commission for a penalty of five percent (5%) of the amount of the check or bank account draft, but in no event shall the penalty be less than five dollars ($5.00) or more than two hundred dollars ($200.00). License agents shall be assessed a penalty of twenty-five percent (25%) of their issuing fee on all remittances to the Commission after the fifteenth day of the month immediately following the month of sale.

(c) Repealed by Session Laws 2005-455, s. 3.2. See notes for contingent effective date.

(d) It is a Class 1 misdemeanor for a license agent to do any of the following:

(1) Withhold or misappropriate funds from the sale of licenses or permits.

(2) Falsify records of licenses or permits sold.

(3) Willfully and knowingly assist or allow a person to obtain a license or permit for which the person is ineligible.

(4) Willfully issue a backdated license or permit.

(5) Willfully include false information or omit material information on records, licenses, or permits regarding either:

a. A person's entitlement to a particular license or permit.

b. The applicability or term of a particular license or permit.

(6) Charge or accept any additional fee, remuneration, or other item of value in association with any activity set out in subdivisions (1) through (5) of this subsection.

(e) through (j) Repealed by Session Laws 2005-455, s. 3.2. See notes for contingent effective date. (1961, c. 352, ss. 4, 9; 1979, c. 830, s. 1; 1985, c. 791, s. 34; 1987, c. 827, s. 98; 1993, c. 539, ss. 852, 853; 1994, Ex. Sess., c. 24, s. 14(c); 2005-455, s. 3.2; 2013-283, s. 15.)

§ 113-270.1A. Hunter safety course required.

(a) Except as provided in subsections (a1) and (d) of this section, on or after July 1, 2013, a person, regardless of age, may not procure a hunting license in this State without producing a hunter education certificate of competency or one of the following issued by the Wildlife Resources Commission:

(1) A North Carolina hunting heritage apprentice permit.

(2) A hunting license issued prior to July 1, 2013.

(a1) A person who qualifies for a disabled license under G.S. 113-270.1C(b)(5) or (6), G.S. 113-270.1D(b)(7) or (8), or G.S. 113-351(c)(3)f. or g. need not comply with the requirements of subsection (a) of this section in order to receive that license, so long as the person does not make use of the license unless:

(1) The disabled hunter is accompanied by an adult of at least 18 years of age who is licensed to hunt; and

(2) The licensed adult maintains a proximity to the disabled hunter which enables the adult to monitor the activities of the disabled hunter by remaining within sight and hearing distance at all times without the use of electronic devices.

(b) The Wildlife Resources Commission shall institute and coordinate a statewide course of instruction in hunter ethics, wildlife laws and regulations, and competency and safety in the handling of firearms, and in so doing, may cooperate with any political subdivision, or with any reputable organization. The course of instruction shall be conducted as follows:

(1) The Wildlife Resources Commission shall designate those persons or agencies authorized to give the course of instruction, and this designation shall be valid until revoked by the Commission. Those designated persons shall submit to the Wildlife Resources Commission validated listings naming all persons who have successfully completed the course of instruction.

(2) The Wildlife Resources Commission may conduct the course in hunter education, using Commission personnel or Commission-approved persons.

(3) The Wildlife Resources Commission shall issue a certificate of competency and safety to each person who successfully completes the course of instruction, and the certificate shall be valid until revoked by the Commission.

(4) Any similar certificate issued outside the State by a governmental agency, shall be accepted as complying with the requirements of subsection (a) above, if the privileges are reciprocal for North Carolina residents.

(5) The Wildlife Resources Commission shall adopt rules and regulations to provide for the course of instruction and the issuance of the certificates consistent with the purpose of this section.

(c) On or after July 1, 2013, any person who obtains a hunting license by presenting a fictitious certificate of competency or who attempts to obtain a certificate of competency or hunting license through fraud shall have his hunting privileges revoked by the Wildlife Resources Commission for a period not to exceed one year.

(d) Notwithstanding the provisions of subsection (a) of this section, the lifetime licenses provided for in G.S. 113-270.1D(b)(1), (2), (3), (4), and (5), and 113-270.2(c)(2), and 113-351(c)(3) may be purchased by or in the name of persons who have not obtained a hunter education certificate of competency, subject to the requirements of this subsection. Pending satisfactory completion of the hunter education course, persons who possess one of the lifetime licenses specified in this subsection may exercise the privileges of the lifetime license only when accompanied by an adult of at least 18 years of age who is licensed to hunt in this State. For the purpose of this section, "accompanied" means that the licensed adult maintains a proximity that enables the adult to monitor the activities of the hunter by remaining within sight and hearing distance at all times without use of electronic devices. (1989, c. 324, s. 1; 1991, c. 70, s. 1; 1997-365, s. 1; 1999-456, s. 27; 2005-438, s. 1; 2013-63, s. 1.)

§ 113-270.1B. License required to hunt, fish, or trap; fees set by Commission.

(a) Except as otherwise specifically provided by law, no person may hunt, fish, trap, or participate in any other activity regulated by the Wildlife Resources Commission for which a license is provided by law without having first procured a current and valid license authorizing the activity.

(b) Except as indicated otherwise, all licenses are annual licenses valid from the date of issue for a period of 12 months.

(c) As used in this section, the term "effective date" means the later of:

(1) The date of purchase of a new license.

(2) The first day after the expiration of a currently valid license of the same type held by the licensee.

(d) For those licenses sold directly through the Commission by telephone, mail, online, or at a service counter, the Commission may charge a fee of two dollars ($2.00) per transaction. A fee may not be charged by the Commission for federal Harvest Information Program (HIP) certification, big game harvest report cards for lifetime license holders, exempt landowners, persons of less than 16 years of age, or for any other license or vessel transactions for which there is no charge.

(e) (Effective January 1, 2015) The Wildlife Resources Commission shall adopt rules to establish fees for the hunting, fishing, trapping, and activity licenses issued and administered by the Wildlife Resources Commission. No rule to increase fees above January 1, 2015, levels may increase a fee in excess of the average increase in the Consumer Price Index for All Urban Consumers over the preceding five years.

The statutory fees for the hunting, fishing, trapping, and activity licenses issued and administered by the Wildlife Resources Commission shall expire when the rules adopted pursuant to this subsection become effective. (1993 (Reg. Sess., 1994), c. 684, s. 1; 2012-81, s. 1; 2013-283, ss. 16, 20(b), (c).)


§ 113-270.1C. Combination hunting and inland fishing licenses.

(a) The combination hunting and inland fishing licenses set forth in subsection (b) of this section entitle the licensee to take, except on game lands, all wild birds and wild animals, other than big game and waterfowl, by all lawful methods and in all open seasons, and to fish with hook and line in all inland and joint fishing waters, except public mountain trout waters. A combination hunting and inland fishing license issued under this section does not entitle the licensee to engage in recreational fishing in coastal fishing waters that are not joint fishing waters.

(b)     Combination hunting and inland fishing licenses issued by the Wildlife Resources Commission are:

(1)     (Effective until August 1, 2014) Resident Annual Combination Hunting and Inland Fishing License - $20.00. This license shall be issued only to an individual resident of the State.

(1)     (Effective August 1, 2014) Resident Annual Combination Hunting and Inland Fishing License - $25.00. This license shall be issued only to an individual resident of the State.

(2),    (3) Repealed by Session Laws 1997-326, s. 2.

(4)     Repealed by Session Laws 2005-455, s. 1.6, effective January 1, 2007.

(5)     Resident Disabled Veteran Lifetime Combination Hunting and Inland Fishing License - $10.00. This license shall be issued only to an individual who is a resident of the State and who is a fifty percent (50%) or more disabled veteran as determined by the United States Department of Veterans Affairs. This license remains valid for the lifetime of the licensee so long as the licensee remains fifty percent (50%) or more disabled. This license entitles the licensee to fish in public mountain trout waters as provided in G.S. 113-272(a).

(6)     Resident Totally Disabled Lifetime Combination Hunting and Inland Fishing License - $10.00. This license shall be issued only to an individual who is a resident of the State and who is totally and permanently disabled as determined by the Social Security Administration. This license remains valid for the lifetime of the licensee. This license entitles the licensee to fish in public mountain trout waters as provided in G.S. 113-272(a). (1993 (Reg. Sess., 1994), c. 684, s. 1; 1997-326, ss. 2, 3; 2001-91, s. 1; 2005-455, s. 1.6; 2013-283, s. 1.)


§ 113-270.1D.  (Effective until August 1, 2014) Sportsman licenses.

(a)     Annual Sportsman License - $40.00. This license shall be issued only to an individual resident of the State and entitles the licensee to take all wild animals and wild birds, including waterfowl, by all lawful methods in all open seasons, including the use of game lands, and to fish with hook and line for all fish in all inland and joint fishing waters, including public mountain trout waters. An annual sportsman license issued under this subsection does not entitle the licensee to engage in recreational fishing in coastal fishing waters that are not joint fishing waters.

(b) Lifetime Sportsman Licenses. Except as provided in subdivision (7) of this subsection, lifetime sportsman licenses are valid for the lifetime of the licensees. Lifetime sportsman licenses entitle the licensees to take all wild animals and wild birds by all lawful methods in all open seasons, including the use of game lands, and to fish with hook and line for all fish in all inland and joint fishing waters, including public mountain trout waters. A lifetime sportsman license issued under this subsection does not entitle the licensee to engage in recreational fishing in coastal fishing waters that are not joint fishing waters. Lifetime sportsman licenses issued by the Wildlife Resources Commission are:

(1) Infant Lifetime Sportsman License - $200.00. This license shall be issued only to an individual under one year of age.

(2) Youth Lifetime Sportsman License - $350.00. This license shall be issued only to an individual under 12 years of age.

(3) Adult Resident Lifetime Sportsman License - $500.00. This license shall be issued only to an individual resident of the State.

(4) Nonresident Lifetime Sportsman License - $1,000. This license shall be issued only to an individual nonresident of the State.

(5) Age 65 Resident Lifetime Sportsman License - $15.00. This license shall be issued only to an individual resident of the State who is at least 65 years of age.

(6) Repealed by Session Laws 2005-455, s. 1.7 effective January 1, 2007.

(7) Resident Disabled Veteran Lifetime Sportsman License - $100.00. This license shall be issued only to an individual who is a resident of the State and who is a fifty percent (50%) or more disabled veteran as determined by the United States Department of Veterans Affairs. This license remains valid for the lifetime of the licensee so long as the licensee remains fifty percent (50%) or more disabled.

(8) Resident Totally Disabled Lifetime Sportsman License - $100.00. This license shall be issued only to an individual who is a resident of the State and who is totally and permanently disabled as determined by the Social Security Administration. (1993 (Reg. Sess., 1994), c. 684, s. 1; 1997-326, s. 1; 1999-339, s. 4; 2005-455, s. 1.7.)

§ 113-270.1D. (Effective August 1, 2014) Sportsman licenses.

(a) Annual Sportsman License - $50.00. This license shall be issued only to an individual resident of the State and entitles the licensee to take all wild animals and wild birds, including waterfowl, by all lawful methods in all open seasons, including the use of game lands, and to fish with hook and line for all fish in all inland and joint fishing waters, including public mountain trout waters. An annual sportsman license issued under this subsection does not entitle the licensee to engage in recreational fishing in coastal fishing waters that are not joint fishing waters.

(b) Lifetime Sportsman Licenses. Except as provided in subdivision (7) of this subsection, lifetime sportsman licenses are valid for the lifetime of the licensees. Lifetime sportsman licenses entitle the licensees to take all wild animals and wild birds by all lawful methods in all open seasons, including the use of game lands, and to fish with hook and line for all fish in all inland and joint fishing waters, including public mountain trout waters. A lifetime sportsman license issued under this subsection does not entitle the licensee to engage in recreational fishing in coastal fishing waters that are not joint fishing waters. Lifetime sportsman licenses issued by the Wildlife Resources Commission are:

(1) Infant Lifetime Sportsman License - $200.00. This license shall be issued only to an individual under one year of age.

(2) Youth Lifetime Sportsman License - $350.00. This license shall be issued only to an individual under 12 years of age.

(3) Adult Resident Lifetime Sportsman License - $500.00. This license shall be issued only to an individual resident of the State.

(4) Nonresident Lifetime Sportsman License - $1,200. This license shall be issued only to an individual nonresident of the State.

(5)     Age 70 Resident Lifetime Sportsman License - $15.00. This license shall be issued only to an individual resident of the State who is at least 70 years of age.

(6)     Repealed by Session Laws 2005-455, s. 1.7 effective January 1, 2007.

(7)     Resident Disabled Veteran Lifetime Sportsman License - $100.00. This license shall be issued only to an individual who is a resident of the State and who is a fifty percent (50%) or more disabled veteran as determined by the United States Department of Veterans Affairs or as established by rules of the Wildlife Resources Commission. This license remains valid for the lifetime of the licensee so long as the licensee remains fifty percent (50%) or more disabled.

(8)     Resident Totally Disabled Lifetime Sportsman License - $100.00. This license shall be issued only to an individual who is a resident of the State and who is totally and permanently disabled as determined by the Social Security Administration or as established by rules of the Wildlife Resources Commission. (1993 (Reg. Sess., 1994), c. 684, s. 1; 1997-326, s. 1; 1999-339, s. 4; 2005-455, s. 1.7; 2013-283, s. 2.)

§ 113-270.2. Hunting licenses.

(a)     The hunting licenses set forth in subdivisions (1), (3), and (6) of subsection (c) of this section entitle the holder to take, except on game lands, wild birds and wild animals, other than big game and waterfowl, by all lawful methods and in all open seasons. The comprehensive hunting licenses of subdivisions (2) and (5) of subsection (c) of this section further entitle the holder to take big game and waterfowl and to use game lands.

(b)     Repealed by Session Laws 1993 (Reg. Sess., 1994), c. 684, s. 2.

(c)     (Effective until August 1, 2014) The hunting licenses issued by the Wildlife Resources Commission are as follows:

(1)     Resident State Hunting License - $15.00. This license shall be issued only to an individual resident of the State.

(2) Lifetime Resident Comprehensive Hunting License - $250.00. This license shall be issued only to an individual resident of the State and is valid for the lifetime of the holder.

(3) Resident County Hunting License - $10.00. This license shall be issued only to an individual resident of the State and is valid only in the county of residence of the license holder.

(4) Controlled Hunting Preserve Hunting License - $15.00. This license shall be issued to an individual resident or nonresident to take only foxes and domestically raised game birds, other than wild turkey, only within a controlled hunting preserve licensed and operated in accordance with G.S. 113-273(g) and implementing rules of the Wildlife Resources Commission.

(5) Resident Annual Comprehensive Hunting License - $30.00. This license shall be issued only to an individual resident of the State.

(6) Nonresident State Hunting License. This license shall be issued only to a nonresident. The nonresident State hunting licenses issued by the Wildlife Resources Commission are:

a. Season License - $60.00.

b. Six-Day License - $40.00. This license is valid for the six consecutive dates indicated on the license.

(c) (Effective August 1, 2014) The hunting licenses issued by the Wildlife Resources Commission are as follows:

(1) Resident State Hunting License - $20.00. This license shall be issued only to an individual resident of the State.

(2) Lifetime Resident Comprehensive Hunting License - $250.00. This license shall be issued only to an individual resident of the State and is valid for the lifetime of the holder.

(3) Repealed by Session Laws 2013-283, s. 3, effective August 1, 2014.

(4) Controlled Hunting Preserve Hunting License - $20.00. This license shall be issued to an individual resident or nonresident to take only foxes and domestically raised game birds, other than wild turkey, only within a controlled

hunting preserve licensed and operated in accordance with G.S. 113-273(g) and implementing rules of the Wildlife Resources Commission.

(5)     Resident Annual Comprehensive Hunting License - $36.00. This license shall be issued only to an individual resident of the State.

(6)     Nonresident State Hunting License. This license shall be issued only to a nonresident. The nonresident State hunting licenses issued by the Wildlife Resources Commission are:

a.      Season License - $80.00.

b.      Ten-Day License - $60.00. This license is valid for the 10 consecutive dates indicated on the license.

(d)     One dollar ($1.00) of the proceeds received from the sale of each nonresident hunting license sold pursuant to subdivision (6) of subsection (c) of this section shall be set aside by the Wildlife Resources Commission and contributed to a proper agency or agencies in the United States for expenditure in Canada for the restoration and management of migratory waterfowl. (1935, c. 486, s. 12; 1937, c. 45, s. 1; 1945, c. 617; 1949, c. 1203, s. 1; 1957, c. 849, s. 1; 1959, c. 304; 1961, c. 384, s. 1; 1967, c. 790; 1969, c. 1030; c. 1042, ss. 1-5, 13; 1971, c. 242; c. 282, s. 1; c. 705, ss. 1, 2; 1973, c. 1262, s. 18; 1975, c. 197, ss. 1-4, 6, 8; c. 673, s. 2; 1977, c. 658; 1979, c. 830, s. 1; 1979, 2nd Sess., c. 1178, s. 1; 1981, c. 482, s. 4; 1981 (Reg. Sess., 1982), c. 1201, s. 1; 1983, c. 140, s. 1; 1987, c. 156, ss. 1, 2; 1987, c. 827, s. 98; 1989, c. 324, s. 2; c. 616, s. 2; 1989 (Reg. Sess., 1990), c. 909, s. 1; 1993 (Reg. Sess., 1994), c. 684, s. 2; 1999-339, s. 5; 2001-91, s. 2; 2013-283, s. 3.)


§ 113-270.2A. Voluntary contribution to hunter education program.

(a)     A person applying for a hunting license may make a voluntary contribution to the Wildlife Resources Commission for the purpose of funding a hunter education program.

(b)     The Wildlife Resources Commission shall devise administrative procedure for the collection of all contributions donated pursuant to the provisions of this act and shall collect and use the contributions to fund and provide for a hunter education program. (1979, c. 764, ss. 1, 2; 1987, c. 827, s. 98; 2013-63, s. 2.)


§ 113-270.2B. Voluntary migratory waterfowl conservation print.

(a) The Wildlife Resources Commission has exclusive production rights for the voluntary migratory waterfowl conservation print, and is authorized to adopt policy for the annual selection of an appropriate design for the print and to have the print produced for sale. This policy may include ownership rights of the original art selected; arrangements for the reproduction, distribution and marketing of prints; and provisions for sharing the resulting revenues.

(b) The proceeds accruing to the Commission from its share of the voluntary migratory waterfowl conservation prints shall be used by the Commission for the benefit of migratory waterfowl management in North Carolina. (1981 (Reg. Sess., 1982), c. 1269; 1987, c. 452, s. 1; c. 827, s. 98.)


§ 113-270.3. (Effective until August 1, 2014) Special activity licenses; big game kill reports.

(a) In addition to any hunting, trapping, or fishing license that may be required pursuant to G.S. 113-270.1B(a), individuals engaging in specially regulated activities must have the appropriate special activity license prescribed in this section before engaging in the regulated activity.

(b) The special activity licenses issued by the Wildlife Resources Commission are as follows:

(1) Resident Big Game Hunting License - $10.00. This license shall be issued only to an individual resident of the State and entitles the holder to take big game by all lawful methods and during all open seasons.

(1a) Nonresident Bear Hunting License - $125.00. This license is valid for use only by an individual within the State and must be procured before taking any bear within the State. Notwithstanding any other provision of law, a nonresident individual may not take any bear within the State without procuring this license; provided, that those persons who have a nonresident lifetime sportsman combination license purchased prior to May 24, 1994, shall not have to purchase this license.

(2) Nonresident Big Game Hunting License. This license shall be issued only to an individual nonresident of the State and entitles the holder to take big game by all lawful methods and during all open seasons. The nonresident big game hunting licenses issued by the Wildlife Resources Commission are:

a. Season License - $60.00.

b. Six-Day License - $40.00. This license is only valid for the six consecutive dates indicated on the license.

(2a) Bonus Antlerless Deer License - $10.00. This license shall be issued to an individual resident or nonresident of the State who holds a valid North Carolina big game hunting license or an individual resident who is exempt from the hunting license requirement in accordance with G.S. 113-276(c) and G.S. 113-276(d) and entitles the holder to take two antlerless deer during seasons and by methods authorized by the Wildlife Resources Commission. This license expires June 30.

(3) Game Land License - $15.00. This license shall be issued to an individual resident or nonresident of the State and entitles the holder to hunt and trap on game lands managed by the Wildlife Resources Commission. The Wildlife Resources Commission may, pursuant to G.S. 113-264(a), designate in its rules other activities on game lands that require purchase of this license and may charge additional fees for use of specially developed facilities.

(4) Falconry License - $10.00. This license shall be issued to an individual resident or nonresident of the State and must be procured before:

a. Taking, importing, transporting, or possessing a raptor; or

b. Taking wildlife by means of falconry.

The Wildlife Resources Commission may issue classes of falconry licenses necessary to participate in the federal/State permit system, require necessary examinations before issuing licenses or permits to engage in various authorized activities related to possession and maintenance of raptors and the sport of falconry, and regulate licenses as required by governing federal law and rules. To defray the costs of administering required examinations, the Wildlife

Resources Commission may charge reasonable fees upon giving them. To meet minimum federal standards plus other State standards in the interests of conservation of wildlife resources, the Wildlife Resources Commission may impose all necessary controls, including those set out in the sections pertaining to collection licenses and captivity licenses, and may issue permits and require reports, but no collection license or captivity license is needed in addition to the falconry license.

(5) Migratory Waterfowl Hunting License - $10.00. This license shall be issued to an individual resident or nonresident of the State and entitles the holder to take migratory waterfowl in accordance with applicable laws and regulations. The Wildlife Resources Commission may implement this license requirement through the sale of an official waterfowl stamp which may be a facsimile, in an appropriate size, of the waterfowl conservation print authorized by G.S. 113-270.2B. An amount not less than one-half of the annual proceeds from the sale of this license shall be used by the Commission for cooperative waterfowl habitat improvement projects through contracts with local waterfowl interests, with the remainder of the proceeds to be used by the Commission in its statewide programs for the conservation of waterfowl.

(c) Any individual who kills any species of big game must report the kill to the Wildlife Resources Commission. The Commission may by rule prescribe the method of making the report, prescribe its contents, and require positive identification of the carcass of the kill, by tagging or otherwise. The Wildlife Resources Commission may administratively provide for the annual issuance of big game tags or other identification for big game authorized by this section to holders of lifetime sportsman licenses and lifetime comprehensive hunting licenses.

(d) Any individual who possesses any of the lifetime sportsman licenses established by G.S. 113-270.1D(b) may engage in specially regulated activities without the licenses required by subdivisions (1), (2), (3), and (5) of subsection (b) of this section. Any individual possessing an annual sportsman license established by G.S. 113-270.1D(a) or a lifetime or annual comprehensive hunting license established by G.S. 113-270.2(c)(2) or (5) may engage in specially regulated activities without the licenses required by subdivisions (1), (3), and (5) of subsection (b) of this section.

(e) When the Wildlife Resources Commission establishes a primitive weapons season pursuant to G.S. 113-291.2(a), all of the combination hunting and fishing licenses established in G.S. 113-270.1C, sportsman licenses established in G.S. 113-270.1D, and hunting licenses established in G.S. 113-270.2(c)(1), (2), (3), (5), and (6) entitle the holder to participate. For purposes of this section, "primitive weapons" include bow and arrow, muzzle-loading firearm, and any other primitive weapon specified in the rules of the Wildlife Resources Commission. (1969, c. 1042, s. 7; 1973, c. 1097, s. 1; 1975, c. 171; c. 197, ss. 5, 7; c. 673, s. 1; 1977, c. 746, s. 1; 1979, c. 830, s. 1; 1979, 2nd Sess., c. 1178, ss. 2, 5; 1981, c. 482, s. 7; c. 620, s. 1; 1981 (Reg. Sess., 1982), c. 1201, s. 2; 1983, c. 140, ss. 2-3; 1987, c. 156, ss. 3-5; c. 452, ss. 2, 3; c. 745, s. 2; c. 827, s. 98; 1991, c. 671, s. 1; 1993 (Reg. Sess., 1994), c. 557, s. 2; 1993 (Reg. Sess., 1994), c. 684, s. 3; 1999-339, s. 6; 2001-91, s. 3; 2006-226, s. 21; 2009-214, s. 1; 2011-369, s. 3.)

§ 113-270.3. (Effective August 1, 2014) Special activity licenses; stamps; big game kill reports.

(a) In addition to any hunting, trapping, or fishing license that may be required pursuant to G.S. 113-270.1B(a), individuals engaging in specially regulated activities must have the appropriate special activity license and stamp prescribed in this section before engaging in the regulated activity.

(b) The special activity licenses and stamp issued by the Wildlife Resources Commission are as follows:

(1) Resident Big Game Hunting License - $13.00. This license shall be issued only to an individual resident of the State and entitles the holder to take big game by all lawful methods and during all open seasons.

(1a) Nonresident Bear Hunting License - $225.00. This license is valid for use only by an individual within the State and must be procured before taking any bear within the State. Notwithstanding any other provision of law, a nonresident individual may not take any bear within the State without procuring this license; provided, that those persons who have a nonresident lifetime sportsman combination license purchased prior to May 24, 1994, shall not have to purchase this license.

(1b) Bear Management Stamp - $10.00. This electronically generated stamp must be procured before taking any bear within the State. Notwithstanding any other provision of law, a resident or nonresident individual may not take any bear within the State without procuring this stamp; provided, that those persons who have purchased a lifetime license established by G.S. 113-270.1D(b), 113-270.2(c)(2), or 113-351(c)(3) prior to July 1, 2014, and those persons exempt from the license requirements as set forth in G.S. 113-276(c) and G.S. 113-276(n) shall obtain this stamp free of charge. All of the revenue generated by this stamp shall be dedicated to black bear research and management.

(2) Nonresident Big Game Hunting License. This license shall be issued only to an individual nonresident of the State and entitles the holder to take big game by all lawful methods and during all open seasons. The nonresident big game hunting licenses issued by the Wildlife Resources Commission are:

a. Season License - $80.00.

b. Ten-Day License - $60.00. This license is only valid for the 10 consecutive dates indicated on the license.

(2a) Bonus Antlerless Deer License - $10.00. This license shall be issued to an individual resident or nonresident of the State who holds a valid North Carolina big game hunting license or an individual resident who is exempt from the hunting license requirement in accordance with G.S. 113-276(c) and G.S. 113-276(d) and entitles the holder to take two antlerless deer during seasons and by methods authorized by the Wildlife Resources Commission. This license expires June 30.

(3) Game Land License - $15.00. This license shall be issued to an individual resident or nonresident of the State and entitles the holder to hunt and trap on game lands managed by the Wildlife Resources Commission. The Wildlife Resources Commission may, pursuant to G.S. 113-264(a), designate in its rules other activities on game lands that require purchase of this license and may charge additional fees for use of specially developed facilities.

(4) Falconry License - $10.00. This license shall be issued to an individual resident or nonresident of the State and must be procured before:

a. Taking, importing, transporting, or possessing a raptor; or

b. Taking wildlife by means of falconry.

The Wildlife Resources Commission may issue classes of falconry licenses necessary to participate in the federal/State permit system, require necessary examinations before issuing licenses or permits to engage in various authorized activities related to possession and maintenance of raptors and the sport of falconry, and regulate licenses as required by governing federal law and rules. To defray the costs of administering required examinations, the Wildlife Resources Commission may charge reasonable fees upon giving them. To meet minimum federal standards plus other State standards in the interests of conservation of wildlife resources, the Wildlife Resources Commission may impose all necessary controls, including those set out in the sections pertaining to collection licenses and captivity licenses, and may issue permits and require reports, but no collection license or captivity license is needed in addition to the falconry license.

(5) Migratory Waterfowl Hunting License - $13.00. This license shall be issued to an individual resident or nonresident of the State and entitles the holder to take migratory waterfowl in accordance with applicable laws and regulations. The Wildlife Resources Commission may implement this license requirement through the sale of an official waterfowl stamp which may be a facsimile, in an appropriate size, of the waterfowl conservation print authorized by G.S. 113-270.2B. An amount not less than one-half of the annual proceeds from the sale of this license shall be used by the Commission for cooperative waterfowl habitat improvement projects through contracts with local waterfowl interests, with the remainder of the proceeds to be used by the Commission in its statewide programs for the conservation of waterfowl.

(c) Any individual who kills any species of big game must report the kill to the Wildlife Resources Commission. The Commission may by rule prescribe the method of making the report, prescribe its contents, and require positive identification of the carcass of the kill, by tagging or otherwise. The Wildlife Resources Commission may administratively provide for the annual issuance of big game tags or other identification for big game authorized by this section to holders of lifetime sportsman licenses and lifetime comprehensive hunting licenses.

(d) Any individual who possesses any of the lifetime sportsman licenses established by G.S. 113-270.1D(b) may engage in specially regulated activities without the licenses required by subdivisions (1), (2), (3), and (5) of subsection (b) of this section. Any individual possessing an annual sportsman license established by G.S. 113-270.1D(a) or a lifetime or annual comprehensive hunting license established by G.S.113-270.2(c)(2) or (5) may engage in specially regulated activities without the licenses required by subdivisions (1), (3), and (5) of subsection (b) of this section.

(e) When the Wildlife Resources Commission establishes a primitive weapons season pursuant to G.S. 113-291.2(a), all of the combination hunting and fishing licenses established in G.S.113-270.1C, sportsman licenses established in G.S. 113-270.1D, and hunting licenses established in G.S. 113-270.2(c)(1), (2), (3), (5), and (6) entitle the holder to participate. For purposes of this section, "primitive weapons" include bow and arrow, muzzle-loading firearm, and any other primitive weapon specified in the rules of the Wildlife Resources Commission. (1969, c. 1042, s. 7; 1973, c. 1097, s. 1; 1975, c. 171; c. 197, ss. 5, 7; c. 673, s. 1; 1977, c. 746, s. 1; 1979, c. 830, s. 1; 1979, 2nd Sess., c. 1178, ss. 2, 5; 1981, c. 482, s. 7; c. 620, s. 1; 1981 (Reg. Sess., 1982), c. 1201, s. 2; 1983, c. 140, ss. 2-3; 1987, c. 156, ss. 3-5; c. 452, ss. 2, 3; c. 745, s. 2; c. 827, s. 98; 1991, c. 671, s. 1; 1993 (Reg. Sess., 1994), c. 557, s. 2; 1993 (Reg. Sess., 1994), c. 684, s. 3; 1999-339, s. 6; 2001-91, s. 3; 2006-226, s. 21; 2009-214, s. 1; 2011-369, s. 3; 2013-283, s. 4.)


§ 113-270.4. Hunting and fishing guide license.

(a) No one may serve for hire as a hunting or fishing guide without having first procured a current and valid hunting and fishing guide license. This license is valid only for use by an individual meeting the criteria set by the Wildlife Resources Commission for issuance of the license subject to the limitations set forth in this section. Possession of the hunting and fishing guide license does not relieve the guide from meeting other applicable license requirements.

(b) (Effective until August 1, 2014) The hunting and fishing guide licenses issued by the Wildlife Resources are:

(1) Resident Hunting and Fishing Guide License - $10.00. This license is valid for use only by an individual resident of the State.

(2) Nonresident Hunting and Fishing Guide License - $ 100.00. This license is valid for use by a nonresident individual in the State.

(b) (Effective August 1, 2014) The hunting and fishing guide licenses issued by the Wildlife Resources are:

(1) Resident Hunting and Fishing Guide License - $15.00. This license is valid for use only by an individual resident of the State.

(2)     Nonresident Hunting and Fishing Guide License - $150.00. This license is valid for use by a nonresident individual in the State.

(c)     The Wildlife Resources Commission may by rule provide for the qualifications and duties of hunting and fishing guides. In implementing this section, the Wildlife Resources Commission may delegate to the Executive Director and his subordinates administrative responsibilities concerning the selection and supervision of hunting and fishing guides, except that provisions relating to revocation of hunting and fishing guide licenses must be substantially set out in the rules of the Wildlife Resources Commission. (1935, c. 486, s. 12; 1937, c. 45, s. 1; 1945, c. 617; 1949, c. 1203, s. 1; 1957, c. 849, s. 1; 1959, c. 304; 1961, c. 834, s. 1; 1967, c. 790; 1969, c. 1030; c. 1042, ss. 1-5; 1971, c. 242, c. 282, s. 1; c. 705, ss. 1, 2; 1973, c. 1262, s. 18; 1975, c. 197, ss. 1-4; 1977, c. 658; 1979, c. 830, s. 1; 1981 (Reg. Sess., 1982), c. 1201, s. 3; 1983, c. 140, s. 4; 1987, c. 156, s. 6; c. 827, s. 98; 1991 (Reg. Sess., 1992), c. 989, s. 1; 1993, c. 553, s. 32.1; 2001-91, s. 4; 2013-283, s. 5.)

§ 113-270.5.  Trapping licenses.

(a)     Except as otherwise specifically provided by law, no one may take fur-bearing animals by trapping, or by any other authorized special method that preserves the pelt from injury, without first having procured a current and valid trapping license. When the trapping license is required, it serves in lieu of a hunting license in the taking of fur-bearing animals. If fur-bearing animals are taken as game, at the times and by the hunting methods that may be authorized, hunting license requirements apply.

(b)     (Effective until August 1, 2014) The trapping licenses issued by the Wildlife Resources Commission are as follows:

(1)     Resident State Trapping License - $25.00. This license is valid only for use by an individual resident of the State.

(2)     Resident County Trapping License - $10.00. This license is valid only for use by an individual resident of the State within the county in which he resides.

(3)     Nonresident State Trapping License - $100.00. This license is valid for use by an individual within the State.

(b) (Effective August 1, 2014) The trapping licenses issued by the Wildlife Resources Commission are as follows:

(1) Resident State Trapping License - $30.00. This license is valid only for use by an individual resident of the State.

(2) Repealed by Session Laws 2013-283, s. 6, effective August 1, 2014.

(3) Nonresident State Trapping License - $125.00. This license is valid for use by an individual within the State. (1929, c. 278, s. 3; 1969, c. 1042, s. 6; 1973, c. 1262, s. 18; 1975, c. 197, ss. 9-11; 1979, c. 830, s. 1; 1981 (Reg. Sess., 1982), c. 1201, s. 4; 1983, c. 140, s. 5; 1987, c. 156, s. 7; c. 827, s. 98; 2001-91, s. 5; 2013-283, s. 6.)


§ 113-271. Hook-and-line licenses in inland and joint fishing waters.

(a) An inland hook-and-line fishing license issued under this section entitles the licensee to fish with hook and line in inland fishing waters and joint fishing waters. An inland hook-and-line fishing license issued under this section does not entitle the licensee to engage in recreational fishing in coastal fishing waters that are not joint fishing waters. An inland hook-and-line fishing license issued under subdivision (1), (3), (6a), (6b), (6c), or (9) of subsection (d) of this section entitles the licensee to fish with hook and line in public mountain trout waters.

(b) Repealed by Session Laws 1993 (Reg. Sess., 1994), c. 684, s. 4.

(c) Repealed by Session Laws 1979, c. 830, s. 1.

(d) (Effective until August 1, 2014) The hook-and-line fishing licenses issued by the Wildlife Resources Commission are as follows:

(1) Resident Annual Comprehensive Inland Fishing License - $20.00. This license shall be issued only to an individual resident of the State.

(2) Resident State Inland Fishing License - $15.00. This license shall be issued only to an individual resident of the State.

(3) Lifetime Resident Comprehensive Inland Fishing License - $250.00. This license shall be issued only to an individual resident of the State and is valid for the lifetime of the licensee.

(4) Resident County Inland Fishing License - $10.00. This license shall be issued only to an individual resident of the State and is valid only within the county of residence of the licensee.

(5) Nonresident State Inland Fishing License - $30.00. This license shall be issued to an individual nonresident of the State.

(6) Short-Term Inland Fishing Licenses. Short-term inland fishing licenses are valid only for the date or consecutive dates indicated on the licenses. Short-term inland fishing licenses issued by the Wildlife Resources Commission are:

a. Resident 10-day Inland Fishing License - $5.00. This license shall be issued only to a resident of the State.

b. Nonresident 10-day Inland Fishing License - $10.00. This license shall be issued only to a nonresident of the State.

c. Repealed by Session Laws 2005-455, s. 1.8, effective January 1, 2007.

(6a) Age 65 Resident Lifetime Inland Fishing License - $15.00. This license shall be issued only to an individual resident of the State who is at least 65 years of age.

(6b) Resident Disabled Veteran Lifetime Inland Fishing License - $10.00. This license shall be issued only to an individual who is a resident of the State and who is a fifty percent (50%) or more disabled veteran as determined by the United States Department of Veterans Affairs. This license remains valid for the lifetime of the licensee so long as the licensee remains fifty percent (50%) or more disabled.

(6c) Resident Totally Disabled Lifetime Inland Fishing License - $10.00. This license shall be issued only to an individual who is a resident of the State and who is totally and permanently disabled as determined by the Social Security Administration. This license remains valid for the lifetime of the licensee.

(7), (8) Repealed by Session Laws 2005-455, s. 1.8, effective January 1, 2007.

(9) Special Landholder and Guest Fishing License - $50.00. This license shall be issued only to the landholder of private property bordering inland or joint fishing waters. This license shall entitle the landholder and guests of the landholder to fish from the shore or any pier or dock originating from the property without any additional fishing license. This license is applicable only to private property and private docks and piers and is not valid for any public property, pier, or dock nor for any private property, pier, or dock operated for any commercial purpose whatsoever. This license shall not be in force unless displayed on the premises of the property and only entitles fishing without additional license to persons fishing from the licensed property and then only when fishing within the private property lines. This license is not transferable as to person or location. For purposes of this subdivision, a guest is any individual invited by the landholder to fish from the property at no charge. A charge includes any fee, assessment, dues, rent, or other consideration which must be paid, whether directly or indirectly, in order to be allowed to fish from the property, regardless of the stated reason for such charge.

(d) (Effective August 1, 2014) The hook-and-line fishing licenses issued by the Wildlife Resources Commission are as follows:

(1) Resident Annual Comprehensive Inland Fishing License - $25.00. This license shall be issued only to an individual resident of the State.

(2) Resident State Inland Fishing License - $20.00. This license shall be issued only to an individual resident of the State.

(3) Lifetime Resident Comprehensive Inland Fishing License - $250.00. This license shall be issued only to an individual resident of the State and is valid for the lifetime of the licensee.

(4) Repealed by Session Laws 2013-283, s. 7, effective August 1, 2014.

(5) Nonresident State Inland Fishing License - $36.00. This license shall be issued to an individual nonresident of the State.

(6) Short-Term Inland Fishing Licenses. Short-term inland fishing licenses are valid only for the date or consecutive dates indicated on the licenses. Short-term inland fishing licenses issued by the Wildlife Resources Commission are:

a. Resident 10-day Inland Fishing License - $7.00. This license shall be issued only to a resident of the State.

b. Nonresident 10-day Inland Fishing License - $18.00. This license shall be issued only to a nonresident of the State.

c. Repealed by Session Laws 2005-455, s. 1.8, effective January 1, 2007.

(6a) Age 70 Resident Lifetime Inland Fishing License - $15.00. This license shall be issued only to an individual resident of the State who is at least 70 years of age.

(6b) Resident Disabled Veteran Lifetime Inland Fishing License - $10.00. This license shall be issued only to an individual who is a resident of the State and who is a fifty percent (50%) or more disabled veteran as determined by the United States Department of Veterans Affairs or as established by rules of the Wildlife Resources Commission. This license remains valid for the lifetime of the licensee so long as the licensee remains fifty percent (50%) or more disabled.

(6c) Resident Totally Disabled Lifetime Inland Fishing License - $10.00. This license shall be issued only to an individual who is a resident of the State and who is totally and permanently disabled as determined by the Social Security Administration or as established by rules of the Wildlife Resources Commission. This license remains valid for the lifetime of the licensee.

(7), (8) Repealed by Session Laws 2005-455, s. 1.8, effective January 1, 2007.

(9) Special Landholder and Guest Fishing License - $100.00. This license shall be issued only to the landholder of private property bordering inland or joint fishing waters. This license shall entitle the landholder and guests of the landholder to fish from the shore or any pier or dock originating from the property without any additional fishing license. This license is applicable only to private property and private docks and piers and is not valid for any public property, pier, or dock nor for any private property, pier, or dock operated for any commercial purpose whatsoever. This license shall not be in force unless displayed on the premises of the property and only entitles fishing without additional license to persons fishing from the licensed property and then only when fishing within the private property lines. This license is not transferable as to person or location. For purposes of this subdivision, a guest is any individual invited by the landholder to fish from the property at no charge. A charge includes any fee, assessment, dues, rent, or other consideration which must be paid, whether directly or indirectly, in order to be allowed to fish from the property, regardless of the stated reason for such charge. (1929, c. 335, ss. 1-

4; 1931, c. 351; 1933, c. 236; 1935, c. 478; 1945, c. 529, ss. 1, 2; c. 567, ss. 1-4; 1949, c. 1203, s. 2; 1953, c. 1147; 1955, c. 198, s. 1; 1957, c. 849, s. 2; 1959, c. 164; 1961, c. 312; c. 834, ss. 3-6; 1965, c. 957, s. 2; 1969, c. 761; c. 1042, s. 9; 1973, c. 476, s. 143; c. 504; 1975, c. 197, s. 15; 1979, c. 737, ss. 1, 2; c. 748, s. 6; c. 830, s. 1; 1979, 2nd Sess., c. 1178, ss. 3, 5; 1981, c. 482, s. 5; 1981 (Reg. Sess., 1982), c. 1201, s. 5; 1983, c. 140, s. 6; 1987, c. 156, ss. 8, 9; c. 827, s. 98; 1989 (Reg. Sess., 1990), c. 909, s. 2; c. 926; 1993 (Reg. Sess., 1994), c. 684, s. 4; 1995, c. 535, s. 6.1; 1997-443, s. 11A.118(a); 1999-456, s. 28.; 2005-455, s. 1.8; 2006-255, s. 8; 2013-283, s. 7.)

§ 113-272. Special trout license; mountain heritage trout waters 3-day fishing license.

(a)     License Required. - Except as provided in G.S. 113-270.1D, G.S. 113-270.1C(b), and G.S. 113-271(a), no one may fish in public mountain trout waters without having first procured a current and valid special trout license in addition to a hook-and-line fishing license required in G.S. 113-271. When public mountain trout waters occur on game lands, this license entitles the holder to use game lands only for the purpose of access to public mountain trout waters to fish with hook and line.

(b)     Repealed by Session Laws 1993 (Reg. Sess., 1994), c. 684, s. 5, effective July 1, 1995.

(c)     Definitions. - As used in this section:

(1)     City has the same meaning as in G.S. 160A-1.

(2)     Mountain heritage trout waters are those waters that have been designated as public mountain trout waters by the Wildlife Resources Commission, and that run through or are adjacent to a city that has been designated as a Mountain Heritage Trout City pursuant to G.S. 113-272.3(e).

(3)     Public mountain trout waters are those waters so designated by the Wildlife Resources Commission which are managed and regulated to sustain a mountain trout fishery.

(d) (Effective until August 1, 2014) Special Trout License: Fee. - $10.00. This license shall be issued to an individual resident or nonresident of the State and entitles the holder to fish with hook and line in public mountain trout waters.

(d) (Effective August 1, 2014) Special Trout License: Fee. - $13.00. This license shall be issued to an individual resident or nonresident of the State and entitles the holder to fish with hook and line in public mountain trout waters.

(e) Mountain Heritage Trout Waters 3-Day Fishing License: Fee. - $5.00. This license shall be issued to an individual resident or nonresident of the State and shall entitle the holder to fish in waters designated by the Wildlife Resources Commission as mountain heritage trout waters for the three consecutive days indicated on the license. An individual who holds a mountain heritage trout waters 3-day fishing license does not need to hold a hook-and-line fishing license issued pursuant to G.S. 113-271 in order to fish in mountain heritage trout waters. (1953, cc. 432, 828; 1955, c. 198, s. 2; 1961, c. 834, s. 2; 1965, c. 957, s. 2; 1969, c. 1042, s. 10; 1973, c. 1262, s. 18; 1975, c. 197, s. 16; 1979, c. 748, s. 7; c. 830, s. 1; 1979, 2nd Sess., c. 1178, ss. 4, 5; 1981, c. 482, s. 6; 1981 (Reg. Sess., 1982), c. 1201, s. 6; 1983, c. 140, s. 7; 1987, c. 156, s. 10; c. 827, s. 98; 1993 (Reg. Sess., 1994), c. 684, s. 5; 2001-91, s. 6; 2007-408, ss. 1, 2; 2013-283, s. 8.)


§ 113-272.1. Repealed by Session Laws 1979, c. 830, s. 1.


§ 113-272.2. Special device licenses.

(a) Except as otherwise specifically provided by law, no one may fish in inland fishing waters with any special device without having first procured a current and valid special device license. Special devices are all devices used in fishing other than hook and line.

(b) Repealed by Session Laws 2001-91, s. 7, effective July 1, 2001.

(c) (Effective until August 1, 2014) The special device licenses issued by the Wildlife Resources Commission are as follows:

(1) Resident Noncommercial Special Device License - $10.00. Except as rules of the Wildlife Resources Commission provide for use of equipment by more than one person, this license is valid only for use by an individual resident of the State. It authorizes the taking of nongame fish from inland fishing waters with no more than three special devices authorized by the rules of the Wildlife Resources Commission for use in specified waters. The Wildlife Resources Commission may restrict the user of the license to specified registered equipment, require tagging of items of equipment, charge up to one dollar ($1.00) per tag issued, and require periodic catch data reports. Unless specifically prohibited, nongame fish lawfully taken under this license may be sold.

(1a) Resident Commercial Special Device License - $100.00. Except as rules of the Wildlife Resources Commission provide for use of equipment by more than one person, this license is valid only for use by an individual resident of the State. It authorizes the taking of nongame fish from inland fishing waters with four or more special devices authorized by the rules of the Wildlife Resources Commission for use in specified waters. The Wildlife Resources Commission may restrict the user of the license to specified registered equipment, require tagging of items of equipment, charge up to one dollar ($1.00) per tag issued, and require periodic catch data reports. Nongame fish lawfully taken under this license may be sold.

(2) Nonresident Noncommercial Special Device License - $50.00. Except as rules of the Wildlife Resources Commission provide for use of equipment by more than one person, this license is valid for use only by an individual within the State. It is otherwise subject to the terms and conditions set out in subdivision (1) of this subsection.

(2a) Nonresident Commercial Special Device License - $200.00. Except as rules of the Wildlife Resources Commission provide for use of equipment by more than one person, this license is valid only for use by an individual within the State. It is otherwise subject to the terms and conditions set out in subdivision (1a) of this subsection.

(3), (4) Repealed by Session Laws 1987, c. 156, s. 11.

(c) (Effective August 1, 2014) The special device licenses issued by the Wildlife Resources Commission are as follows:

(1) Repealed by Session Laws 2013-283, s. 9, effective August 1, 2014.

(1a) Resident Special Device License - $75.00. Except as rules of the Wildlife Resources Commission provide for use of equipment by more than one person, this license is valid only for use by an individual resident of the State. It authorizes the taking of nongame fish from inland fishing waters with special devices authorized by the rules of the Wildlife Resources Commission for use in specified waters. The Wildlife Resources Commission may restrict the user of the license to specified registered equipment, require tagging of items of equipment, charge up to one dollar ($1.00) per tag issued, and require periodic catch data reports. Nongame fish lawfully taken under this license may be sold.

(2) Repealed by Session Laws 2013-283, s. 9, effective August 1, 2014.

(2a) Nonresident Special Device License - $500.00. Except as rules of the Wildlife Resources Commission provide for use of equipment by more than one person, this license is valid only for use by an individual within the State. It is otherwise subject to the terms and conditions set out in subdivision (1a) of this subsection.

(3), (4) Repealed by Session Laws 1987, c. 156, s. 11.

(d) Repealed by Session Laws 1995, c. 36, s. 2. (1979, c. 830, s. 1; 1981, c. 620, s. 2; 1981 (Reg. Sess., 1982), c. 1201, s. 7; 1983, c. 140, s. 8; 1987, c. 156, ss. 11, 12; c. 827, s. 98; 1993 (Reg. Sess., 1994), c. 778, s. 1; 1995, c. 36, s. 2; 2001-91, s. 7; 2013-283, s. 9.)


§ 113-272.3. Special provisions respecting fishing licenses; grabbling; taking bait fish; use of landing nets; lifetime licenses issued from Wildlife Resources Commission headquarters; personalized lifetime sportsman combination licenses.

(a) The Wildlife Resources Commission by rule may define the meaning of "hook and line" and "special device" as applied to fishing techniques. Any technique of fishing that may be lawfully authorized which employs neither the use of any special device nor hook and line must be pursued under the appropriate hook-and-line fishing license.

(b) In accordance with established fishing customs and the orderly conservation of wildlife resources, the Wildlife Resources Commission may by rule provide for use of nets or other special devices which it may authorize as an incident to hook-and-line fishing or for procuring bait fish without requiring a special device license. In this instance, however, the individual fishing must meet applicable hook-and-line license requirements.

(c) Lifetime licenses are issued from the Wildlife Resources Commission headquarters. Each application for an Infant Lifetime Sportsman or Youth Lifetime Sportsman License must be accompanied by a certified copy of the birth certificate, adoption order containing the date of birth, or other proof of age satisfactory to the Commission, of the individual to be named as the licensee.

(d) In issuing lifetime licenses, the Wildlife Resources Commission is authorized to adopt rules to establish a personalized series for certain license types and to charge a five dollar ($5.00) administrative fee, to be deposited in the Wildlife Fund, to defray the cost of issuance of the personalized license. (1979, c. 830, s. 1; 1981, c. 482, s. 8; c. 620, s. 3; 1987, c. 827, s. 98; 1993 (Reg. Sess., 1994), c. 684, s. 6.1; 2005-455, s. 1.9; 2006-255, s. 9.)

§ 113-272.4. Collection licenses.

(a) In the interest of the orderly and efficient conservation of wildlife resources, the Wildlife Resources Commission may provide for the licensing of qualified individuals to take any of the wildlife resources of the State under a collection license that may serve in lieu of any other license required in this Article. This license authorizes incidental transportation and possession of the wildlife resources necessary to implement the authorized purposes of the taking, but the Wildlife Resources Commission in its discretion may additionally impose permit requirements under subsection (d) below and G.S. 113-274.

(b) The Wildlife Resources Commission may delegate to the Executive Director the authority to impose time limits during which the license is valid and restrictions as to what may be taken and method of taking and possession, in the interests of conservation objectives. The Executive Director through his responsible agents must determine whether a particular license applicant meets the standards and qualifications for licensees set by the Wildlife Resources Commission. Methods of taking under a collection license need not be restricted to those applicable to ordinary hunting, trapping, or fishing, but the licensee must observe the restrictions as to taking, transportation, and possession imposed by the Executive Director upon the granting of the license.

(c) When a more limited duration period is not set by the Executive Director in implementing the rules of the Wildlife Resources Commission, collection licenses are valid from January 1 through December 31 in any year. This license is issued upon payment of five dollars ($5.00), but the Wildlife Resources Commission may provide for issuance without charge to licensees who represent educational or scientific institutions or some governmental agency.

(d) As necessary, the Executive Director may administratively impose on licensees under this section restrictions upon individuals taking, transporting, or possessing under the license which will permit ready identification and control of those involved in the interest of efficient administration of laws pertaining to wildlife resources. Restrictions may include requirements as to record keeping, tagging, marking packages, cages, or containers and exhibition of additional limited-purpose and limited-time permits that may be issued without charge to cover particular activities and other actions that may be administratively required in the reasonable implementation of the objectives of this Subchapter.

(e) If the Executive Director deems it administratively appropriate and convenient to do so, in the interests of simplifying the administration of licensing requirements, he may grant particular licensees under this section the privilege of utilizing assistants in taking, transporting, or possessing wildlife resources who themselves are not licensed. Any assistants so taking, transporting, or possessing wildlife resources must have readily available for inspection a written authorization from the licensee to engage in the activity in question. The written authorization must contain information administratively required by the Executive Director, and a copy of the authorization must be placed in the mail addressed to the Executive Director or his designated agent before any assistant acts under the authorization. In his discretion the Executive Director may refuse to issue, refuse to renew, or revoke the privilege conferred in this subsection. If this is done, each individual engaged in taking, transporting, or possessing wildlife resources under this section must meet all applicable licensing and permit requirements. (1979, c. 830, s. 1; 1987, c. 827, s. 98.)

§ 113-272.5. Captivity license.

(a) In the interests of humane treatment of wild animals and wild birds that are lawfully taken, crippled, tame, or unfit for immediate release into their natural habitat, the Wildlife Resources Commission may license qualified individuals to hold at a specified location one or more of any particular species of wild animal or wild bird alive in captivity for scientific, educational, exhibition, or other purposes. Before issuing this license, the Executive Director must satisfy himself that issuance of the license is appropriate under the objectives of this Subchapter, and that the wild animal or wild bird was not acquired unlawfully or merely as a pet. Upon refusing to issue the captivity license, the Executive Director may either take possession of the wild animal or wild bird for appropriate disposition or issue a captivity permit under G.S. 113-274(c)(1b) for a limited period until the holder makes proper disposition of the wild animal or wild bird.

(b) Unless a shorter time is set for a license upon its issuance under the provisions of subsection (c), captivity licenses are annual licenses issued beginning January 1 each year and running until the following December 31. This license is issued upon payment of five dollars ($5.00) to the Wildlife Resources Commission.

(c) The Wildlife Resources Commission may require standards of caging and care and reports to and supervision by employees of the Wildlife Resources Commission as necessary to insure humane treatment and furtherance of the objectives of this Subchapter. The Executive Director in implementing the provisions of this section may administratively impose through responsible agents and employees restrictions upon the mode of captivity that he deems necessary, including prescribing methods of treatment and handling designed, if possible, to enable the wild animal or wild bird to become self-sufficient and requiring that the wild animal or wild bird be set free when self-sufficiency is attained. To this end, the Executive Director may issue the captivity license with an expiration date earlier than December 31 and may also act to terminate any captivity license earlier than the expiration date for good cause.

(d) Any substantial deviation from reasonable requirements imposed by rule or administratively under the authority of this section renders possession of the wild animal or wild bird unlawful.

(e) No captivity license may be issued for any cougar (Felis concolor), except to:

(1) A bona fide publicly supported zoo.

(2) An educational or scientific research institution.

(3)     An individual who lawfully possessed the cougar on June 29, 1977. The license may not be granted, however, for possession of a cougar within a municipality which prohibits such possession by ordinance.

(4)     An individual who holds a cougar without caging under conditions simulating a natural habitat, the development of which is in accord with plans and specifications developed by the holder and approved by the Wildlife Resources Commission.

(f)     The licensing provisions of this section apply to black bears held in captivity, but, to the extent that it differs from this section, Article 2 of Chapter 19A of the General Statutes governs the keeping of black bears in captivity. (1979, c. 830, s. 1; 1979, 2nd Sess., c. 1285, s. 3; 1981, c. 575, s. 1; 1987, c. 827, s. 98; 2013-3, s. 1.)


§ 113-272.6.  Transportation of cervids and licensing of captive cervid facilities.

(a)     The Wildlife Resources Commission shall regulate the transportation, including importation and exportation, and possession of cervids, including game carcasses and parts of game carcasses extracted by hunters. The Commission shall adopt rules to implement this section, including requirements for captivity licenses, captivity permits, and transportation permits. The rules adopted pursuant to this section shall establish standards of care for the transportation and possession of cervids, including requirements for fencing, tagging, record keeping, and inspection of captive cervid facilities. Notwithstanding any other provision of law, the Commission may charge a fee of up to fifty dollars ($50.00) for the processing of applications for captivity licenses, captivity permits, and transportation permits, and the renewal or modification of those licenses and permits. The fees collected shall be applied to the costs of administering this section.

(b)     The Wildlife Resources Commission shall notify every applicant for a transportation permit that any permit issued is subject to the applicant's compliance with the Department of Agriculture and Consumer Services' requirements for transportation pursuant to Article 34 of Chapter 106 of the General Statutes.

(c)     The Department of Agriculture and Consumer Services shall regulate the production and sale of farmed cervids for commercial purposes pursuant to G.S. 106-549.97.

(d)     Notwithstanding any other provision of law, the North Carolina Wildlife Resources Commission shall issue captivity licenses, captivity permits, or transportation permits to any person possessing cervids that were held in captivity by that person prior to May 17, 2002, if the Executive Director finds that the applicant has come into compliance with all applicable rules related to the holding of cervids in captivity by January 1, 2004, and that issuance of such license or permit does not pose unreasonable risk to the conservation of wildlife resources.

(e)     Any captivity license, captivity permit, or cervids held contrary to the provisions of this section may be subject to forfeiture and disposition in accordance with the provisions of G.S. 113-137 or G.S. 113-276.2. (2003-344, s. 5.)


§ 113-273.  Dealer licenses.

(a)     "Dealer" Defined; All Licenses Annual. - As used in this section, the word "dealer" includes all persons or individuals required to be licensed under the terms of this section. Except when indicated otherwise, dealer licenses are annual licenses issued beginning January 1 each year running until the following December 31.

(b)     License Required; Rules Governing Licensee. - Except as otherwise provided, no person may engage in any activity for which a dealer license is provided under this section without first having procured a current and valid dealer license for that activity. In implementing the provisions of this section, the Wildlife Resources Commission may by rule govern every aspect of the licensee's dealings in wildlife resources. Specifically, these rules may require dealers to:

(1)     Implement a system of tagging or otherwise identifying and controlling species regulated under the license and pay a reasonable fee, not to exceed two dollars and twenty-five cents ($2.25), for each tag furnished by the Wildlife Resources Commission;

(2) Keep records and statistics in record books furnished by the Wildlife Resources Commission, and pay a reasonable charge to defray the cost of furnishing the books;

(3) Be subject to inspection at reasonable hours and audit of wildlife resources and pertinent records and equipment;

(4) Make periodic reports;

(5) Post performance bonds payable to the Wildlife Resources Commission conditioned upon faithful compliance with provisions of law; and

(6) Otherwise comply with reasonable rules and administrative requirements that may be imposed under the authority of this section.

(c) Repealed by Session Laws 1993, c. 18, s. 3.

(d) Repealed by Session Laws 1979, c. 830, s. 1.

(e) Repealed by Session Laws 1993, c. 18, s. 3.

(f) Fur-Dealer License. - Except as otherwise provided in this subsection, any individual in this State who deals in furs must obtain an appropriate fur-dealer license. For the purposes of this subsection, "dealing in furs" is engaging in the business of buying or selling fur-bearing animals or other wild animals that may lawfully be sold, the raw furs, pelts, or skins of those animals, or the furs, pelts, or skins of wild animals which may not themselves be sold but whose fur, pelt, or skin may lawfully be sold. A hunter or trapper who has lawfully taken wild animals whose fur, pelt, or skin is permitted to be sold under this subsection is not considered a fur dealer if he exclusively sells the animals or the furs, pelts, and skins, as appropriate, to licensed fur dealers. All fur-dealer licenses are annual licenses issued beginning July 1 each year running until the following June 30. Fur-dealer licenses issued by the Wildlife Resources Commission are as follows:

(1) Resident fur-dealer license, sixty dollars ($60.00). Authorizes an individual resident of the State to deal in furs in accordance with the rules of the Wildlife Resources Commission.

(2) Nonresident fur-dealer license, three hundred dollars ($300.00). Authorizes an individual within the State to deal in furs in accordance with the rules of the Wildlife Resources Commission.

(3) Fur-dealer station license, one hundred twenty dollars ($120.00). Authorizes a person or individual to deal in furs at an established location where fur dealings occur under the supervision of a responsible individual manager named in the license. Individual employees of the business dealing in furs solely at the established location under the supervision of the manager need not acquire an individual license. Any employee who also deals in furs outside the established location must obtain the appropriate individual license. Individuals dealing in furs at an established location may elect to do so under their individual licenses.

The Executive Director may administratively provide for reissuance of a station license without charge for the remainder of the year when either a business continues at an established location under a new supervising manager or the business changes to a new location. Before reissuing the license, however, the Executive Director must satisfy himself that there is a continuation of essentially the same business previously licensed and that any new supervising manager meets the qualifications imposed by rules of the Wildlife Resources Commission. The supervising manager must file the names of all employees of the business covered by a fur-dealer station license, whether temporary or permanent, including employees who process or skin the animals.

The Executive Director must furnish supervising managers and individual licensees with forms or record books for recording required information as to purchase, sale, importation, exportation, and other dealings, and make a reasonable charge to cover the costs of any record books furnished. It is unlawful for anyone dealing in furs to fail to submit reports required by rules or reasonable administrative directives.

(g) Controlled Hunting Preserve Operator License. - The Wildlife Resources Commission is authorized by rule to set standards for and to license the operation of controlled hunting preserves operated by private persons. Controlled hunting preserves are of two types: one is an area marked with appropriate signs along the outside boundaries on which only domestically raised game birds other than wild turkeys are taken; the other is an area enclosed with a dog-proof fence on which foxes and coyotes may be hunted with dogs only. A controlled fox and coyote hunting preserve operated for private use may be of any size; a controlled hunting preserve operated for commercial purposes shall be an area of not less than 500 acres or of such size as set by regulation of the Wildlife Resources Commission, which shall take into account differences in terrain and topography, as well as the welfare of the wildlife.

Operators of controlled fox hunting preserves may purchase live foxes and coyotes from licensed trappers who live-trap foxes and coyotes during any open season for trapping them and may, at any time, take live foxes from their preserves for sale to other licensed operators. The controlled hunting preserve operator license may be purchased for a fee of fifty dollars ($50.00), and is an annual license issued beginning 1 July each year running until the following 30 June.

(h)     Game Bird Propagation License. - No person may propagate game birds in captivity or possess game birds for propagation without first procuring a license under this subsection. The Wildlife Resources Commission may by rule prescribe the activities to be covered by the propagation license, which species of game birds may be propagated, and the manner of keeping and raising the birds, in accordance with the overall objectives of conservation of wildlife resources. Except as limited by this subsection, propagated game birds may be raised and sold for purposes of propagation, stocking, food, or taking in connection with dog training as authorized in G.S. 113-291.1(d). Migratory game bird operations authorized under this subsection must also comply with any applicable provisions of federal law and rules. The Wildlife Resources Commission may impose requirements as to shipping, marking packages, banding, tagging, or wrapping the propagated birds and other restrictions designed to reduce the change of illicit game birds being disposed of under the cover of licensed operations. The Wildlife Resources Commission may make a reasonable charge for any bands, tags, or wrappers furnished propagators. The game bird propagation license is issued by the Wildlife Resources Commission upon payment of a fee of five dollars ($5.00). It authorizes a person or individual to propagate and sell game birds designated in the license, in accordance with the rules of the Wildlife Resources Commission, except:

(1)     Wild turkey and ruffed grouse may not be sold for food.

(2)     Production and sale of pen-raised quail for food purposes is under the exclusive control of the Department of Agriculture and Consumer Services. The Wildlife Resources Commission, however, may regulate the possession, propagation, and transportation of live pen-raised quail.

Wild turkey acquired or raised under a game bird propagation license shall be confined in a cage or pen approved by the Wildlife Resources Commission and no such wild turkey shall be released for any purpose or allowed to range free. It is a Class 3 misdemeanor to sell wild turkey or ruffed grouse for food purposes, to sell quail other than lawfully acquired pen-raised quail for food purposes, or to release or allow wild turkey to range free.

(i)     Furbearer Propagation License. - No person may engage in propagation in captivity or possess any species of furbearers for propagation for the purpose of selling the animals or their pelts for use as fur without first procuring a license under this subsection. The furbearer propagation license is issued by the Wildlife Resources Commission upon payment of a fee of twenty-five dollars ($25.00). It authorizes the propagation or sale of the pelts or carcasses of the species of furbearing animals named therein, including bobcats, opossums and raccoons, or red and silver foxes (Vulpes vulpes), for use as fur. The Wildlife Resources Commission may by rule prescribe the activities covered by the license, the manner of keeping and raising the animals and the manner of killing them prior to sale, in accordance with overall objectives of conservation of wildlife resources and humane treatment of wild animals raised in captivity. The Wildlife Resources Commission may require tagging of the pelts or carcasses of the animals prior to sale in accordance with the provisions of G.S. 113-276.1(5) and G.S. 113-291.4(g). It is unlawful for any person licensed under this subsection to sell any pelt or carcass of any furbearing animal or fox to any other person who is not lawfully authorized to buy and possess the same, or to sell or deliver a live specimen of any such animal to any person who is not authorized to buy or receive and to hold the animal in captivity.

(j)     [Reserved.]

(k)     Taxidermy License. - Any individual who engages in taxidermy involving wildlife for any compensation, including reimbursement for the cost of materials, must first procure a taxidermy license. This license is an annual license issued by the Wildlife Resources Commission for ten dollars ($10.00). The Wildlife Resources Commission must require a licensee to keep records concerning any wildlife taken or possessed by him; to keep records of the names and addresses of persons bringing him wildlife, the names and addresses of persons taking the wildlife if different, and other information concerning the origin of the wildlife; to inspect any applicable licenses or permits pertaining to the taking and possession of wildlife brought to him; to restrict him to taxidermy upon lawfully acquired wildlife; and to keep other pertinent records. No taxidermist subject to license requirements may sell any game or game fish in which he deals except that a taxidermist may acquire a valid possessory lien upon game or game fish under the terms of Chapter 44A of the General Statutes and, with a permit from the Executive Director, may sell the game or game fish under the procedure authorized in Chapter 44A. Wildlife acquired by a taxidermist is deemed "personal property" for the purposes of Chapter 44A. (1929, c. 333, ss. 1-7; c. 198, ss. 1, 2, 4; 1933, c. 337, ss. 1-4; c. 430, s. 1; 1935, c. 471, ss. 1-3; c. 486, ss. 4, 12, 21; 1937, c. 45, s. 1; 1945, c. 617; 1949, c. 1203, s. 1; 1957, cc. 386, 841; c. 849, s. 1; 1959, c. 304; 1961, c. 311; c. 834, s. 1; c. 1056; 1965, c. 957, s. 2; 1967, c. 790; 1969, c. 1030; c. 1042, ss. 1-5; 1971, c. 242; c. 282, s. 1; c. 515, s. 5; c. 705, ss. 1, 2; 1973, c. 1098; c. 1262, ss. 18, 86; 1975, c. 197, ss. 1-4, 13, 14; 1977, c. 658; 1979, c. 830, s. 1; 1981, c. 620, ss. 4-6; 1983, c. 140, s. 9; 1985, c. 476, s. 1; 1987, c. 133; c. 827, s. 98; 1989, c. 616, s. 3; 1993, c. 18, s. 3; c. 539, s. 854; 1994, Ex. Sess., c. 24, s. 14(c); 1997-261, s. 81; 2003-96, s. 1.)

§ 113-274. Permits.

(a) As used in this Article, the word "permit" refers to a written authorization issued without charge by an employee or agent of the Wildlife Resources Commission to an individual or a person to conduct some activity over which the Wildlife Resources Commission has jurisdiction. When sale of wildlife resources is permitted, rules or the directives of the Executive Director may require the retention of invoices or copies of invoices in lieu of a permit.

(b) Except as otherwise specifically provided, no one may engage in any activity for which a permit is required without having first procured a current and valid permit.

(c) The Wildlife Resources Commission may issue the following permits:

(1) Repealed by Session Laws 1979, c. 830, s. 1.

(1a) Depredation Permit. - Authorizes the taking, destruction, transfer, removal, transplanting, or driving away of undesirable, harmful, predatory, excess, or surplus wildlife or wildlife resources. Livestock or poultry owners shall be issued a depredation permit for coyotes upon request. The permit must state the manner of taking and the disposition of wildlife or wildlife resources authorized or required and the time for which the permit is valid, plus other restrictions that may be administratively imposed in accordance with rules of the

Wildlife Resources Commission. No depredation permit or any license is needed for the owner or lessee of property to take wildlife while committing depredations upon the property. The Wildlife Resources Commission may regulate the manner of taking and the disposition of wildlife taken without permit or license, including wildlife killed accidentally by motor vehicle or in any other manner.

(1b)    Captivity Permit. - Authorizes the possession of live wildlife that may lawfully be permitted to be retained alive, in accordance with governing rules of the Wildlife Resources Commission. This permit may not substitute for any required collection license or captivity license, but may be temporarily issued for possession of wild animals or wild birds for scientific, educational, exhibition, or other purposes pending action on a captivity license or following its denial or termination. If this permit is issued for fish to be held indefinitely, the Wildlife Resources Commission may provide for periodic renewals of the permit, at least once each three years, to insure a review of the circumstances and conditions under which fish are kept. Wild animals and wild birds kept temporarily in captivity under this permit must be humanely treated and in accordance with any stipulations in the permit, but the standards of caging and care applicable to species kept under the captivity license do not apply unless specified in the permit. Any substantial deviation from reasonable requirements imposed by rule or administratively under the authority of this section renders the possession of the wildlife unlawful.

(1c)    Possession Permit. - Authorizes the possession of dead wildlife or other wildlife resources lawfully acquired. The Wildlife Resources Commission may by rule implement the issuance and supervision of this permit, in accordance with governing laws and rules respecting the possession of wildlife. Any substantial deviation from reasonable requirements imposed by rule or administratively under the authority of this section renders the possession of the wildlife unlawful.

(2)    Transportation Permit. - The Wildlife Resources Commission may require the use of transportation permits by persons required to be licensed under this Article, or by persons and individuals exempt from license requirements, while transporting wildlife resources within the State - as necessary to discourage unlawful taking or dealing in wildlife resources and to control and promote the orderly and systematic transportation of wildlife resources within, into, through, and out of the State. Transportation permits may be issued for wildlife transported either dead or alive, in accordance with restrictions that may be reasonably imposed. When convenient, rules or

administrative directives may require the retention and use of an invoice or memorandum of sale, or the license or permit authorizing the taking or acquisition of the wildlife resources, as a transportation permit. When circumstances warrant, however, a separate additional transportation permit may be required. Any substantial deviation from reasonable requirements imposed by rule or administratively under the authority of this section renders the transportation of the wildlife resources unlawful.

(3)     Exportation or Importation Permit. - Authorizes the exportation or importation of wildlife resources from or into the State or from county to county. The Wildlife Resources Commission may by rule implement the issuance and supervision of this permit, in accordance with governing laws and rules respecting the exportation and importation of wildlife resources. Any substantial deviation from reasonable requirements imposed by rule or administratively under the authority of this section renders the importation or exportation of the wildlife resources unlawful.

(3a)     Trophy Wildlife Sale Permit. - Authorizes the owner of lawfully taken and possessed dead wildlife specimens or their parts that are mounted, stuffed, or otherwise permanently preserved to sell identified individual specimens that may lawfully be sold under applicable laws and rules.

(3b)     Repealed by Session Laws 1993, c. 18, s. 4.

(3c)     Hunting Heritage Apprentice Permit. - Authorizes a person who does not meet the hunter education course requirements under G.S. 113-270.1A(a) to purchase a hunting license and hunt if accompanied by an adult at least 18 years of age who is licensed to hunt in this State or if accompanied by an adult landholder or spouse exempted from the hunting license requirement as defined by G.S. 113-276(c), provided the licensee is hunting on the landholder's land. For purposes of this section, "accompanied" means that the licensed adult maintains a proximity that enables the adult to monitor the activities of the apprentice by remaining within sight and hearing distance at all times without use of electronic devices. This permit is valid only for the term of the hunting license purchased under the authority of the permit. Any person who hunts with a permit issued under this subdivision without complying with all the requirements of this subdivision is guilty of hunting without having first procured a current and valid license, in violation of G.S. 113-270.1B.

(4)     Other Permits. - In implementing the provisions of this Subchapter, the Wildlife Resources Commission may issue permits for taking, purchase, or sale

of wildlife resources if the activity is lawfully authorized, if there is a need for control of the activity, and no other license or permit is applicable. In addition, if a specific statute so provides, a permit under this subdivision may be required in addition to a license when there is a need for closer control than provided by the license. (1935, c. 486, ss. 4, 22; 1941, c. 231, s. 1; 1965, c. 957, s. 2; 1971, c. 423, s. 2; c. 809, s. 1; 1973, c. 1262, s. 18; 1977, c. 794, s. 1; 1979, c. 830, s. 1; 1987, c. 827, s. 98; 1993, c. 18, s. 4; 2010-156, s. 2; 2013-3, s. 2; 2013-63, s. 3.)

§ 113-275. General provisions respecting licenses and permits.

(a) The Wildlife Resources Commission is authorized to make agreements with other jurisdictions as to reciprocal honoring of licenses in the best interests of the conservation of wildlife resources.

(a1) Notwithstanding the fees specified for nonresident individuals by G.S. 113-270.2, 113-270.3, 113-270.5, 113-271, 113-272, 113-272.2, and 113-273, if the Wildlife Resources Commission finds that a state has a nonresident license fee related to wildlife resources that exceeds the fee for a comparable nonresident license in North Carolina, the Wildlife Resources Commission may, by resolution in official session, increase the nonresident license fee applicable to citizens of that state to an amount equal to the fee a North Carolina resident is required to pay in that state.

The action of the Wildlife Resources Commission to increase a fee pursuant to this subsection is not subject to the provisions of Article 2A of Chapter 150B of the General Statutes. The action of the Wildlife Resources Commission to increase a fee pursuant to this subsection becomes effective on the date specified by the Wildlife Resources Commission.

(b) Every license issued under the provisions of this Article is effective beginning upon its date of issuance unless the license expressly provides to the contrary, in accordance with rules of the Wildlife Resources Commission and such administrative authority to set future effective dates in particular types of cases as may be delegated by the Wildlife Resources Commission to responsible employees or agents.

(b1) No hunting or fishing license issued to a resident under the provisions of G.S. 113-270.1C, 113-270.1D, 113-270.2, 113-270.3, 113-271, or 113-272 becomes invalid for use during the term for which it is issued by reason of a removal of the residence of the licensee to another state.

(c) Every license issued under the provisions of this Article must be sold for the full prescribed amount notwithstanding that a portion of the prescribed license period may have elapsed prior to the license application.

(c1) Upon receipt of a proper application together with a fee of five dollars ($5.00), the Wildlife Resources Commission may issue a new license or permit to replace one that has been lost or destroyed before its expiration. The application must be on a form of the Wildlife Resources Commission setting forth information in sufficient detail to allow ready identification of the lost or destroyed license or permit and ascertainment of the applicant's continued entitlement to it.

(d) In implementing the sale and distribution of licenses issued under this Article, the Wildlife Resources Commission may require license applicants to disclose such information as necessary for determining the applicant's eligibility for a particular license. Such information as deemed desirable to assist in enforcement of license requirements may be required to be recorded on the face of any license. Fixing the form of the license may be by reasonable administrative directive, and requirements as to such form need not be embodied in rules of the Wildlife Resources Commission in order to be validly required.

(e) Where employees of the Wildlife Resources Commission sell licenses of a type also sold through license agents, such employees must sell the licenses for the full amount and remit such full amount to the Wildlife Resources Commission without any deduction of the stipulated license agent's fee.

(f) Except as otherwise specifically provided by statute or except as the Wildlife Resources Commission may by rule prescribe to the contrary:

(1) All licenses and permits under this Article must be kept ready at hand by or about the person of individual licensees and permittees while engaged in the regulated operations;

(2) All licenses and permits under this Article are nontransferable; and

(3) All individuals engaged in operations subject to license or permit requirements must have an individual license or permit - except where such individuals are in the employ of and under the supervision of someone who has the license or permit or acceptable evidence of the same at hand and the activity is one for which a person not an individual may acquire a license.

(g) It is unlawful to buy, sell, lend, borrow, or in any other way transfer or receive or attempt to do any such things with respect to any nontransferable license or permit for the purpose of circumventing the requirements of this Article.

(h) It is unlawful for any person engaged in regulated operations under this Article to refuse to exhibit or display any required license, permit, or identification upon the request of any employee or agent of the Wildlife Resources Commission or of any officer authorized to enforce the provisions of this Article.

(i) It is unlawful to refuse to comply with any provisions of this Article or of rules and administrative requirements reasonably promulgated under the authority of this Article.

(j) It is a Class 1 misdemeanor for any person:

(1) Knowingly to engage in any activity regulated under this Article with an improper, false, or altered license or permit;

(2) Knowingly to make any application for a license or permit to which he is not entitled;

(3) Knowingly to make any false, fraudulent, or misleading statement in applying for a license or permit under this Article; or

(4) To counterfeit, alter, or falsify any application, license, or permit under this Article.

(k) A person may use a bow and arrow to take nongame fish in inland and joint fishing waters subject to any applicable rule of the Wildlife Resources Commission regarding seasons, creel limits, type of weapon or subsidiary gear, or any other restriction necessary for the conservation of wildlife under the authority of the following licenses:

(1) All of the combination hunting and fishing licenses issued pursuant to G.S. 113-270.1C;

(2) All of the sportsman licenses issued pursuant to G.S. 113-270.1D;

(3) The hunting licenses issued pursuant to G.S. 113- 270.2(c)(1), (2), (3), (5), and (6);

(4) The hook-and-line fishing licenses issued pursuant to G.S. 113-271(d)(1), (2), (3), (4), (5), (6), (8), and (9); and

(5) All of the special device fishing licenses issued pursuant to G.S. 113-272.2. (1929, c. 335, ss. 6, 10, 11; 1945, c. 567, ss. 5, 6; 1961, c. 329; 1965, c. 957, s. 2; 1973, c. 1262, s. 18; 1979, c. 830, s. 1; 1981, c. 620, ss. 7, 8; 1987, c. 745, s. 1; c. 827, s. 98; 1993, c. 539, s. 855; 1994, Ex. Sess., c. 24, s. 14(c); 1993 (Reg. Sess., 1994), c. 684, s. 7; 1995, c. 36, s. 1; 2000-189, s. 10; 2005-455, s. 1.10.)

§ 113-276. Exemptions and exceptions to license and permit requirements.

(a), (b) Repealed by Session Laws 1979, c. 830, s. 1.

(c) (Effective until August 1, 2014) Except as otherwise provided in this Subchapter, every landholder, his spouse, and dependents under 18 years of age residing with him may take wildlife upon the land held by the landholder without any license required by G.S. 113-270.1B or G.S. 113-270.3(a), except that such persons are not exempt from the falconry license described in G.S. 113-270.3(b)(4).

(c) (Effective August 1, 2014) Except as otherwise provided in this Subchapter, every landholder, his spouse, and dependents under 18 years of age residing with him may take wildlife upon the land held by the landholder without any license required by G.S. 113-270.1B or G.S. 113-270.3(a), except that such persons are not exempt from the bear management stamp established in G.S. 113-270.3(b)(1b) and the falconry license described in G.S. 113-270.3(b)(4).

(d) Except as otherwise provided in this Subchapter, individuals under 16 years of age are exempt from the hunting and trapping license requirements of G.S. 113-270.1B(a) and G.S. 113-270.3(a), except the falconry license described in G.S. 113-270.3(b)(4). Individuals under 16 may hunt under this exemption, provided that the hunter is accompanied by an adult of at least 18 years of age who is licensed to hunt in this State. For purposes of this section, "accompanied" means that the licensed adult maintains a proximity that enables the adult to monitor the activities of the hunter by remaining within sight and hearing distance at all times without use of electronic devices. Upon successfully obtaining the hunter education certificate of competency required by G.S. 113-270.1A(a), a hunter may hunt under the license exemption until age 16 without adult accompaniment. Individuals under 16 years of age are exempt from the fishing license requirements of G.S. 113-270.1B(a), 113-272, and 113-271.

(e) Repealed by Session Laws 2005-455, s. 1.11.

(f) A special device license is not required when a landing net is used:

(1) To take nongame fish in inland fishing waters; or

(2) To assist in taking fish in inland fishing waters when the initial and primary method of taking is by the use of hook and line - so long as applicable hook-and-line fishing-license requirements are met.

As used in this subsection, a "landing net" is a net with a handle not exceeding eight feet in length and with a hoop or frame to which the net is attached not exceeding 60 inches along its outer perimeter.

(g) Bow nets covered by a special device license may be used in waters and during the seasons authorized in the rules of the Wildlife Resources Commission by an individual other than the licensee with the permission of the licensee. The individual using another's bow net must also secure the net owner's special device license and keep it on or about his person while fishing in inland fishing waters.

(h) Repealed by Session Laws 1979, c. 830, s. 1.

(i) A food server may prepare edible wildlife lawfully taken and possessed by a patron for serving to the patron and any guest he may have. The Executive Director may provide for the keeping of records by the food server necessary for administrative control and supervision with respect to wildlife brought in by patrons.

(j) A migrant farm worker who has in his possession a temporary certification of his status as such by the Rural Employment Service of the Division of Employment Security on a form provided by the Wildlife Resources Commission is entitled to the privileges of a resident of the State and of the county indicated on such certification during the term thereof for the purposes of purchasing and using the resident fishing licenses provided by G.S. 113-271(d)(2), (4), and (6)a.

(k)     A person may participate in a field trial for beagles without a hunting license if approved in advance by the Executive Director, conducted without the use or possession of firearms, and on an area of not more than 100 acres of private land which is completely and permanently enclosed with a metal fence through which rabbits may not escape or enter at any time.

(l)     The fishing license provisions of this Article do not apply upon the lands held in trust by the United States for the Eastern Band of the Cherokee Indians.

(l1)     The licensing provisions of this Article do not apply to a member of an Indian tribe recognized under Chapter 71A of the General Statutes for purposes of hunting, trapping, or fishing on tribal land. A person taking advantage of this exemption shall possess and produce proper identification confirming the person's membership in a State-recognized tribe upon request by a wildlife enforcement officer. For purposes of this section, "tribal land" means only real property owned by an Indian tribe recognized under Chapter 71A of the General Statutes.

(l2)     A resident of this State who is a member of the Armed Forces of the United States serving outside the State, or who is serving on full-time active military duty outside the State in a reserve component of the Armed Forces of the United States as defined in 10 U.S.C. 10101, is exempt from the hunting and fishing license requirements of G.S. 113-270.1B, G.S. 113-270.3(b)(1), G.S. 113-270.3(b)(3), G.S. 113-270.3(b)(5), G.S. 113-271, G.S. 113-272, G.S. 113-272.2(c)(1), and the Coastal Recreational Fishing License requirements of G.S. 113-174.2 while that person is on leave in this State for 30 days or less. In order to qualify for the exemption provided under this subsection, the person shall have on his or her person at all times during the hunting or fishing activity the person's military identification card and a copy of the official document issued by the person's service unit confirming that the person is on authorized leave from a duty station outside this State.

A person exempted from licensing requirements under this subsection is responsible for complying with any reporting requirements prescribed by rule of the Wildlife Resources Commission, complying with the hunter education requirements of G.S. 113-270.1A, purchasing any federal migratory waterfowl stamps as a result of waterfowl hunting activity, and complying with any other requirements that the holder of a North Carolina license is subject to.

(m) The fourth day of July of each year is declared a free fishing day to promote the sport of fishing and no hook-and-line fishing license is required to fish in any of the public waters of the State on that day. All other laws and rules pertaining to hook-and-line fishing apply.

(n) (Effective until August 1, 2014) The Wildlife Resources Commission may adopt rules to exempt individuals from the hunting and fishing license requirements of G.S. 113-270.1B, 113-270.3(b)(1), 113-270.3(b)(3), 113-270.3(b)(5), 113-271, 113-272, and 113-272.2(c)(1) who participate in organized hunting and fishing events for the specified time and place of the event when the purpose of the event is consistent with the conservation objectives of the Commission. A person exempted from licensing requirements under this subsection is responsible for complying with any reporting requirements prescribed by rule of the Wildlife Resources Commission, purchasing any federal migratory waterfowl stamps as a result of waterfowl hunting activity, and complying with any other requirements that the holder of a North Carolina license is subject to. Those exempted persons shall comply with the hunter education requirements of G.S. 113-270.1A or shall be accompanied by a properly licensed adult of at least 18 years of age who maintains a proximity that enables the adult to monitor the activities of the hunter by remaining within sight and hearing distance at all times without use of electronic devices.

(n) (Effective August 1, 2014) The Wildlife Resources Commission may adopt rules to exempt individuals from the hunting and fishing license requirements of G.S. 113-270.1B, 113-270.3(b)(1), 113-270.3(b)(1a), 113-270.3(b)(1b), 113-270.3(b)(2), 113-270.3(b)(3), 113-270.3(b)(5), 113-271, 113-272, and 113-272.2(c)(1) who participate in organized hunting and fishing events for the specified time and place of the event when the purpose of the event is consistent with the conservation objectives of the Commission. A person exempted from licensing requirements under this subsection is responsible for complying with any reporting requirements prescribed by rule of the Wildlife Resources Commission, purchasing any federal migratory waterfowl stamps as a result of waterfowl hunting activity, and complying with any other requirements that the holder of a North Carolina license is subject to. Those exempted persons shall comply with the hunter safety requirements of G.S. 113-270.1A or shall be accompanied by a properly licensed adult who maintains a proximity to the license exempt individual which enables the adult to monitor the activities of, and communicate with, the individual at all times. (1929, c. 335, ss. 1, 10; 1935, c. 486, s. 12; 1937, c. 45, s. 1; 1945, c. 567, ss. 1, 6; c. 617; 1949, c. 1203, s. 1; 1951, c. 1112, s. 2; 1957, c. 849, s. 1; 1959, c. 304; 1961, cc. 312, 329; c. 834, s. 1; 1963, c. 170; 1965, c. 957, s. 2; 1967, cc. 127, 654, 790; 1969, c. 1030; c. 1042, ss. 1-5; 1971, c. 242; c. 282, s. 1; c. 705, ss. 1, 2; c. 1231, s. 1; 1973, c. 1262, s. 18; 1975, c. 197, ss. 1-4; 1977, c. 191, s. 1; c. 658; 1979, c. 830, s. 1; 1987, c. 827, s. 98; 1993 (Reg. Sess., 1994), c. 684, ss. 6, 8, 9; 1999-456, ss. 29, 30; 2005-285, s. 1; 2005-438, s. 2; 2005-455, ss. 1.11, 1.12, 1.13, 1.14; 2009-25, s. 1; 2009-248, s. 1; 2011-401, s. 3.15; 2013-63, s. 4; 2013-283, s. 14.)

§ 113-276.1. Regulatory authority of Wildlife Resources Commission as to license requirements and exemptions.

In its discretion and in accordance with the best interests of the conservation of wildlife resources, the Wildlife Resources Commission may implement the provisions of this Article with rules that:

(1) [Reserved.]

(2) Regulate license requirements and exemptions applying to the taking of wildlife on particular waters forming or lying across a county boundary where there may be confusion as to the location of the boundary, hardship imposed as to the location of the boundary, or difficulty of administering or enforcing the law with respect to the actual boundary location.

(3) Require persons subject to license requirements, and persons exempt from license requirements, to carry, display, or produce identification that may be necessary to substantiate the person's entitlement to a particular license or to a particular exemption from license requirements.

(4) Require individuals aboard vessels or carrying weapons or other gear that may be used to take wildlife resources, and in an area at a time wildlife resources may be taken, to exhibit identification that includes the individual's name and current address. More than one piece of identification, including a vehicle driver license, may be required to be exhibited, if available.

(5) Implement a system of tagging and reporting fur-bearing animals and big game. Upon the implementation of a tagging system for any species of fur-bearing animal, the Wildlife Resources Commission may charge a reasonable

fee to defray its costs, not to exceed two dollars twenty-five cents ($2.25) per tag, for each tag furnished. The price of the big game hunting license includes the cost of big game tags. (1979, c. 830, s. 1; 1987, c. 827, s. 98.)

§ 113-276.2. Licensees and permittees subject to administrative control; refusal to issue or reissue, suspension, and revocation of their licenses and permits; court orders of suspension.

(a) This section applies to the administrative control of:

(1) Persons, other than individual hunters and fishermen taking wildlife as sportsmen, holding permits under this Article;

(2) Individuals holding special device licenses under G.S. 113-272.2(c)(1), (1a), (2), and (2a);

(3) Individuals holding collection licenses under G.S. 113-272.4;

(4) Individuals holding captivity licenses under G.S. 113-272.5 and G.S. 113-272.6; and

(5) Persons holding dealer licenses under G.S. 113-273.

(b) Before issuing any license or permit to persons subject to administrative control under this section, the Executive Director must satisfy himself that the person meets the qualifications set by statute, rule, or his administrative guidelines. If the person fails to meet the qualifications or if the Executive Director learns of some other cause for believing that issuing the license or permit would be contrary to the best interests of the conservation of wildlife resources, he must refuse to issue the license or permit.

(c) Before reissuing any license or permit to any person subject to administrative control, the Executive Director must review all available information and apply the same standards that governed initial issuance of the license or permit before he may reissue it.

(d) Upon refusing to issue or reissue a license or permit under this section, the Executive Director must notify the person in writing of the reasons for his action and inform him that if he is dissatisfied with the Executive Director's decision he may commence a contested case on the refusal by filing a petition under G.S. 150B-23 within 10 days of receiving the notice. The notice must be personally served by a law enforcement officer or an agent of the Wildlife Resources Commission or sent by mail with return receipt requested.

(e) The Executive Director shall revoke a license or permit issued to a person subject to administrative control if he finds that the person does not meet the qualifications for the license or permit, has committed a substantial criminal violation of this Subchapter or a rule adopted under the Subchapter, or has seriously or persistently failed to comply with the terms and conditions upon which the license or permit was issued. Before revoking a license or permit, the Executive Director shall notify the licensee or permittee of his findings and his intention to revoke the license or permit. The notice must be personally served by a law enforcement officer or an agent of the Wildlife Resources Commission or sent by mail with return receipt requested. A licensee or permittee who disagrees with the Executive Director's findings may commence a contested case on revocation by filing a petition under G.S. 150B-23 within 10 days of receiving the notice. Revocation or suspension of a license or permit by a court under G.S. 113-277 runs concurrently with a revocation under this section.

(f) Repealed by Session Laws 1987, c. 827, s. 8.

(g) Upon revocation of a license or permit, the Executive Director or his agent must request return of the license or permit and all associated forms, tags, record books, inventories, invoice blanks, and other property furnished by the Wildlife Resources Commission or required to be kept by the Commission solely in connection with the license or permit. If the person needs to retain a copy of the property returned to the Wildlife Resources Commission for tax purposes or other lawful reason, the person may copy items returned if the copies are clearly marked in a manner that they could not be mistaken for the originals. In securing property to be returned or in otherwise closing out the affairs conducted under the license or permit, agents of the Wildlife Resources Commission may enter at reasonable hours the premises of the person in which wildlife resources or items of property pertaining to the license or permit are kept, or reasonably believed to be kept, to inspect, audit, inventory, remove, or take other appropriate action. Any wildlife resources in the possession of the person which he may no longer possess must be disposed of in accordance with the most nearly appropriate provision of G.S. 113-137. If a person fails to return to an agent of the Wildlife Resources Commission all wildlife resources and other property covered by this subsection; refuses to allow entry by the agent to inspect, audit, remove property, or perform other duties; or otherwise obstructs an agent of the Wildlife Resources Commission in performing his duties under this subsection, he is guilty of a Class 2 misdemeanor. Each day's violation is a separate offense.

(h) No person refused issuance or reissuance of a license or permit under this section, or whose license or permit was revoked, is eligible to apply again for that or any similar license or permit for two years. Upon application, the Executive Director may not grant the license or permit unless the person produces clear evidence, convincing to the Executive Director, that he meets all standards and qualifications and will comply with all requirements of statutes, rules, and reasonable administrative directives pertaining to the license or permit.

(i) The Executive Director is required to make necessary investigations and cause necessary disclosure of information by all persons subject to administrative control, and all applicants for a license or permit that would place them in this category, to determine that the real party in interest is seeking or has been issued the license or permit. Any attempt to circumvent the provisions of this section is a Class 1 misdemeanor.

(j) If the Executive Director determines that the effective conservation of wildlife resources would be seriously impaired by continued unfettered operations or by continued possession of property by the person subject to administrative control, the Executive Director may apply to the appropriate court for an order:

(1) Placing special reporting and inspection requirements on the person; or

(2) Impounding some or all of the records or other property associated with the license or permit; or

(3) Limiting the scope of operations under the license or permit; or

(4) If there is clear evidence of a serious threat to the conservation of wildlife resources, suspending the operations of the person under the license or permit; or

(5) Placing other appropriate restrictions, prohibitions, or requirements upon the person. (1979, c. 830, s. 1; 1987, c. 827, ss. 8, 98; 1993, c. 539, ss. 856, 857; 1994, Ex. Sess., c. 24, s. 14(c); 1999-456, s. 31; 2003-344, s. 6.)

§ 113-276.3. Mandatory suspension of entitlement to license or permit for fixed period upon conviction of specified offenses.

(a)     Upon conviction of a suspension offense under this section, the defendant's entitlement to any license or permit applicable to the type of activity he was engaging in that resulted in the conviction is suspended for the period stated in subsection (d). The period of suspension begins:

(1)     Upon the surrender to an authorized agent of the Wildlife Resources Commission of all applicable licenses and permits; or

(2)     If no licenses or permits are possessed, the defendant fails or refuses to surrender all licenses or permits, or any license or permit is lost or destroyed, upon the Executive Director's placing in the mail the notification required by subsection (c).

(b)     If the defendant does not wish to appeal, the presiding judge may order surrender of all applicable licenses and permits to an agent of the Wildlife Resources Commission. If the presiding judge does not order the surrender, or if there is for any other reason a failure by the defendant to surrender all applicable licenses and permits, an authorized agent of the Wildlife Resources Commission must demand surrender. Each day's failure or refusal to surrender a license or permit upon demand, in the absence of satisfactorily accounting for the failure to do so, is a separate offense. A charge under this subsection does not affect the power of the court to institute contempt proceedings if a failure or refusal to surrender a license or permit also violates a court order. Any agent of the Wildlife Resources Commission accepting surrender of licenses and permits, in the courtroom or at a subsequent time and place, must transmit them to the Executive Director with a written notation of the date of surrender and a report of other pertinent circumstances required by the Executive Director.

(c)     The Executive Director must institute a procedure for the systematic reporting to him by protectors or other authorized agents of the Wildlife Resources Commission of all convictions of suspension offenses under this section. Upon obtaining information concerning conviction of a suspension offense and receiving any surrendered licenses and permits, the Executive Director must determine if all appropriate licenses and permits possessed by the defendant have been surrendered; if not, the Executive Director must notify the appropriate agent of the Wildlife Resources Commission to demand surrender or renew a demand for surrender under the terms of subsection (b) if it is feasible to do so. Upon satisfying himself that he has received all licenses and permits for which surrender may feasibly be obtained, if any, the Executive Director must mail the defendant a notice of the suspension of his entitlement to possess or procure any license or permit of the type applicable to the activity engaged in that resulted in conviction of the suspension offense. The notice must specify the commencement and termination dates of the period of suspension that apply under the terms of this section.

(d) Any violation of this Subchapter or of any rule adopted by the Wildlife Resources Commission under the authority of this Subchapter which is subject to a penalty greater than the one provided in G.S. 113-135(a)(1) is a suspension offense. Conviction of any of the following suspension offenses results in a suspension for a period of two years:

(1) A violation of G.S. 113-294(b).

(2) A violation of G.S. 113-294(c).

(2a) A violation of G.S. 113-294(c1).

(3) A violation of G.S. 113-294(e).

(4) Repealed by Session Laws 1999-120, s. 2, effective October 1, 1999.

(5) A violation of G.S. 113-291.1A.

A conviction of any other suspension offense results in a suspension for a period of one year.

(e) Unless otherwise provided in the judgment, any action by a court under G.S. 113-277 to suspend entitlement to a license or permit or to suspend or revoke a license or permit supersedes any suspension of entitlement to a license or permit mandated by this section. If the judgment of the court after a conviction for suspension offense does not include any suspension or revocation action, the provisions of this section apply. (1979, c. 830, s. 1; 1981, c. 424, s. 1; 1987, c. 827, s. 98; 1999-120, s. 2; 2005-62, s. 3.)

§ 113-277. Suspension and revocation of licenses and permits in the discretion of the court; suspension of entitlement; court's power concurrent; definition of "conviction"; penalties.

(a) Upon conviction of any licensee or permittee under this Article of a violation of any law or rule administered by the Wildlife Resources Commission under the authority of this Subchapter, the court in its discretion may order surrender of that license or permit plus any other license or permit issued by the Wildlife Resources Commission. The court may order suspension of any license or permit for some stipulated period or may order revocation of any license or permit for the remainder of the period for which it is valid. A period of suspension may extend past the expiration date of a license or permit, but no period of suspension longer than two years may be imposed. During any period of suspension or revocation, the licensee or permittee is not entitled to purchase or apply for any replacement, renewal, or additional license or permit regulating the same activity covered by the suspended or revoked license or permit. The Wildlife Resources Commission may by administrative action and by rule devise procedures designed to implement license or permit suspensions and revocations that may be ordered by the courts.

(a1) Upon conviction of any person who is not a licensee or permittee under this Article of a violation of any law or rule administered by the Wildlife Resources Commission under the authority of this Subchapter, the court in its discretion may suspend the entitlement of the defendant to possess or procure any specified licenses and permits issued by the Wildlife Resources Commission for a period not to exceed two years.

(a2) A suspension or revocation by a court under this section may be ordered to run concurrently or consecutively with any suspension under G.S. 113-276.3 or any action under G.S. 113-276.2. If no provision is made, G.S. 113-276.3(e) applies, but action by the Executive Director or the Wildlife Resources Commission under G.S. 113-276.2 may not be preempted.

(a3) As used in this Article, the term "conviction" has the same meaning assigned to it in G.S. 113-171.

(a4) The Wildlife Resources Commission shall order the surrender of any license or permit issued under this Article to a person whose licensing privileges have been forfeited under G.S. 15A-1331.1 for the period specified by the court.

(b) It is a Class 1 misdemeanor for any person during a period of suspension or revocation under the terms of this Article:

(1) To engage in any activity licensed in this Article without the appropriate license or permit;

(2)   Knowingly to make any application for a license or permit to which he is not entitled;

(3)   Knowingly to make any false, fraudulent, or misleading statement in applying for a license or permit under this Article;

(4)   To counterfeit, alter, or falsify any application, license, or permit under this Article;

(5)   Knowingly to retain and use any license or permit which has been ordered revoked or suspended under the terms of this Article; or

(6)   Willfully to circumvent the terms of suspension or revocation in any manner whatsoever. (1965, c. 957, s. 2; 1973, c. 1262, s. 18; 1979, c. 830, s. 1; 1981, c. 424, s. 2; 1987, c. 827, s. 98; 1993, c. 539, s. 858; 1994, Ex. Sess., c. 20, s. 4; c. 24, s. 14(c); 1998-225, s. 3.10; 2012-194, s. 45(d).)

§ 113-278. Reserved for future codification purposes.

§ 113-279. Reserved for future codification purposes.

§ 113-280. Reserved for future codification purposes.


Article 21A.

Regulating Hunting and Fishing on the Registered Property of Another.

§ 113-281. Definitions.

In addition to the definitions in Article 12 of this Chapter, the following definitions apply in this Article:

(1)   Entry Permit. - The permit described in G.S. 113-283.

(2)   Posted Property. - Registered property that is posted in substantial compliance with G.S. 113-282(d).

(3) Registered Property. - Property that has been accepted for registration by the Wildlife Resources Commission as provided in G.S. 113-282, and has not been deleted from registration.

(4) Registrant. - A current applicant of record for a tract of registered property. (1981, c. 854, s. 1.)


§ 113-282. Registration and posting of property.

(a) A person who controls the hunting, fishing, or hunting and fishing rights to a tract of property and wishes to register it under this Article must apply to the Wildlife Resources Commission in accordance with this section.

(b) The registration application must contain:

(1) A statement under oath by the applicant that he has the right to control hunting or fishing, or both, on the tract of property to be registered. If the applicant is not a landholder, he must file a copy of his lease or other document granting him control of hunting, fishing, or hunting and fishing rights on the tract.

(2) Three copies of a description of the tract that will allow law-enforcement officers to determine in the field, and prove in court, whether an individual is within the boundaries of the tract. This description may take the form of a map, plat, aerial photograph showing boundaries, diagram keyed to known landmarks, or any other document or description that graphically demarks the boundaries with sufficient accuracy for use by officers in court and in the field. Any amendment of the boundaries of a registered tract must be accomplished by a new registration application meeting the requirements of this subsection.

(3) An agreement by the applicant to post the tract in accordance with the requirements of this section and to make a continuing effort to maintain posted notices for the tract.

(4) An agreement by the applicant to issue or cause issuance of an entry permit to all individuals to whom he or his authorized agent gives permission to hunt or fish on the tract. The applicant must file the name and signature of any agent authorized by him to issue the entry permit, and a registrant must amend his application to rescind the agent's authority and to substitute or add an authorized agent.

(5) A fee of ten dollars ($10.00) to cover the administrative costs of processing the registration application.

(c) The Executive Director must examine any submitted application to determine whether the requirements of subsection (b) have been fully met. If he determines that these requirements have been met and if his inquiries of persons with knowledge of the locality of the tract corroborate the truthfulness and accuracy of the information in the application, he must register the tract of property and notify the registrant of his action. Registration consists of filing the application in a central registry open to the public with an indication whether the property is registered as to hunting, fishing, or both. Upon registration, the Executive Director must send, for the information of protectors and other law-enforcement officers, the two duplicate copies of the description of the tract as follows: (i) to the sheriff of the county in which the tract is located, or to the chief of the county police department if such a department is the primary agency enforcing the criminal laws in a county; and (ii) to an appropriate protector stationed in the area where the tract is located. The Executive Director must also furnish officers with copies of the signatures of registrants and their authorized agents and other pertinent information for enforcement of this Article.

(d) A registrant must post his registered property as soon as practicable after receiving notice that the tract was accepted for registration. Posted notices must measure at least 120 square inches; contain the word "POSTED" in letters at least three inches high; state that the property is registered with the Wildlife Resources Commission and that hunting or fishing, or both, are prohibited without an entry permit; and set out the name and address and, if feasible, the telephone number of the person to contact for an entry permit. At least one notice must be conspicuously posted on the registered property not more than 200 yards apart close to and along the boundaries. In any event at least one notice must be placed on each side of the registered property, one at each corner, and one at each point of entry. A point of entry is where a roadway, trail, path, or other way likely to be used by entering sportsmen leads into the tract. If registered property is posted only with respect to fishing, it is sufficient if the notices prohibit fishing without permission, and are posted at intervals of not more than 200 yards along the stream or shoreline and at points of entry likely to be used by fishermen. Notices posted along the boundaries of a tract must face in the direction that they will be most likely seen by persons entering the tract. Notices posted along a stream or shoreline must face in the direction that they will most likely be seen by anyone intending to fish. With respect to any particular hunter or fisherman, or person who has entered to hunt or fish, there is substantial compliance with this subsection, notwithstanding that one or more of the required notices may be absent, illegible, or improperly placed, if any notice is or has been reasonably visible to him while he was within or approaching the registered tract.

(e)     If a registrant loses his proprietary interest or his control of the hunting, fishing, or hunting and fishing rights as to which he has registered the property, he must within 20 days notify the Executive Director. If a new person who controls those rights wishes to continue the registration of the tract, he must make application under the terms of subsection (b), except that no copies of the tract's description need be filed if there is no change of boundaries. When the Executive Director receives the notice under this subsection, or otherwise learns that a registrant has lost his proprietary control of the applicable hunting, fishing, or hunting and fishing rights, and there is no pending application to continue registration of the tract, the Executive Director must immediately delete registration of the tract, notify the presently responsible landholder, and require him to remove any remaining posted notices.

(f)     A person who controls the hunting, fishing, or hunting and fishing rights to registered property may apply to the Wildlife Resources Commission in writing to delete the registration of the tract. If he is not the registrant, he must satisfy the Executive Director of his present right to control the applicable hunting and fishing rights. If he is the registrant, his statement that he still controls the applicable rights on the tract is sufficient unless the Executive Director has reason to require further evidence on this point. Upon determination that an application to delete is proper, the Executive Director must immediately delete registration of the tract, notify the presently responsible landholder, and require him to remove any remaining posted notices.

(g)     Any law-enforcement officer or any employee of the Wildlife Resources Commission who determines that a registrant has failed to keep registered property posted in compliance with subsection (d) must so notify the registrant or his agent. If within a reasonable time after notice the registrant fails to take steps to post or repost the tract, or if without regard to notice a registrant is inexcusably or repeatedly negligent in failing to keep the tract properly posted, the Executive Director must immediately delete registration of the tract, notify the presently responsible landholder, and require him to remove any remaining posted notices.

(h)     A landholder's failure to cause the removal of all posted signs within a reasonable time after receipt of notice that the tract has been deleted from registration is a misdemeanor punishable as provided in G.S. 113-135. (1981, c. 854, s. 1.)

§ 113-283. Entry permits furnished by Wildlife Resources Commission.

(a) Upon registration of property, the Executive Director must furnish the registrant with a reasonable number of standardized permit forms to be carried by individuals given permission to hunt or fish on the registered property. The Executive Director must establish a procedure for resupplying registrants with entry permits for their registered property as needed.

(b) To be valid, the entry permit must be issued and dated within the previous 12 months and signed by the registrant or an authorized agent whose signature is on file with the Wildlife Resources Commission. (1981, c. 854, s. 1.)

§ 113-284. Affirmative duty of sportsmen to determine if property is registered and posted.

Every individual who enters the property of another to hunt or fish without first having obtained permission from an authorized person in control of hunting and fishing rights or his agent is under a duty to look for posted notices. In the apparent absence of such notices, the individual intending to enter is nevertheless under a duty to determine if practicable whether the property is registered under the terms of this Article. (1981, c. 854, s. 1.)

§ 113-285. Hunting or fishing on registered property of another without permission.

(a) No one may hunt or fish, or enter to hunt or fish, on the registered and posted property of another without having in possession a valid entry permit issued to him.

(b) No one may hunt or fish, or enter to hunt or fish, on the registered property of another without having in possession a valid entry permit issued to him if he has reason to know the property had been posted.

(c) A violation of this section is a misdemeanor punishable as provided in G.S. 113-135. (1981, c. 854, s. 1.)

§ 113-286. Removal, destruction, or mutilation of posted notices.

Unauthorized removal, destruction, or mutilation of posted notices on registered property is a Class 2 misdemeanor. (1981, c. 854, s. 1; 1993, c. 539, s. 859; 1994, Ex. Sess., c. 24, s. 14(c).)

§ 113-287. General provisions pertaining to enforcement of Article.

(a) If property is registered, the original or a true copy of the application and all supporting items are admissible in evidence. The registrant's affidavit that he has the right to control hunting, fishing, or hunting and fishing on the registered property constitutes prima facie evidence of the facts so asserted. The description filed with the application constitutes prima facie evidence of the boundaries of the registered property.

(b) If an individual hunts or fishes, or enters to hunt or fish, on registered property that is or had been posted, any registrant or his agent, any landholder of that property, and any protector or other law-enforcement officer may request that the individual produce a valid entry permit.

(c) In addition to protectors, it is the duty of sheriffs and their deputies, county police officers, and other law-enforcement officers with general enforcement jurisdiction to investigate reported violations of this Article and to initiate prosecutions when they determine that violations have occurred.

(d) Any entry permit issued to an individual does not substitute for any required hunting or fishing license. (1981, c. 854, s. 1.)

§ 113-288. Reserved for future codification purposes.

§ 113-289. Reserved for future codification purposes.

Article 21B.

Criminally Negligent Hunting.

§ 113-290. Unlawful use of firearms.

It is unlawful for any person, while hunting or taking wild animals or wild birds as those terms are defined in G.S. 113-129 and G.S. 113-130, to discharge a firearm:

(1)     Carelessly and heedlessly in wanton disregard for the safety of others; or

(2)     Without due caution or circumspection, and in a manner so as to endanger any person or property;

and resulting in property damage or bodily injury. (1991, c. 748, s. 1.)


§ 113-290.1. Penalties.

(a)     A person who violates the provisions of this Article is guilty of a misdemeanor punishable as follows:

(1)     If property damage only results from the unlawful activity, a Class 2 misdemeanor, and the court shall order the payment of restitution to the property owner;

(2)     If bodily injury not leading to the disfigurement or total or partial permanent disability of another person results from the unlawful activity, a Class 1 misdemeanor; if property damage also results from the unlawful activity, the court shall order the payment of restitution to the property owner;

(3)     If bodily injury leading to the disfigurement or total or partial permanent disability of another person results from the unlawful activity, a Class 1 misdemeanor; if property damage also results from the unlawful activity, the court shall order the payment of restitution to the property owner;

(4)     If death results from the unlawful activity, a Class 1 misdemeanor; if property damage also results from the unlawful activity, the court shall order the payment of restitution to the property owner.

(b)  The fact that a person was impaired at the time of a violation of this Article shall be an aggravating factor and the court shall impose an additional fine and/or imprisonment in accordance with (a)(2) above in cases not resulting in bodily injury and in accordance with (a)(4) above in cases resulting in bodily injury. For purposes of this section, "impaired" means being under the influence of an impairing substance, or having consumed sufficient alcohol so that the person has, at any relevant time after the offense, an alcohol concentration of .10 or above.

(c)  In addition to the penalties provided in (a), upon conviction of a violation of this Article, the Wildlife Resources Commission shall suspend all hunting privileges of:

(1)  A person convicted under (a)(1) for one year;

(2)  A person convicted under (a)(2) for three years; and

(3)  A person convicted under (a)(3) or (a)(4) for five years.

(d)  A person convicted of hunting or taking wild animals or wild birds while his hunting license is suspended under this section shall be guilty of a Class 1 misdemeanor, and shall have all hunting privileges suspended for an additional five years. The person shall not be issued another hunting license until he has satisfactorily completed the hunter safety course established in G.S. 113-270.1A.

(e)  This Article shall be enforced by law enforcement officers of the Wildlife Resources Commission, by sheriffs and deputy sheriffs, and by peace officers with general subject matter jurisdiction.

(f)  A violation of this Article resulting in the death of another person constitutes a separate and distinct offense from, and is not a lesser included offense of, the crime of involuntary manslaughter. (1991, c. 748; 1993, c. 539, ss. 860, 861; 1994, Ex. Sess., c. 24, s. 14(c).)


Article 22.

Regulation of Wildlife.

§ 113-291. General restrictions.

Except as specifically permitted in this Subchapter or in rules made under the authority of this Subchapter, no person may take, possess, buy, sell, or transport any wildlife - whether dead or alive, in whole or in part. Nor may any person take, possess, buy, sell, or transport any nests or eggs of wild birds except as so permitted. No person may take, possess, buy, sell, or transport any wildlife resources in violation of the rules of the Wildlife Resources Commission. (1965, c. 957, s. 2; 1979, c. 830, s. 1; 1987, c. 827, s. 98.)

§ 113-291.1. Manner of taking wild animals and wild birds.

(a) Except as otherwise provided, game may only be taken between a half hour before sunrise and a half hour after sunset and only by one or a combination of the following methods:

(1) With a rifle, except that rifles may not be used in taking wild turkeys.

(2) With a shotgun not larger than number 10 gauge.

(3) With a bow and arrow of a type prescribed in the rules of the Wildlife Resources Commission.

(4) With the use of dogs.

(5) By means of falconry.

Fur-bearing animals may be taken at any time during open trapping season with traps authorized under G.S. 113-291.6 and as otherwise authorized pursuant to this subsection, and rabbits may be box-trapped in accordance with rules of the Wildlife Resources Commission. The Wildlife Resources Commission may adopt rules prescribing the manner of taking wild birds and wild animals not classified as game. Use of pistols in taking wildlife is governed by subsection (g). The Wildlife Resources Commission may prescribe the manner of taking wild animals and wild birds on game lands and public hunting grounds.

(b) No wild animals or wild birds may be taken:

(1) From or with the use of any vehicle; vessel, other than one manually propelled; airplane; or other conveyance except that the use of vehicles and vessels is authorized:

a. As hunting stands, subject to the following limitations. No wild animal or wild bird may be taken from any vessel under sail, under power, or with the engine running or while still in motion from such propulsion. No wild animal or wild bird may be taken from any vehicle if it is in motion, the engine is running, or the passenger area of the vehicle is occupied. The prohibition of occupying the passenger area of a vehicle does not apply to a disabled individual whose mobility is restricted.

b. For transportation incidental to the taking.

(2) With the use or aid of any artificial light, net, trap, snare, electronic or recorded animal or bird call, or fire, except as may be otherwise provided by statute[;] provided, however, that the Wildlife Resources Commission may adopt rules prescribing seasons and the manner of taking of wild animals and wild birds with the use of artificial light and electronic calls. No wild birds may be taken with the use or aid of salt, grain, fruit, or other bait. No black bear may be taken with the use or aid of any salt, salt lick, grain, fruit, honey, sugar-based material, animal parts or products, or other bait, except as provided by the rules of the Wildlife Resources Commission. However, no rule established by the Wildlife Resources Commission shall allow for the taking of a black bear with the use and aid of bear bait attractants, including scented sprays, aerosols, scent balls, and scent powders, and no rule established by the Wildlife Resources Commission shall allow for the taking of a black bear while it is consuming bait. No wild turkey may be taken from an area in which bait has been placed until the expiration of 10 days after the bait has been consumed or otherwise removed. The taking of wild animals and wild birds with poisons, drugs, explosives, and electricity is governed by G.S. 113-261, G.S. 113-262, and Article 22A of this Subchapter.

Upon finding that the placement of processed food products in areas frequented by black bears is detrimental to the health of individual black bears or is attracting and holding black bears in an area to the extent that the natural pattern of movement and distribution of black bears is disrupted and bears' vulnerability to mortality factors, including hunting, is increased to a level that causes concern for the population, the Wildlife Resources Commission may adopt rules to regulate, restrict, or prohibit the placement of those products and prescribe time limits during which hunting is prohibited in areas where those products have been placed.

Any person who is convicted of unlawfully taking bear with the use or aid of any type of bait as provided by this subsection or by rules adopted pursuant to this subsection is punishable as provided by G.S. 113-294(c1).

(c) It is a Class 1 misdemeanor for any person taking wildlife to have in his possession any:

(1) Repealed by Session Laws 2013-369, s. 23, effective October 1, 2013.

(2) Weapon of mass death and destruction as defined in G.S. 14-288.8, other than a suppressor or other device designed to muffle or minimize the report of a firearm that is lawfully possessed by a person in compliance with 26 U.S.C. Chapter 53 §§ 5801-5871.

The Wildlife Resources Commission may prohibit individuals training dogs or taking particular species from carrying axes, saws, tree-climbing equipment, and other implements that may facilitate the unlawful taking of wildlife, except tree-climbing equipment may be carried and used by persons lawfully taking raccoons and opossums during open season.

(d) In accordance with governing rules of the Wildlife Resources Commission imposing further restrictions that may be necessary, hunters may conduct field trials with dogs in areas and at times authorized with the use of approved weapons and ammunition. The Wildlife Resources Commission may authorize organized retriever field trials, utilizing domestically raised waterfowl and game birds, to be held under its permit.

(d1) Except in areas closed to protect sensitive wildlife populations, and subject to conditions and restrictions contained in rules of the Wildlife Resources Commission, hunters may train dogs during the closed season:

(1) With the use of weapons and ammunition approved by the Wildlife Resources Commission;

(2) If reasonable control is exercised to prevent the dogs from running unsupervised at large and from killing wild animals and wild birds;

(3) On land owned or leased by the dog trainer or upon which the person has written permission to train dogs; and

(4) Using domestically raised waterfowl and game birds, provided the birds are marked and sources are documented as required by the Wildlife Resources Commission.

(e) Raccoons and opossum may be taken at night with dogs during seasons set by rules of the Wildlife Resources Commission with the use of artificial lights of a type designed or commonly used to aid in taking raccoon and opossum. No conveyance may be used in taking any raccoon or opossum at night, but incidental transportation of hunters and dogs to and from the site of hunting is permitted. The Wildlife Resources Commission may by rule prescribe restrictions respecting the taking of frogs, or other creatures not classified as wildlife which may be found in areas frequented by game, with the use of an artificial light, and may regulate the shining of lights at night in areas frequented by deer as provided in subsection (e1).

(e1) After hearing sufficient evidence and finding as a fact that an area frequented by deer is subject to substantial unlawful night deer hunting or that residents in the area have been greatly inconvenienced by persons shining lights on deer, the Wildlife Resources Commission may by rule prohibit the intentional sweeping of that area with lights, or the intentional shining of lights on deer, during the period either:

(1) From 11:00 p.m. until one-half hour before sunrise; or

(2) From one-half hour after sunset until one-half hour before sunrise.

Before adopting this rule, the Wildlife Resources Commission must propose it at a public hearing in the area to be closed and seek the reactions of the local inhabitants. The rule must exempt necessary shining of lights by landholders, motorists engaged in normal travel on the highway, and campers and others legitimately in the area, who are not attempting to attract wildlife. This subsection does not limit the right of hunters to take raccoon and opossum with dogs lawfully at night with a light under the terms of subsection (e).

(e2) If the Wildlife Resources Commission has enacted a rule under the authority of subsection (e1) prohibiting the shining of lights from 11:00 p.m. until one-half hour before sunrise in any county or area of a county, the Wildlife Resources Commission is authorized, without holding an additional public hearing, to extend the applicability of that rule to the period one-half hour after sunset to one-half hour before sunrise upon receipt of a resolution from the board of commissioners of the county requesting extension of the period.

(f) To keep North Carolina provisions respecting migratory game birds in substantial conformity with applicable federal law and rules, the Wildlife Resources Commission may by rule, or as provided in subsection (f1) of this section, expand or modify provisions of this Article if necessary to achieve such conformity, including allowing the use of electronic calls. In particular, the Commission may prohibit the use of rifles, unplugged shotguns, live decoys, and sinkboxes in the taking of migratory game birds; vary shooting hours; adopt specific distances, not less than 300 yards, hunters must maintain from areas that have been baited, and fix the number of days afterwards during which it is still unlawful to take migratory game birds in the area; and adopt similar provisions with regard to the use of live decoys. In the absence of rules of the Wildlife Resources Commission to the contrary, the rules of the United States Department of the Interior prohibiting the use of rifles, unplugged shotguns, toxic shot and sinkboxes in taking migratory game birds in North Carolina shall apply, and any violation of such federal rules is unlawful.

(f1) The Commission is authorized to issue proclamations to allow the use of electronic calls or unplugged shotguns to achieve substantial conformity with applicable federal law and rules established by the United States Department of Interior or any successor agency. The Commission may delegate this authority to the Executive Director. Each proclamation shall state the hour and date upon which it becomes effective and shall be issued at least 48 hours prior to the effective date and time. A permanent file of the text of all proclamations shall be maintained in the office of the Executive Director. Certified copies of proclamations are entitled to judicial notice in any civil or criminal proceeding.

The Executive Director shall make a reasonable effort to give notice of the terms of any proclamation to persons who may be affected by it. This effort shall include press releases to communications media, posting of notices at boating access areas and other places where persons affected may gather, personal communication by agents of the Wildlife Resources Commission, and other measures designed to reach persons who may be affected. Proclamations under this subsection shall remain in force until rescinded following the same procedure established for enactment.

(g) If a season is open permitting such method of taking for the species in question, a hunter may take rabbits, squirrels, opossum, raccoons, fur-bearing animals, and nongame animals and birds open to hunting with a pistol. In addition, a hunter or trapper lawfully taking a wild animal or wild bird by another lawful method may use a knife, pistol, or other swift method of killing the animal or bird taken. The Wildlife Resources Commission may, however, restrict or prohibit the carrying of firearms during special seasons or in special areas reserved for the taking of wildlife with primitive weapons or other restricted methods.

(g1)  The Wildlife Resources Commission may by rule prescribe the types of handguns and handgun ammunition that may be used in taking big game animals other than wild turkey. During the regular gun seasons for taking bear, deer and wild boar these animals may be taken with types of handguns and handgun ammunition that shall be approved for such use by the rules of the Wildlife Resources Commission. The Commission shall not provide any special season for the exclusive use of handguns in taking wildlife.

(h)  In the interests of enhancing the enjoyment of sportsmen, and if consistent with conservation objectives, the Wildlife Resources Commission may by rule relax requirements of this section on controlled shooting preserves and in other highly controlled situations.

(i)  The intentional destruction or substantial impairment of wildlife nesting or breeding areas or other purposeful acts to render them unfit is unlawful. These prohibitions include cutting down den trees, shooting into nests of wild animals or birds, and despoliation of dens, nests, or rookeries.

(j)  It is unlawful to take deer swimming or in water above the knees of the deer.

(k)  If a hunter kills or wounds a big game animal during the hunting hours authorized by subsection (a) of this section, the hunter may use a portable light source and a single dog on a leash to assist the hunter in retrieving the dead or wounded big game animal, and may dispatch a wounded big game animal using only a .22-caliber rimfire pistol, archery equipment, or a handgun otherwise legal for that hunting season. Pursuit and retrieval under this subsection may occur between the hours of one-half hour after sunset and 11:00 p.m. if necessary, but such pursuit and retrieval may not be accomplished using a motorized vehicle.

For purposes of this section, the term "dispatch" means the quick and humane killing of a wounded animal to prevent further suffering through infection, starvation, or other distress in the wild. (C.S., s. 2124; 1935, c. 486, s. 20;

1939, c. 235, s. 1; 1949, c. 1205, s. 3; 1955, c. 104; 1959, cc. 207, 500; 1961, c. 1182; 1963, c. 381; c. 697, ss. 1, 3½; 1967, c. 858, s. 1; c. 1149, s. 1.5; 1969, cc. 75, 140; 1971, c. 439, ss. 1-3; c. 899, s. 1; 1973, c. 1096; c. 1262, s. 18; 1975, c. 669; 1977, c. 493; 1979, c. 830, s. 1; 1979, 2nd Sess., c. 1285, ss. 4-6; 1983, c. 137, ss. 1, 2; c. 492; 1985, c. 360; c. 554, ss. 1, 2; 1987, cc. 97, 134, 827, s. 98; 1993, c. 539, s. 862; 1994, Ex. Sess., c. 24, s. 14(c); 1995, c. 64, s. 1; 1999-120, s. 1; 2003-160, s. 1; 2005-76, ss. 1, 2; 2005-298, s. 1; 2007-401, s. 6; 2009-221, ss. 2, 3; 2011-22, s. 1; 2011-369, s. 4; 2013-283, s. 12; 2013-369, s. 23.)


§ 113-291.1A. Computer-assisted remote hunting prohibited.

(a)     It is unlawful for a person to engage in computer-assisted remote hunting or provide or operate a facility that allows others to engage in computer-assisted remote hunting if the wild animal or wild bird being hunted or shot is located in this State.

(b)     For purposes of this section "computer-assisted remote hunting" means the use of a computer or other device, equipment, or software, to remotely control the aiming and discharging of a firearm or other weapon, that allows a person, not physically present at the location of that firearm or other weapon, to hunt or shoot a wild animal or wild bird. (2005-62, s. 1.)


§ 113-291.2. Seasons and bag limits on wild animals and birds; including animals and birds taken in bag; possession and transportation of wildlife after taking.

(a)     In accordance with the supply of wildlife and other factors it determines to be of public importance, the Wildlife Resources Commission may fix seasons and bag limits upon the wild animals and wild birds authorized to be taken that it deems necessary or desirable in the interests of the conservation of wildlife resources. The authority to fix seasons includes the closing of seasons completely when necessary and fixing the hours of hunting. The authority to fix bag limits includes the setting of season and possession limits. Different seasons and bag limits may be set in differing areas; early or extended seasons and different or unlimited bag limits may be authorized on controlled shooting preserves, game lands, and public hunting grounds; and special or extended seasons may be fixed for those engaging in falconry, using primitive weapons, or taking wildlife under other special conditions.

Unless modified by rules of the Wildlife Resources Commission or as provided in subsection (f) of this section, the seasons, shooting hours, bag limits, and possession limits fixed by the United States Department of Interior or any successor agency for migratory game birds in North Carolina must be followed, and a violation of the applicable federal rules is hereby made unlawful. When the applicable federal rules require that the State limit participation in seasons and/or bag limits for migratory game birds, the Wildlife Resources Commission may schedule managed hunts for migratory game birds. Participants in such hunts shall be selected at random by computer, and each applicant 16 years of age or older shall have the required general hunting license and the waterfowl hunting license prior to the drawing for the managed hunt. Each applicant under 16 years of age shall either have the required general hunting license and the waterfowl hunting license or shall apply as a member of a party that includes a properly licensed adult. All applications for managed waterfowl hunts shall be screened prior to the drawing for compliance with these requirements. A nonrefundable fee of ten dollars ($10.00) shall be required of each applicant to defray the cost of processing the applications.

(a1) When the Executive Director of the Wildlife Resources Commission receives a petition from the State Health Director declaring a rabies emergency for a particular county or district pursuant to G.S. 130A-201, the Executive Director of the Wildlife Resources Commission shall develop a plan to reduce the threat of rabies exposure to humans and domestic animals by foxes, raccoons, skunks, or bobcats in the county or district. The plan shall be based upon the best veterinary and wildlife management information and techniques available. The plan may involve a suspension or liberalization of any regulatory restriction on the taking of foxes, raccoons, skunks, or bobcats, except that the use of poisons, other than those used with dart guns, shall not be permitted under any circumstance. If the plan involves a suspension or liberalization of any regulatory restriction on the taking of foxes, raccoons, skunks, or bobcats, the Executive Director of the Wildlife Resources Commission shall prepare and adopt temporary rules setting out the suspension or liberalization pursuant to G.S. 150B-21.1(a)(1). The Executive Director shall publicize the plan and the temporary rules in the major news outlets that serve the county or district to inform the public of the actions being taken and the reasons for them. Upon notification by the State Health Director that the rabies emergency no longer exists, the Executive Director of the Wildlife Resources Commission shall cancel the plan and repeal any rules adopted to implement the plan. The Executive

Director of the Wildlife Resources Commission shall publicize the cancellation of the plan and the repeal of any rules in the major news outlets that serve the county or district.

(b) Any individual hunter or trapper who in taking a wild animal or bird has wounded or otherwise disabled it must make a reasonable effort to capture and kill the animal or bird. All animals and birds taken that can be retrieved must be retrieved and counted with respect to any applicable bag limits governing the individual taking the animal or bird.

(c) An individual who has lawfully taken game within applicable bag, possession, and season limits may, except as limited by rules adopted pursuant to subsection (c1) of this section, after the game is dead, possess and personally transport it for his own use by virtue of his hunting license, and without any additional permit, subject to tagging and reporting requirements that may apply to the fox and big game, as follows:

(1) In an area in which the season is open for the species, the game may be possessed and transported without restriction.

(2) The individual may possess and transport the game lawfully taken on a trip:

a. To his residence;

b. To a preservation or processing facility that keeps adequate records as prescribed in G.S. 113-291.3(b)(3) or a licensed taxidermist;

c. From a place authorized in subparagraph b to his residence.

(3) The individual may possess the game indefinitely at his residence, and may there accumulate lawfully-acquired game up to the greater of:

a. The applicable possession limit for each species; or

b. One half of the applicable season limit for each species.

The above subdivisions apply to an individual hunter under 16 years of age covered by the license issued to his parent or guardian, if he is using that license, or by the license of an adult accompanying him. An individual who has lawfully taken game as a landholder without a license may possess and transport the dead game, taken within applicable bag, possession, and season limits, to his residence. He may indefinitely retain possession of such game, within aggregate possession limits for the species in question, in his residence.

(c1)     In the event that the Executive Director finds that game carcasses or parts of game carcasses are known or suspected to carry an infectious or contagious disease that poses an imminent threat to the health or habitat of wildlife species, the Wildlife Resources Commission shall adopt rules to regulate the importation, transportation, or possession of those carcasses or parts of carcasses that, according to wildlife disease experts, may transmit such a disease.

(d)     Except in the situations specifically provided for above, the Wildlife Resources Commission may by rule impose reporting, permit, and tagging requirements that may be necessary upon persons:

(1)     Possessing dead wildlife taken in open season after the close of that season.

(2)     Transporting dead wildlife from an area having an open season to an area with a closed season.

(3)     Transporting dead wildlife lawfully taken in another state into this State.

(4)     Possessing dead wildlife after such transportation.

The Wildlife Resources Commission in its discretion may substitute written declarations to be filed with agents of the Commission for permit and tagging requirements.

(e)     Upon application of any landholder or agent of a landholder accompanied by a fee of fifty dollars ($50.00), the Executive Director may issue to such landholder or agent a special license and a number of special antlerless or antlered deer tags that in the judgment of the Executive Director is sufficient to accommodate the landholder or the landholder's agent's deer population management objectives or correct any deer population imbalance that may occur on the property. Subject to applicable hunting license requirements, the special deer tags may be used by any person or persons selected by the landholder or his agent as authority to take antlerless deer, including male deer with "buttons" or spikes not readily visible, or antlered deer on the tract of land concerned during any established deer hunting season. The Executive Director or designee may stipulate on the license that special deer tags for antlered deer, if applicable, may only be valid for deer that meet certain minimum harvest criteria. The Executive Director or designee may also define on the license valid hunt dates that fall outside of the general deer hunting season. Harvested antlerless or antlered deer for which special tags are issued shall be affixed immediately with a special deer tag and shall be reported immediately in the wildlife cooperator tagging book supplied with the special deer tags. This tagging book and any unused tags shall be returned to the Commission within 15 days of the close of the season. The Wildlife Resources Commission may offer an alternate reporting system when the Commission determines that such an alternate system is appropriate. Antlerless or antlered deer taken under this program and tagged with the special tags provided shall not count as part of the daily bag, possession, and season limits of the person taking the deer.

(f) The Commission is authorized to issue proclamations to set seasons, shooting hours, bag limits, and possession limits that are congruent with the season framework established by the United States Department of Interior or any successor agency. The Commission may delegate this authority to the Executive Director. Each proclamation shall state the hour and date upon which it becomes effective and shall be issued at least 48 hours prior to the effective date and time. A permanent file of the text of all proclamations shall be maintained in the office of the Executive Director. Certified copies of proclamations are entitled to judicial notice in any civil or criminal proceeding.

The Executive Director shall make a reasonable effort to give notice of the terms of any proclamation to persons who may be affected by it. This effort shall include press releases to communications media, posting of notices at boating access areas and other places where persons affected may gather, personal communication by agents of the Wildlife Resources Commission, and other measures designed to reach persons who may be affected. Proclamations under this subsection shall remain in force until rescinded following the same procedure established for enactment. (1935, c. 486, ss. 16, 17; 1949, c. 1205, s. 1; 1973, c. 1262, s. 18; 1977, c. 499, s. 1; 1979, c. 830, s. 1; 1979, 2nd Sess., c. 1285, s. 7; 1981, c. 681, s. 1; 1987, c. 38; c. 827, s. 98; 1989, c. 642, s. 2; 1995, c. 181, s. 1; 1997-402, s. 2; 1999-339, s. 7; 2003-344, ss. 7, 8; 2005-82, s. 2; 2007-401, s. 3; 2009-221, s. 1.)

§ 113-291.3. Possession, sale, and transportation of wildlife.

(a) Live wildlife and the nests and eggs of wild birds may be taken, possessed, transported, bought, sold, imported, exported, or otherwise acquired or disposed of only as specifically authorized in this Subchapter or its implementing rules. The Wildlife Resources Commission may impose necessary reporting, permit, and tagging requirements in regulating activities involving live wildlife and the nests and eggs of wild birds. The Wildlife Resources Commission may charge a reasonable fee to defray the cost of any tagging procedure.

(b) With respect to dead wildlife:

(1) Lawfully taken wildlife may be possessed and transported as provided in G.S. 113-291.2. Wildlife possessed under any dealer license may be possessed and transported in accordance with the provisions of law and rules applicable to the license, and wildlife may be sold to qualified persons if authorized under provisions governing the license. In other situations, except as this Subchapter may expressly provide, possession and transportation of wildlife may be regulated by the Wildlife Resources Commission.

(2) Unless there is a specific restriction on the transfer of the species in question, an individual may accept the gift of wildlife lawfully taken within North Carolina if taking possession does not cause him to exceed applicable possession limits. If he notes and preserves in writing the name and address of the donor and under what license or exemption from license requirements the wildlife was taken, he may possess that wildlife without a permit in the places possession without a permit would be authorized in G.S. 113-291.2 had he taken the wildlife.

(3) A licensed taxidermist or other licensed dealer taking temporary possession of wildlife of another may possess the wildlife that he is authorized to handle under his license in accordance with the rules of the Wildlife Resources Commission. A person not a dealer operating a preservation or processing facility, whether commercially or not, may possess the wildlife owned by another without any permit or license if he ascertains that the wildlife was lawfully taken within the State and keeps a written record of:

a. The name and address of the owner of the wildlife and an adequate description of the wildlife left with him. If the description of the wildlife changes as the result of processing, the new description must be recorded.

b. The date, serial number, and type of the license under which the wildlife was taken or the applicable exemption from license requirements which the taker met.

c. The date all wildlife left with him is received and returned to the owner. If the receiving or returning of possession is to an agent or common carrier or otherwise occurs under circumstances in which permit requirements may apply, the type and date of the permit which authorizes the transaction must also be recorded.

(4) The sale of rabbits and squirrels and their edible parts not for resale is permitted. If the Wildlife Resources Commission finds that affected game populations would not be endangered, it may authorize the sale of heads, antlers, horns, hides, skins, plumes, feet, and claws of one or more game animals or birds. In addition, it may authorize the sale of bobcats, opossums, and raccoons, and their parts, following their taking as game animals. No part of any bear or wild turkey may be sold under the above provisions, however, and no part of any fox taken in North Carolina may be sold except as provided in G.S. 113-291.4. In regulating sales, the Wildlife Resources Commission may impose necessary permit requirements.

(5) Lawfully taken fur-bearing animals and their parts, including furs and pelts, may, subject to any tagging and reporting requirements, be possessed, transported, bought, sold, given or received as a gift, or otherwise disposed of without restriction. The Wildlife Resources Commission may regulate the importation of wildlife from without the State by fur dealers, and may regulate the sale of fox fur and other wildlife hides taken within the State if sale of them is authorized. Fox furs lawfully taken without the State may be imported, possessed, transported, bought, sold, and exported in accordance with reasonable rules of the Wildlife Resources Commission. Processed furs acquired through lawful channels within or without the State by persons other than fur dealers are not subject to rule.

(6) Nongame animals and birds open to hunting and nongame fish lawfully taken, except as this Subchapter and its implementing rules expressly provide otherwise, may be possessed, transported, bought, sold, given or received as a gift, or otherwise disposed of without restriction.

(7) The possession and disposition of wild animals and wild birds killed accidentally or to prevent or halt depredations to property are governed by G.S. 113-274(c)(1a).

(8) The edible parts of deer raised domestically in another state may be transported into this State and resold as a meat product for human consumption when the edible parts have passed inspection in the other state by that state's inspection agency or the United States Department of Agriculture.

(c) The Wildlife Resources Commission may make reasonable rules governing the marking of packages, crates, and other containers in which wildlife may be shipped.

(d) Any person hiring a hunter or trapper to take game is deemed to be buying game. Any hunter or trapper who may be hired is deemed to be selling game. (1935, c. 486, ss. 19, 22; 1941, c. 231, s. 1; 1973, c. 1262, s. 18; 1979, c. 830, s. 1; 1979, 2nd Sess., c. 1285, s. 8; 1987, c. 827, s. 98; 1997-142, s. 15; 1997-456, s. 44.)

§ 113-291.4. Regulation of foxes; study of fox and fur-bearer populations.

(a) All of the regulatory powers granted the Wildlife Resources Commission generally with respect to game, wild animals, and wildlife apply to foxes unless there are specific overriding restrictions in this section.

(b) Except for any closed season under subsection (h), foxes may be taken with dogs both night and day on a year-round basis.

(c) Foxes may not be taken with firearms except:

(1) As provided in subsection (f) or (i) of this section or G.S. 113-291.4A(a).

(2) As an incidental method of humanely killing them following any lawful method of taking that does not result in death.

(3) When they are lawfully shot under laws and rules pertaining to the destruction of animals committing depredations to property.

(d) Foxes may not be taken with the aid of any electronic calling device.

(e) The Wildlife Resources Commission is directed to improve its capabilities for studying fox and fur-bearer populations generally and, on the basis of its present knowledge and future studies, to implement management methods and impose controls designed to produce optimum fox and fur-bearer populations in the various areas of the State.

(f) If, on the basis of its studies and other information available, the Wildlife Resources Commission determines the population of foxes in an area is fully adequate to support a harvesting of that population, the Wildlife Resources Commission may, upon passage of local legislation permitting same, open a season for taking foxes by trapping. When the season is open for trapping, foxes may also be taken by the use of methods lawful for taking game animals, including the use of firearms. Any bag, possession, or season limits imposed on foxes taken from the area in question will apply in the aggregate to all foxes killed without regard to the method of taking.

(f1) In those counties in which open seasons for taking foxes with weapons and by trapping were established between June 18, 1982, and July 1, 1987, in accordance with the procedure then set forth in subsection (f) of this section, the Wildlife Resources Commission is authorized to continue such seasons from year to year so long as the fox populations of such counties remain adequate to support the resulting harvest. The counties referred to in this subsection are as follows: Caswell, Clay, Graham, Henderson, Hyde, Macon, and Tyrrell.

(g) The Wildlife Resources Commission may provide for the sale of foxes lawfully taken in areas of open season as provided in subsection (f), under a system providing strict controls. The Wildlife Resources Commission must implement a system of tagging foxes and fox furs with a special fox tag, and the Commission may charge two dollars and twenty-five cents ($2.25) for each tag furnished to hunters, trappers, and fur dealers. The fox tag or tags must be procured before taking foxes by any method designed to kill foxes or when the intent is to harvest foxes. The number of tags furnished to any individual may be limited as to area and as to number in accordance with area, bag, possession, or season limits that may be imposed on foxes. No person may continue to hunt or trap foxes under this fox harvesting provision unless he still has at least one valid unused fox tag lawful for use in the area in question. A person hunting foxes with dogs not intending to kill them need not have any fox tag, but any fox accidentally killed by that hunter must be disposed of without sale as provided below, and no foxes not tagged may be sold. The Wildlife Resources Commission may by rule provide reporting and controlled-disposition requirements, not including sale, of foxes killed accidentally by dog hunters, motor vehicles, and in other situations; it may also impose strict controls on the disposition of foxes taken by owners of property under the laws and rules relating to depredations, and authorize sale under controlled conditions of foxes taken under depredation permits.

(h)     In any area of the State in which the Wildlife Resources Commission determines that hunting of foxes with dogs has an appreciably harmful effect upon turkey restoration projects, it may declare a closed season for an appropriate length of time upon the taking with dogs of all species of wild animals and birds. Except as otherwise provided in G.S. 113-291.1(d) or (d1), this subsection does not prohibit lawful field trials or the training of dogs.

(i)     Upon notification by the State Health Director of the presence of a contagious animal disease in a local fox population, the Commission is authorized to establish such population control measures as are appropriate until notified by public health authorities that the problem is deemed to have passed. (1979, c. 830, s. 1; 1981 (Reg. Sess., 1982), c. 1203, ss. 1-3; 1985, c. 476, s. 2; 1987, c. 726, s. 1; c. 827, s. 98; 1989, c. 504, s. 2; c. 616, s. 4; c. 727, s. 113; 1991, c. 483, s. 1(a), (b); 1993, c. 208, s. 4; 2008-102, s. 3.)


§ 113-291.4A. Open seasons for taking foxes with firearms.

(a)     There is an open season for the taking of foxes with firearms in all areas of the State east of Interstate Highway 77 and in Mitchell and Caldwell Counties from the beginning of the season established by the Wildlife Resources Commission for the taking of rabbits and quail through January 1 of each year. The selling, buying, or possessing for sale of any fox or fox part taken pursuant to this subsection is prohibited, and is punishable as provided by G.S. 113-294(a) or (j).

(b)     The Wildlife Resources Commission shall establish appropriate bag and season limits that may be imposed upon the taking of foxes pursuant to this act, and may make reasonable rules governing the possession of foxes killed by motor vehicles or other accidental means. (1989, c. 616, s. 1; 1989 (Reg. Sess., 1990), c. 811; 1995, c. 32, s. 1; 1999-456, s. 32.)


§ 113-291.5. Regulation of dogs used in hunting; limitations on authority of Wildlife Resources Commission; control of dogs on game lands; control of dogs chasing deer; other restrictions.

(a) Except as provided in G.S. 113-291.4, in the area described below, the Wildlife Resources Commission may regulate the use of dogs taking wildlife with respect to seasons, times, and places of use. The area covered by this subsection is that part of the State in and west of the following counties or parts of counties: Rockingham; Guilford; that part of Alamance and Orange lying south of Interstate Highway 85; Chatham; that part of Wake lying south of N.C. Highway 98; Lee; Randolph; Montgomery; Stanly; Union; and that part of Anson lying west of N.C. Highway 742.

(b) In the area of the State lying east of that described in subsection (a), the Wildlife Resources Commission may not restrict or prohibit the use of dogs in hunting or the training of dogs, in season or out, except during the breeding and raising seasons for game during the period April 15 through June 15.

(c) On game lands, wildlife refuges, and public hunting grounds the Wildlife Resources Commission may regulate the possession and use of dogs and may impound dogs found running at large without supervision or, if unsupervised, without means of identification.

(d) The Wildlife Resources Commission may not by its rules anywhere in the State restrict the number of dogs used in hunting or require that any particular breed of dog be used in hunting.

(e) It is unlawful to allow dogs not under the control of the owner or the individual in possession of the dogs to run or chase deer during the closed deer season.

(f) Nothing in this section is intended to require the leashing or confining of pet dogs. (1979, c. 830, s. 1; 1987, c. 827, s. 98.)


§ 113-291.6. Regulation of trapping.

(a) No one may take wild animals by trapping upon the land of another without having in his possession written permission issued and dated within the previous year by the owner of the land or his agent. This subsection does not apply to public lands on which trapping is not specifically prohibited, including tidelands, marshlands, and any other untitled land.

(b) No one may take wild animals by trapping with any steel-jaw, leghold, or conibear trap unless it:

(1) Has a jaw spread of not more than seven and one-half inches.

(2) Is horizontally offset with closed jaw spread of at least three sixteenths of an inch for a trap with a jaw spread of more than five and one-half inches. This subdivision does not apply if the trap is set in the water with quick-drown type of set.

(3) Is smooth edged and without teeth or spikes.

(4) Has a weather-resistant permanent tag attached legibly giving the trapper's name and address.

A steel-jaw or leghold trap set on dry land with solid anchor may not have a trap chain longer than eight inches from trap to anchor unless fitted with a shock-absorbing device approved by the Wildlife Resources Commission.

(c) No person may set or otherwise use a trap so that animals or birds when caught will be suspended. No hook of any type may be used to take wild animals or wild birds by trapping.

(d) Conibear type traps that have an inside jaw spread or opening (width or height) greater than seven and one-half inches and no larger than 26 inches in width and 12 inches in height may only be set in the water and in areas in which beaver and otter may be lawfully trapped. For the purposes of this section:

(1) A water-set trap is one totally covered by water with the anchor secured in water deep enough to drown the animal trapped quickly.

(2) In areas of tidal waters, the mean high water is considered covering water.

(3) In reservoir areas, covering water is the low water level prevailing during the preceding 24 hours.

(4) Marshland, as defined in G.S. 113-229(n)(3), is not considered dry land.

(e)   With respect to any lawfully placed trap of another set in compliance with the provisions of this section, no one without the express permission of the trapper may:

(1)   Remove or disturb any trap; or

(2)   Remove any fur-bearing animal from the trap.

This subsection does not apply to wildlife protectors or other law-enforcement officers acting in the performance of their duties.

(f)   Nothing in this section prohibits the use of steel- or metal-jaw traps by county or State public health officials or their agents to control the spread of disease when the use of these traps has been declared necessary by the State Health Director.

(g)   The Wildlife Resources Commission must include the trapping requirements of this section in its annual digest of hunting and trapping rules provided to each person upon purchase of a license.

(h)   A person who has been issued a depredation permit for coyotes under G.S. 113-274(c) may use a Collarumm™ trap, or similar trap approved by the Wildlife Resources Commission, solely for the purpose of taking coyotes under that permit. The person authorized to use these traps pursuant to this subsection shall provide information on the effectiveness and efficiency of the traps as requested by the Commission. To minimize the risk of harm to nontargeted species, any such trap set shall be attended daily and any nontarget animal caught released. (1977, c. 933, ss. 2, 7; 1979, c. 830, s. 1; 1981, c. 729; 1987, c. 827, s. 98; 1989, c. 727, s. 114; 1997-418, s. 5; 2009-120, s. 1; 2010-156, s. 1.)


§ 113-291.7.  Regulation of bears; limited retention of local acts closing bear seasons.

Local acts closing the season on bears are exempted from the provisions of G.S. 113-133.1(b) until July 1, 1981. After that date any local acts setting a year-round closed season on bears which have not by their terms expired are temporarily retained until the Wildlife Resources Commission supersedes them by adopting rules either opening a season in the county affected or carrying forward the closed-season provision. (1979, c. 830, s. 1; 1987, c. 827, s. 98.)

§ 113-291.8. Requirement to display hunter orange.

(a) Any person hunting game animals other than foxes, bobcats, raccoons, and opossum, or hunting upland game birds other than wild turkeys, or hunting feral swine, with the use of firearms, must wear a cap or hat on his head made of hunter orange material or an outer garment of hunter orange visible from all sides. Any person hunting deer during a deer firearms season shall wear hunter orange. Hunter orange material is a material that is a daylight fluorescent orange color.

This section does not apply to a landholder, his spouse, or children, who are hunting on land held by the landholder. This subsection shall be enforced by warning ticket only until October 1, 1992, with respect to those hunting rabbit, squirrel, grouse, pheasant, and quail.

(b) Any person violating this section during the 1987 big game hunting season shall be given a warning of violation only. Thereafter, any person violating this section has committed an infraction and shall pay a fine of twenty-five dollars ($25.00). An infraction is an unlawful act that is not a crime. The procedure for charging and trying an infraction is the same as for a misdemeanor, but conviction of an infraction has no consequence other than payment of a fine. A person convicted of an infraction may not be assessed court costs.

Wildlife Enforcement Officers are authorized to charge persons with the infraction created by this section.

(c) Failure to wear hunter orange material in violation of this section shall not constitute negligence per se or contributory negligence per se. (1987, c. 72, s. 1; 1991, c. 71, s. 1; 2007-401, s. 4; 2011-369, s. 5.)

§ 113-291.9. Taking of beaver.

(a) Notwithstanding any other law, there is an open season for taking beaver with firearms or bow and arrow during any open season for the taking of wild animals, provided that permission has been obtained from the owner or lessee of the land on which the beaver is being taken.

(b) Notwithstanding any other law, it is lawful to use or sell beaver parts taken under a depredation permit issued by the Wildlife Resources Commission.

(c) Notwithstanding G.S. 113-291.6(d) or any other law, it is lawful to set traps of the conibear type that have an inside jaw spread or opening (width or height) no larger than 26 inches in width and 12 inches in height if at least one-half of the trap is covered by water, when trapping beaver during the season for trapping beaver as established by the Wildlife Resources Commission.

(d) Notwithstanding G.S. 113-291.1(b)(2) or any other law, it is lawful to use snares when trapping beaver during the season for trapping beaver as established by the Wildlife Resources Commission.

(e) Repealed by Session Laws 1993, c. 33, s. 1.

(f) Notwithstanding any other provision of law, landowners whose property is or has been damaged or destroyed by beaver may take beaver on their property by any lawful method without obtaining a depredation permit from the Wildlife Resources Commission, and may obtain assistance from other persons in taking the depredating beaver by giving those persons permission to take beaver on the landowner's property.

(g) Repealed by Session Laws 1997-456, s. 53. (1991, c. 483, s. 3; 1993, c. 33, s. 1; 1995, c. 509, s. 56; 1997-97, s. 1; 1997-456, s. 53; 2007-401, s. 2; 2009-120, s. 2.)


§ 113-291.10. Beaver Damage Control Advisory Board.

(a) There is established the Beaver Damage Control Advisory Board. The Board shall consist of nine members, as follows:

(1) The Executive Director of the North Carolina Wildlife Resources Commission, or his designee, who shall serve as chair;

(2) The Commissioner of Agriculture, or a designee;

(3) The Assistant Commissioner of the North Carolina Forest Service of the Department of Agriculture and Consumer Services, or a designee;

(4) The Director of the Division of Soil and Water Conservation of the Department of Agriculture and Consumer Services, or a designee;

(5) The Director of the North Carolina Cooperative Extension Service, or a designee;

(6) The Secretary of Transportation, or a designee;

(7) The State Director of the Wildlife Services Division of the Animal and Plant Health Inspection Service, U.S. Department of Agriculture, or a designee;

(8) The President of the North Carolina Farm Bureau Federation, Inc., or a designee, representing private landowners; and

(9) A representative of the North Carolina Forestry Association.

(b) The Beaver Damage Control Advisory Board shall develop a statewide program to control beaver damage on private and public lands. The Beaver Damage Control Advisory Board shall act in an advisory capacity to the Wildlife Resources Commission in the implementation of the program. In developing the program, the Board shall:

(1) Orient the program primarily toward public health and safety and toward landowner assistance, providing some relief to landowners through beaver control and management rather than eradication;

(2) Develop a priority system for responding to complaints about beaver damage;

(3) Develop a system for documenting all activities associated with beaver damage control, so as to facilitate evaluation of the program;

(4) Provide educational activities as a part of the program, such as printed materials, on-site instructions, and local workshops; and

(5) Provide for the hiring of personnel necessary to implement beaver damage control activities, administer the program, and set salaries of personnel.

No later than March 15 of each year, the Board shall issue a report to the Wildlife Resources Commission, the Senate and House Appropriations Subcommittees on Natural and Economic Resources, and the Fiscal Research Division on the results of the program during the preceding year.

(c) The Wildlife Resources Commission shall implement the program, and may enter a cooperative agreement with the Wildlife Services Division of the Animal and Plant Health Inspection Service, United States Department of Agriculture, to accomplish the program.

(d) Notwithstanding G.S. 113-291.6(d) or any other law, it is lawful to use snares when trapping beaver pursuant to the beaver damage control program developed pursuant to this section. The provisions of Chapter 218 of the 1975 Session Laws; Chapter 492 of the 1951 Session Laws, as amended by Chapter 506 of the 1955 Session Laws; and Chapter 1011 of the 1983 Session Laws do not apply to trapping carried out in implementing the beaver damage control program developed pursuant to this section.

(e) In case of any conflict between G.S. 113-291.6(a) and G.S. 113-291.6(b) and this section, this section prevails.

(f) Each county that volunteers to participate in this program for a given fiscal year shall provide written notification of its wish to participate no later than September 30 of that year and shall commit the sum of four thousand dollars ($4,000) in local funds no later than September 30 of that year. Funds, as appropriated for this program each fiscal year of the biennium, shall be paid from funds available to the Wildlife Resources Commission to provide the State share necessary to support this program, provided the sum of at least twenty-five thousand dollars ($25,000) in federal funds is available each fiscal year of the biennium to provide the federal share. (1991 (Reg. Sess., 1992), c. 1044, s. 69; 1993, c. 561, s. 111; 1993 (Reg. Sess., 1994), c. 769, s. 27.3; 1995, c. 358, s. 7; c. 437, s. 5; c. 467, s.4; c. 507, s. 26.6; 1996 Second Ex. Sess., c. 18, s. 27.15; 1997-256, s. 10; 1997-347, s. 6; 1997-401, s. 6; 1997-418, s. 5; 1997-443, c. 15.44; 1998-23, s. 16; 1998-212, s. 14.18(a)-(c), (e); 1999-237, s. 15.1(b), (c); 2005-386, s. 1.7; 2007-484, s. 13; 2009-451, s. 13.10; 2011-145, ss. 13.22A(bb), 13.25(rr), 13.29; 2013-155, s. 18.)

§ 113-291.11. Feeding of alligators prohibited.

It is unlawful to intentionally feed alligators outside of captivity. (2007-401, s. 5.)

§ 113-291.12. Unlawful to remove live feral swine from traps.

It is unlawful to remove feral swine from a trap while the swine is still alive or to transport the live swine after that removal. (2011-369, s. 6(a).)

§ 113-292. Authority of the Wildlife Resources Commission in regulation of inland fishing and the introduction of exotic species.

(a) The Wildlife Resources Commission is authorized to authorize, license, regulate, prohibit, prescribe, or restrict all fishing in inland fishing waters, and the taking of inland game fish in coastal fishing waters, with respect to:

(1) Time, place, character, or dimensions of any methods or equipment that may be employed in taking fish;

(2) Seasons for taking fish;

(3) Size limits on and maximum quantities of fish that may be taken, possessed, bailed to another, transported, bought, sold, or given away.

(b) The Wildlife Resources Commission is authorized to authorize, license, regulate, prohibit, prescribe, or restrict:

(1) The opening and closing of inland fishing waters, whether entirely or only as to the taking of particular classes of fish, use of particular equipment, or as to other activities within the jurisdiction of the Wildlife Resources Commission; and

(2) The possession, cultivation, transportation, importation, exportation, sale, purchase, acquisition, and disposition of all inland fisheries resources and all related equipment, implements, vessels, and conveyances as necessary to implement the work of the Wildlife Resources Commission in carrying out its duties.

To the extent not in conflict with provisions enforced by the Department, the Wildlife Resources Commission may exercise the powers conferred in this subsection in coastal fishing waters pursuant to its rule of inland game fish in such waters.

(c) The Wildlife Resources Commission is authorized to make such rules pertaining to the acquisition, disposition, transportation, and possession of fish in connection with private ponds as may be necessary in carrying out the provisions of this Subchapter and the overall objectives of the conservation of wildlife resources.

(c1) The Wildlife Resources Commission is authorized to issue proclamations suspending or extending the hook-and-line season for striped bass in the inland and joint waters of coastal rivers and their tributaries, and the Commission may delegate this authority to the Executive Director. Each proclamation shall state the hour and date upon which it becomes effective, and shall be issued at least 48 hours prior to the effective date and time. A permanent file of the text of all proclamations shall be maintained in the office of the Executive Director. Certified copies of proclamations are entitled to judicial notice in any civil or criminal proceeding.

The Executive Director shall make reasonable effort to give notice of the terms of any proclamation to persons who may be affected by it. This effort shall include press releases to communications media, posting of notices at boating access areas and other places where persons affected may gather, personal communication by agents of the Wildlife Resources Commission, and other measures designed to reach persons who may be affected. Proclamations under this subsection shall remain in force until rescinded following the same procedure established for enactment.

(d) The Wildlife Resources Commission is authorized to authorize, license, regulate, prohibit, prescribe, or restrict anywhere in the State the acquisition, importation, possession, transportation, disposition, or release into public or private waters or the environment of zoological or botanical species or specimens that may threaten the introduction of epizootic disease or may create a danger to or an imbalance in the environment inimical to the conservation of wildlife resources. This subsection is not intended to give the Wildlife Resources Commission the authority to supplant, enact any conflicting rules, or otherwise take any action inconsistent with that of any other State agency acting within its jurisdiction.

(e) It is unlawful for any person to:

(1) Release or place exotic species of wild animals or wild birds in an area for the purpose of stocking the area for hunting or trapping;

(2) Release or place species of wild animals or wild birds not indigenous to that area in an area for the purpose of stocking the area for hunting or trapping;

(3) Take by hunting or trapping any animal or bird released or placed in an area in contravention of subdivisions (1) and (2) of this subsection, except under a permit to hunt or trap which may be issued by the Wildlife Resources Commission for the purpose of eradicating or controlling the population of any species of wildlife that has been so released or placed in the area. (1965, c. 957, s. 2; 1973, c. 1262, s. 18; 1979, c. 830, s. 1; 1983, cc. 555, 615; 1987, c. 827, s. 98; 1991, c. 104, s. 1; c. 636, s. 8; 2003-344, s. 9.)


§ 113-293. Obstructing rivers or creeks; keeping open fishways in dams.

(a), (b) Repealed by Session Laws 1979, c. 830, s. 1.

(c) It is unlawful for any person in inland fishing waters:

(1) To set a net of any description across the main channel of any river or creek;

(2) To erect so as to extend more than three fourths of the distance across any river or creek any stand, dam, weir, hedge, or other obstruction to the passage of fish;

(3) To erect any stand, dam, weir, or hedge in any part of a river or creek required to be left open for the passage of fish; or,

(4) Having erected any dam where the same was allowed, to fail to make and keep open such slope or fishway as may be required by law to be kept open for the free passage of fish.

The provisions of this section may not be construed to conflict in any way with the laws and rules of any other agency with jurisdiction over the activity or subject matter in question. (Code, ss. 3387-3389; Rev., s. 2457; 1909, c. 466, s.

1; 1915, c. 84, s. 21; 1917, c. 290, s. 7; C.S., ss. 1878, 1974; 1925, c. 168, s. 2; 1935, c. 35; 1945, c. 776; 1951, c. 1045, s. 1; 1953, cc. 774, 1251; 1963, c. 1097, s. 1; 1965, c. 957, s. 2; 1973, c. 1262, s. 18; 1979, c. 830, s. 1; 1987, c. 827, s. 98.)

§ 113-294. Specific violations.

(a) Any person who unlawfully sells, possesses for sale, or buys any wildlife is guilty of a Class 2 misdemeanor, punishable by a fine of not less than two hundred fifty dollars ($250.00), unless a greater penalty is prescribed for the offense in question.

(b) Any person who unlawfully sells, possesses for sale, or buys any deer or wild turkey is guilty of a Class 2 misdemeanor, punishable by a fine of not less than five hundred dollars ($500.00) in addition to such other punishment prescribed for the offense in question.

(c) Any person who unlawfully takes, possesses, or transports any wild turkey is guilty of a Class 2 misdemeanor, punishable by a fine of not less than two hundred fifty dollars ($250.00) in addition to such other punishment prescribed for the offense in question.

(c1) Any person who unlawfully takes, possesses, transports, sells, possesses for sale, or buys any bear or bear part is guilty of a Class 1 misdemeanor, punishable by a fine of not less than two thousand dollars ($2,000) in addition to such other punishment prescribed for the offense in question. Each of the acts specified shall constitute a separate offense.

(c2) Any person who unlawfully takes, possesses, transports, sells, possesses for sale, or buys any cougar (Felis concolor) is guilty of a Class 1 misdemeanor, unless a greater penalty is prescribed for the offense in question.

(c3) Any person who unlawfully takes, possesses, or transports any elk is guilty of a Class 1 misdemeanor, punishable by a fine of not less than two thousand five hundred dollars ($2,500) in addition to such other punishment prescribed for the offense in question.

(d) Any person who unlawfully takes, possesses, or transports any deer is guilty of a Class 3 misdemeanor, punishable by a fine of not less than two hundred fifty dollars ($250.00) in addition to such other punishment prescribed for the offense in question.

(d1)   Any person who unlawfully takes, possesses, or transports any deer from land that has been posted in accordance with the provisions of G.S. 14-159.7 without written permission of the landowner, lessee, or the agent of the landowner or lessee is guilty of a Class 2 misdemeanor, punishable by a fine of not less than five hundred dollars ($500.00).

(e)   Any person who unlawfully takes deer between a half hour after sunset and a half hour before sunrise with the aid of an artificial light is guilty of a Class 2 misdemeanor, punishable by a fine of not less than five hundred dollars ($500.00) in addition to such other punishment prescribed for the offense in question.

(f)   Any person who unlawfully takes, possesses, transports, sells, or buys any beaver, or violates any rule of the Wildlife Resources Commission adopted to protect beavers, is guilty of a Class 3 misdemeanor, unless a greater penalty is prescribed for the offense in question.

(g)   Any person who unlawfully takes wild animals or birds from or with the use of a vessel equipped with a motor or with motor attached is guilty of a Class 2 misdemeanor, unless a greater penalty is prescribed for the offense in question.

(h)   Any person who willfully makes any false or misleading statement in order to secure for himself or another any license, permit, privilege, exemption, or other benefit under this Subchapter to which he or the person in question is not entitled is guilty of a Class 1 misdemeanor.

(i)   Any person who violates any provision of G.S. 113-291.6, regulating trapping, is guilty of a Class 2 misdemeanor, unless a greater penalty is prescribed for the offense in question.

(j)   Any person who unlawfully sells, possesses for sale, or buys a fox, or who takes any fox by unlawful trapping or with the aid of any electronic calling device is guilty of a Class 2 misdemeanor, unless a greater penalty is prescribed for the offense in question.

(k)   Repealed by Session Laws 1995, c. 209, s. 1.

(l) Any person who unlawfully takes, possesses, transports, sells or buys any bald eagle or golden eagle, alive or dead, or any part, nest or egg of a bald eagle or golden eagle is guilty of a Class 1 misdemeanor, unless a greater penalty is prescribed for the offense in question.

(m) Any person who unlawfully takes any migratory game bird with a rifle; or who unlawfully takes any migratory game bird with the aid of live decoys or any salt, grain, fruit, or other bait; or who unlawfully takes any migratory game bird during the closed season or during prohibited shooting hours; or who unlawfully exceeds the bag limits or possession limits applicable to any migratory game bird; or who violates any of the migratory game bird permit or tagging rules of the Wildlife Resources Commission is guilty of a Class 2 misdemeanor, punishable by a fine of not less than two hundred fifty dollars ($250.00) in addition to any other punishment prescribed for the offense in question.

(n) Any person who violates any rule of the Commission that restricts access by vehicle on game lands to a person who holds a special vehicular access identification card and permit issued by the Commission to persons who have a handicap that limits physical mobility shall be guilty of a Class 2 misdemeanor and shall be fined not less than one hundred dollars ($100.00) in addition to any other punishment prescribed for the offense.

(o) Any person who willfully transports or attempts to transport live coyotes (Cania latrans) into this State for any purpose, or who breeds coyotes for any purpose in this State, is guilty of a Class 1 misdemeanor, and upon conviction the Wildlife Resources Commission shall suspend any controlled hunting preserve operator license issued to that person for two years.

(p) Any person who willfully imports or possesses black-tailed or mule deer (Odocoileus hemionus and all subspecies) in this State for any purpose is guilty of a Class 1 misdemeanor.

(q) Any person who violates any provision of G.S. 113-291.1A is guilty of a Class 1 misdemeanor.

(r) It is unlawful to place processed food products as bait in any area of the State where the Wildlife Resources Commission has set an open season for taking black bears. For purposes of this subsection, the term "processed food products" means any food substance or flavoring that has been modified from its raw components by the addition of ingredients or by treatment to modify its chemical composition or form or to enhance its aroma or taste. The term includes substances modified by sugar, honey, syrups, oils, salts, spices, peanut butter, grease, meat, bones, or blood, as well as extracts of such substances. The term also includes sugary products such as candies, pastries, gums, and sugar blocks, as well as extracts of such products. Nothing in this subsection prohibits the lawful disposal of solid waste or the legitimate feeding of domestic animals, livestock, or birds. The prohibition against taking bears with the use and aid of bait shall not apply to the release of dogs in the vicinity of any food source that is not a processed food product as defined herein. Violation of this subsection constitutes a Class 2 misdemeanor, punishable by a fine of not less than two hundred fifty dollars ($250.00).

(s) Any person who violates the provisions of G.S. 113-291.12 by unlawfully removing feral swine from a trap while the swine is still alive or by transporting such swine after that removal is guilty of a Class 2 misdemeanor, punishable by a fine of not less than two hundred fifty dollars ($250.00). The acts of removal from a trap and of transporting the swine after removal shall constitute separate offenses. (1935, c. 486, s. 25; 1939, c. 235, s. 2; c. 269; 1941, c. 231, s. 2; c. 288; 1945, c. 635; 1949, c. 1205, s. 4; 1953, c. 1141; 1963, c. 147; c. 697, ss. 2, 31/2; 1965, c. 616; 1967, c. 729; c. 1149, s. 1; 1971, c. 423, s. 1; c. 524; c. 899, s. 2; 1973, c. 677; 1975, c. 213; 1977, c. 705, s. 4; c. 794, s. 2; c. 933, s. 8; 1979, c. 830, s. 1; 1985, c. 303; c. 554, s. 3; 1987, c. 452, s. 4; c. 827, s. 98; 1989, c. 327, s. 2; 1991, c. 366, s. 1; 1993, c. 539, s. 863; 1994, Ex. Sess., c. 24, s. 14(c); 1995, c. 209, ss. 1, 2; 2003-96, s. 2; 2003-344, s. 10; 2005-62, s. 2; 2007-96, s. 1; 2011-369, s. 6(b); 2013-380, s. 11.)

§ 113-294.1. Wildlife Poacher Reward Fund.

(a) There is established in the Office of the State Treasurer the Wildlife Poacher Reward Fund. Monies in the Fund shall be used to pay rewards to persons who provide information to the Wildlife Resources Commission or to law enforcement authorities that results in the arrest and conviction of persons who have committed criminal offenses involving the taking, injury, removal, damage, or destruction of wildlife resources. The Wildlife Resources Commission shall adopt rules for the administration of the Fund for these purposes.

(b) The assets of the Wildlife Poacher Reward Fund shall be derived from the following:

(1) A percentage of the compensation paid annually to the Commission as special conditions of offenders' probation in criminal cases involving the taking, injury, removal, damage, or destruction of wildlife pursuant to G.S. 15A-1343(b1)(5), to be set by the Commission at not less than ten percent (10%) of those amounts paid as replacement costs and investigative costs.

(2) All amounts paid to the Commission under G.S. 15A-1343(b1)(5) as compensation for rewards paid from the Fund.

(3) The proceeds of any gifts, grants, and contributions to the State which are specifically designated for inclusion in the Fund.

(4) Any other sources specified by law. (2013-380, s. 1.)


§ 113-295. Unlawful harassment of persons taking wildlife resources.

(a) It is unlawful for a person to interfere intentionally with the lawful taking of wildlife resources or to drive, harass, or intentionally disturb any wildlife resources for the purpose of disrupting the lawful taking of wildlife resources. It is unlawful to take or abuse property, equipment, or hunting dogs that are being used for the lawful taking of wildlife resources. This subsection does not apply to a person who incidentally interferes with the taking of wildlife resources while using the land for other lawful activity such as agriculture, mining, or recreation. This subsection also does not apply to activity by a person on land he owns or leases.

Violation of this subsection is a Class 2 misdemeanor for a first conviction and a Class 1 misdemeanor for a second or subsequent conviction.

(b) The Wildlife Resources Commission may, either before or after the institution of any other action or proceeding authorized by this section, institute a civil action for injunctive relief to restrain a violation or threatened violation of subsection (a) of this section pursuant to G.S. 113-131. The action shall be brought in the superior court of the county in which the violation or threatened violation is occurring or about to occur and shall be in the name of the State upon the relation of the Wildlife Resources Commission. The court, in issuing any final order in any action brought pursuant to this subsection may, in its discretion, award costs of litigation including reasonable attorney and expert-witness fees to any party. (1987, c. 636, s. 3; 1993, c. 539, s. 864; 1994, Ex. Sess., c. 24, s. 14(c).)

§ 113-296. Disabled Sportsman Program.

(a) The Disabled Sportsman Program is established, to be developed and administered by the Wildlife Resources Commission. The Disabled Sportsman Program shall consist of special hunting and fishing activities adapted to the needs of persons with the disabilities described in subsection (b) of this section.

(b) In order to be eligible for participation in the Disabled Sportsman Program established by this section, an individual must be a holder of a Resident Disabled Veteran or Resident Totally Disabled license or must be able to certify through competent medical evidence one of the following disabilities:

(1) Missing fifty percent (50%) or more of one or more limbs, whether by amputation or natural causes.

(2) Paralysis of one or more limbs.

(3) Dysfunction of one or more limbs rendering the individual unable to perform the tasks of grasping and lifting with the hands and arms or unable to walk without mechanical assistance, other than a cane.

(4) Disease, injury, or defect confining the individual to a wheelchair, walker, or crutches.

(5) Legal deafness.

(6) Legal blindness, for purposes of participation in disabled fishing only.

The disability must be permanent, and an individual loses eligibility to participate in the Disabled Sportsman Program when the specified disability ceases to exist.

(c) A person who qualifies under subsection (b) of this section may apply for participation in the Disabled Sportsman Program by completing an application supplied by the Wildlife Resources Commission and by supplying the medical evidence necessary to confirm the person's disability. In order to participate in activities under the Program, each disabled participant may be accompanied by an able-bodied companion, who may also participate in the hunting, fishing, or other activity. The Commission shall charge each disabled participant an application fee of ten-dollars ($10.00) to defray the cost of processing the application and administering the special activities provided under the Program. An applicant may apply for any or all available Disabled Sportsman hunts at the time of application for a single fee. Any subsequent applications shall be accompanied by an additional ten-dollar ($10.00) application fee. The participant and the participant's companion shall also obtain any applicable hunting, fishing, or other special license required for the activities.

(d) In developing the Disabled Sportsman Program, the Wildlife Resources Commission shall:

(1) Establish special seasons and bag limits for hunting all or selected species of wildlife;

(2) Authorize the manner for taking wildlife, consistent with State law;

(3) Permit the use of vehicles and other means of conveyance in areas normally closed to such use;

(4) Set special fishing seasons and size and creel limits for inland fish; and

(5) Permit the use of crossbows or other specially equipped bows by persons incapable of arm movement sufficient to operate a longbow, recurve bow, or compound bow, but only during a season for hunting with bow and arrow and only during a special hunt organized and supervised by the Wildlife Resources Commission for the Disabled Sportsman Program; and

(6) Alter any other established rules of the Wildlife Resources Commission pertaining to hunting, fishing, or special activities, as generally applicable or as applicable to game lands, for the purpose of providing access to disabled persons participating in the Disabled Sportsman Program.

The Wildlife Resources Commission may use its game lands for purposes of conducting special activities for the Disabled Sportsman Program, and may enter into agreements with other landholders for purposes of conducting special activities on private lands.

(e) The Wildlife Resources Commission may establish special activities under the Disabled Sportsman Program for any class or classes of disability described in subsection (b) of this section. The Commission shall publicize these activities through the public media and in the Commission's publications to ensure that disabled persons are notified of the activities and informed about the application process.

(f)     The Wildlife Resources Commission shall hold at least four special hunting activities under the Disabled Sportsman Program per calendar year. The Commission shall alternate the location of these special activities so as to provide equal access to disabled persons in all regions of the State. (1993 (Reg. Sess., 1994), c. 557, s. 1; 2005-438, s. 3; 2005-455, s. 1.15; 2008-205, s. 2.)

§ 113-297.  Method exemptions for disabled persons.

(a)     Any person whose physical disability makes it impossible for the person to hunt or fish by conventional methods for one year or more may apply to the Wildlife Resources Commission for a hunting or fishing methods exemption allowing that person to hunt or fish in a manner that would otherwise be prohibited by rules adopted by the Commission. The application shall be accompanied by a signed statement from a physician containing the following information:

(1)     The nature of the person's disability;

(2)     The necessity of the exemption in order to allow the person to hunt or fish; and

(3)     Whether the disability is permanent or temporary and, if temporary, the length of time after which the physician anticipates that the person may be able to hunt or fish without the exemption.

The Wildlife Resources Commission may authorize any reasonable exemption in order to permit a disabled person complying with the requirements of this section to hunt or fish and may issue a permit describing the exemption made in each case. The permit may be permanent or, if the disability is temporary, the permit may coincide with the length of time the signed physician's statement indicates the disability is expected to last. A person issued a permit under this section shall possess the permit while hunting or fishing in the exempted manner.

(b) In addition to providing disabled persons reasonable exemptions from rules adopted by the Wildlife Resources Commission, the Commission may permit a person complying with the application procedure outlined in subsection (a) of this section to use a crossbow or other specially equipped bow if the physician's statement indicates that the person is incapable of arm movement sufficient to operate a longbow, recurve bow, or compound bow. (1995, c. 62, s. 1.)

§ 113-298. Unlawful use of facilities provided for disabled sportsman.

Any person who knowingly uses facilities or participates in activities provided by the Wildlife Resources Commission for disabled sportsmen, when that person does not meet the qualifications for use of those facilities or participation in those activities, is guilty of a Class 3 misdemeanor. (1997-326, s. 5.)

§ 113-299. Reserved for future codification purposes.

§ 113-300. Reserved for future codification purposes.

Article 22A.

Use of Poisons and Pesticides.

§ 113-300.1. Use of poisons and pesticides in general.

No one may take any wild animal or bird with the use of any poison or pesticide except as provided in this Article. The taking of fish by the use of poison is governed by G.S. 113-261 and G.S. 113-262, and the prohibitions of those sections against the taking of wildlife by poison apply unless specifically permitted under this Article. Otherwise, the Wildlife Resources Commission may, by rules consistent with the North Carolina Pesticide Law of 1971 and the Structural Pest Control Act of 1955, regulate, prohibit, or restrict the use of poisons or pesticides upon or severely affecting wildlife resources. (1979, c. 830, s. 1; 1979, 2nd Sess., c. 1285, s. 9; 1987, c. 827, s. 98.)

§ 113-300.2. Declaring wild animal or bird a pest; concurrence of Wildlife Resources Commission required before poison or pesticide may be used.

(a)     When there is a factual basis for the declaration, any wild animal or bird may be declared a pest by:

(1)     The Commissioner of Agriculture under the Structural Pest Control Act of North Carolina of 1955, as amended, in Article 4C of Chapter 106 of the General Statutes, in accordance with any regulations or restrictions imposed by the Structural Pest Control Committee; or

(2)     The Pesticide Board under the North Carolina Pesticide Law of 1971, as amended, in Article 52 of Chapter 143 of the General Statutes.

(b)     When a wild animal or bird is declared a pest, the Commissioner of Agriculture or the Pesticide Board, as the case may be, must notify the Wildlife Resources Commission in writing of the action taken; the areas in which the declaration is effective; the type, amount, and mode of application of any poison or pesticide proposed for use against the pest; and other information pertinent to the declaration.

(c)     Upon receiving notification under subsection (b), the Wildlife Resources Commission may:

(1)     Hold a timely public hearing on the question whether it should concur in the declaration that the wild animal or bird is a pest and should be open to taking with the type or types of poison or pesticide specified or authorized in the notice, in the areas and under the circumstances specified. After holding the public hearing the Wildlife Resources Commission must decide, within 60 days after receiving the notice under subsection (b), whether it concurs or refuses to concur in the declaration that the wild animal or bird is a pest.

(2)     Take no action. In this event, 60 days after the Wildlife Resources Commission receives notice of the declaration under subsection (b), the concurrence of the Wildlife Resources Commission will occur automatically.

(d)     Upon the concurrence of the Wildlife Resources Commission in the declaration under subsection (b), the wild animal or bird may be taken with the use of any poison or pesticide specified in the notice in accordance with applicable restrictions in statutes and regulations and in accordance with any special restrictions imposed by the Commissioner of Agriculture, the Structural

Pest Control Committee, or the Pesticide Board. If the Wildlife Resources Commission refuses to concur, no poison or pesticide may be used to take the wild animal or bird.

(e) After holding a public hearing on the subject, the Wildlife Resources Commission may rescind its concurrence to a declaration under subsection (b) or grant its concurrence previously withheld.

(f) With the approval of the Structural Pest Control Committee or the Pesticide Board, as the case may be, the Wildlife Resources Commission may grant a qualified concurrence to a declaration, imposing further restrictions as to the use of poison or pesticide in taking the wild animal or bird in question. (1979, c. 830, s. 1.)


§ 113-300.3. Penalties for violations of Article; repeated offenses.

(a) Each day in which poisons or pesticides are used unlawfully in taking wild animals or birds constitutes a separate offense.

(b) Any taking of a wild animal or bird in willful violation of this Article or in willful violation of any restrictions imposed by the Commissioner of Agriculture, the Structural Pest Control Committee, the Pesticide Board, or the Wildlife Resources Commission is punishable under G.S. 113-262(a). For the purposes of prosecutions under that subsection, the term "poison" includes pesticides.

(c) Any person taking a wild animal or bird declared a pest with the use of poison or pesticide who neglects to observe applicable restrictions imposed by the Commissioner of Agriculture, the Structural Pest Control Committee, the Pesticide Board, or the Wildlife Resources Commission is guilty of a Class 3 misdemeanor, unless a greater penalty is prescribed for the offense in question. (1979, c. 830, s. 1; 1993, c. 539, s. 865; 1994, Ex. Sess., c. 24, s. 14(c).)


§ 113-300.4. Reserved for future codification purposes.


Article 22B.

Interstate Wildlife Violator Compact.

§ 113-300.5. Short title.

This Article may be cited as the "Interstate Wildlife Violator Compact." (2008-120, s. 1.)

§ 113-300.6. Governor to execute compact; form of compact.

The Governor shall execute an Interstate Wildlife Violator Compact on behalf of the State of North Carolina with any state of the United States legally joining therein in the form substantially as follows:

Article I.

Findings, Declaration of Policy, and Purpose.

(a) The party states find that:

(1) Wildlife resources are managed in trust by the respective states for the benefit of all residents and visitors.

(2) The protection of their respective wildlife resources can be materially affected by the degree of compliance with state statute, law, regulation, ordinance, or administrative rule relating to the management of those resources.

(3) The preservation, protection, management, and restoration of wildlife contributes immeasurably to the aesthetic, recreational, and economic aspects of these natural resources.

(4) Wildlife resources are valuable without regard to political boundaries; therefore, all persons should be required to comply with wildlife preservation, protection, management, and restoration laws, ordinances, and administrative rules and regulations of all party states as a condition precedent to the continuance or issuance of any license to hunt, fish, trap, or possess wildlife.

(5)     Violation of wildlife laws interferes with the management of wildlife resources and may endanger the safety of persons and property.

(6)     The mobility of many wildlife law violators necessitates the maintenance of channels of communication among the various states.

(7)     In most instances, a person who is cited for a wildlife violation in a state other than the person's home state:

a.      Must post collateral or bond to secure appearance for a trial at a later date; or

b.      If unable to post collateral or bond, is taken into custody until the collateral or bond is posted; or

c.      Is taken directly to court for an immediate appearance.

(8)     The purpose of the enforcement practices described in subdivision (7) of this subsection is to ensure compliance with the terms of a wildlife citation by the person who, if permitted to continue on the person's way after receiving the citation, could return to the person's home state and disregard the person's duty under the terms of the citation.

(9)     In most instances, a person receiving a wildlife citation in the person's home state is permitted to accept the citation from the officer at the scene of the violation and to immediately continue on the person's way after agreeing or being instructed to comply with the terms of the citation.

(10)    The practice described in subdivision (7) of this subsection causes unnecessary inconvenience and, at times, a hardship for the person who is unable at the time to post collateral, furnish a bond, stand trial, or pay the fine, and thus is compelled to remain in custody until some alternative arrangement can be made.

(11)    The enforcement practices described in subdivision (7) of this subsection consume an undue amount of law enforcement time.

(b)     It is the policy of the party states to:

(1) Promote compliance with the statutes, laws, ordinances, regulations, and administrative rules relating to management of wildlife resources in their respective states.

(2) Recognize the suspension of wildlife license privileges of any person whose license privileges have been suspended by a party state and treat this suspension as if it had occurred in their state.

(3) Allow violators to accept a wildlife citation, except as provided in subsection (b) of Article III, and proceed on the violator's way without delay whether or not the person is a resident in the state in which the citation was issued, provided that the violator's home state is party to this compact.

(4) Report to the appropriate party state, as provided in the compact manual, any conviction recorded against any person whose home state was not the issuing state.

(5) Allow the home state to recognize and treat convictions recorded for their residents which occurred in another party state as if they had occurred in the home state.

(6) Extend cooperation to its fullest extent among the party states for obtaining compliance with the terms of a wildlife citation issued in one party state to a resident of another party state.

(7) Maximize effective use of law enforcement personnel and information.

(8) Assist court systems in the efficient disposition of wildlife violations.

(c) The purposes of this compact are to:

(1) Provide a means through which the party states may participate in a reciprocal program to effectuate policies enumerated in subsection (b) of this Article in a uniform and orderly manner.

(2) Provide for the fair and impartial treatment of wildlife violators operating within party states in recognition of the person's right of due process and the sovereign status of a party state.

Article II.

Definitions.

Unless the context requires otherwise, the definitions in this Article apply through this compact and are intended only for the implementation of this compact:

(1)     "Citation" means any summons, complaint, ticket, penalty assessment, or other official document issued by a wildlife officer or other peace officer for a wildlife violation containing an order which requires the person to respond.

(2)     "Collateral" means any cash or other security deposited to secure an appearance for trial, in connection with the issuance by a wildlife officer or other peace officer of a citation for a wildlife violation.

(3)     "Compliance" with respect to a citation means the act of answering the citation through appearance at a court, a tribunal, or payment of fines, costs, and surcharges, if any, or both such appearance and payment.

(4)     "Conviction" means a conviction, including any court conviction, of any offense related to the preservation, protection, management, or restoration of wildlife which is prohibited by state statute, law, regulation, ordinance, or administrative rule, or a forfeiture of bail, bond, or other security deposited to secure appearance by a person charged with having committed any such offense, or payment of a penalty assessment, or a plea of nolo contendere, or the imposition of a deferred or suspended sentence by the court.

(5)     "Court" means a court of law, including Magistrate's Court and the Justice of the Peace Court.

(6)     "Home state" means the state of primary residence of a person.

(7)     "Issuing state" means the party state which issues a wildlife citation to the violator.

(8)     "License" means any license, permit, or other public document which conveys to the person to whom it was issued the privilege of pursuing, possessing, or taking any wildlife regulated by statute, law, regulation, ordinance, or administrative rule of a party state.

(9) "Licensing authority" means the department or division within each party state which is authorized by law to issue or approve licenses or permits to hunt, fish, trap, or possess wildlife.

(10) "Party state" means any state which enacts legislation to become a member of this wildlife compact.

(11) "Personal recognizance" means an agreement by a person made at the time of issuance of the wildlife citation that the person will comply with the terms of that citation.

(12) "State" means any state, territory, or possession of the United States, including the District of Columbia and the Commonwealth of Puerto Rico.

(13) "Suspension" means any revocation, denial, or withdrawal of any or all license privileges, including the privilege to apply for, purchase, or exercise the benefits conferred by any license.

(14) "Terms of the citation" means those conditions and options expressly stated upon the citation.

(15) "Wildlife" means all species of animals, including but not necessarily limited to mammals, birds, fish, reptiles, amphibians, mollusks, and crustaceans, which are defined as "wildlife" and are protected or otherwise regulated by statute, law, regulation, ordinance, or administrative rule in a party state. "Wildlife" includes all species of animals that are protected or regulated by the Wildlife Resources Commission, the Marine Fisheries Commission, or the Division of Marine Fisheries in the Department of Environment and Natural Resources. "Wildlife" also means food fish and shellfish as defined by statute, law, regulation, ordinance, or administrative rule in a party state. Species included in the definition of "wildlife" vary from state to state and determination of whether a species is "wildlife" for the purposes of this compact shall be based on local law.

(16) "Wildlife law" means any statute, law, regulation, ordinance, or administrative rule developed and enacted to manage wildlife resources and the use thereof.

(17) "Wildlife officer" means any individual authorized by a party state to issue a citation for a wildlife violation.

(18) "Wildlife violation" means any cited violation of a statute, law, regulation, ordinance, or administrative rule developed and enacted to manage wildlife resources and the use thereof.

Article III.

Procedures for Issuing State.

(a) When issuing a citation for a wildlife violation, a wildlife officer shall issue a citation to any person whose primary residence is in a party state in the same manner as if the person were a resident of the home state and shall not require the person to post collateral to secure appearance, subject to the exceptions contained in subsection (b) of this Article, if the officer receives the person's personal recognizance that the person will comply with the terms of the citation.

(b) Personal recognizance is acceptable:

(1) If not prohibited by local law or the compact manual; and

(2) If the violator provides adequate proof of the violator's identification to the wildlife officer.

(c) Upon conviction or failure of a person to comply with the terms of a wildlife citation, the appropriate official shall report the conviction or failure to comply to the licensing authority of the party state in which the wildlife citation was issued. The report shall be made in accordance with procedures specified by the issuing state and shall contain the information specified in the compact manual as minimum requirements for effective processing by the home state.

(d) Upon receipt of the report of conviction or noncompliance required by subsection (c) of this Article, the licensing authority of the issuing state shall transmit to the licensing authority in the home state of the violator the information in a form and content as contained in the compact manual.

Article IV.

Procedures for Home State.

(a) Upon receipt of a report of failure to comply with the terms of a citation from the licensing authority of the issuing state, the licensing authority of the home state shall notify the violator, shall initiate a suspension action in accordance with the home state's suspension procedures, and shall suspend the violator's license privileges until satisfactory evidence of compliance with the terms of the wildlife citation has been furnished by the issuing state to the home state licensing authority. Due process safeguards will be accorded.

(b) Upon receipt of a report of conviction from the licensing authority of the issuing state, the licensing authority of the home state shall enter such conviction in its records and shall treat such conviction as if it occurred in the home state for the purposes of the suspension of license privileges.

(c) The licensing authority of the home state shall maintain a record of actions taken and make reports to issuing states as provided in the compact manual.

Article V.

Reciprocal Recognition of Suspension.

All party states shall recognize the suspension of license privileges of any person by any state as if the violation on which the suspension is based had in fact occurred in their state and could have been the basis for suspension of license privileges in their state.

Article VI.

Applicability of Other Laws.

Except as expressly required by provisions of this compact, nothing herein shall be construed to affect the right of any party state to apply any of its laws relating to license privileges to any person or circumstance or to invalidate or prevent any agreement or other cooperative arrangements between a party state and a nonparty state concerning wildlife law enforcement.

Article VII.

Compact Administrator Procedures.

(a) For the purpose of administering the provisions of this compact and to serve as a governing body for the resolution of all matters relating to the operation of this compact, a Board of Compact Administrators is established. The Board of Compact Administrators shall be composed of one representative from each of the party states to be known as the Compact Administrator. The Compact Administrator shall be appointed by the head of the licensing authority of each party state and will serve and be subject to removal in accordance with the laws of the state the Compact Administrator represents. A Compact Administrator may provide for the discharge of the Compact Administrator's duties and the performance of the Compact Administrator's functions as a Board member by an alternate. An alternate shall not be entitled to serve unless written notification of the alternate's identity has been given to the Board of Compact Administrators.

(b) Each member of the Board of Compact Administrators shall be entitled to one vote. No action of the Board of Compact Administrators shall be binding unless taken at a meeting at which a majority of the total number of votes on the board are cast in favor thereof. Action by the Board of Compact Administrators shall be only at a meeting at which a majority of the party states are represented.

(c) The Board of Compact Administrators shall elect annually, from its membership, a Chair and Vice-Chair.

(d) The Board of Compact Administrators shall adopt bylaws, not inconsistent with the provisions of this compact or the laws of a party state, for the conduct of its business and shall have the power to amend and rescind its bylaws.

(e) The Board of Compact Administrators may accept for any of its purposes and functions under this compact all donations and grants of money, equipment, supplies, materials, and services, conditional or otherwise, from any state, the United States, or any governmental agency, and may receive, utilize, and dispose of the same.

(f)     The Board of Compact Administrators may contract with or accept services or personnel from any governmental or intergovernmental agency, individual, firm, corporation, or any private nonprofit organization or institution.

(g)     The Board of Compact Administrators shall formulate all necessary procedures and develop uniform forms and documents for administering the provisions of this compact. All procedures and forms adopted pursuant to Board of Compact Administrators action shall be contained in the compact manual.

Article VIII.

Entry into Compact and Withdrawal.

(a)     This compact shall become effective when it has been adopted by at least two states.

(b)     (1)     Entry into the compact shall be made by resolution of ratification executed by the authorized officials of the applying state and submitted to the Chair of the Board of Compact Administrators.

(2)     The resolution shall be in a form and content as provided in the compact manual and shall include statements that in substance are as follows:

a.     A citation of the authority by which the state is empowered to become a party to this compact;

b.     Agreement to comply with the terms and provisions of the compact; and

c.     That compact entry is with all states then party to the compact and with any state that legally becomes a party to the compact.

(3)     The effective date of entry shall be specified by the applying state, but shall not be less than 60 days after notice has been given by the Chair of the Board of Compact Administrators or by the secretariat of the Board to each party state that the resolution from the applying state has been received.

(c)     A party state may withdraw from this compact by official written notice to the other party states, but a withdrawal shall not take effect until 90 days after notice of withdrawal is given. The notice shall be directed to the Compact

Administrator of each member state. No withdrawal shall affect the validity of this compact as to the remaining party states.

Article IX.

Amendments to the Compact.

(a) This compact may be amended from time to time. Amendments shall be presented in resolution form to the Chair of the Board of Compact Administrators and may be initiated by one or more party states.

(b) Adoption of an amendment shall require endorsement by all party states and shall become effective 30 days after the date of the last endorsement.

Article X.

Construction and Severability.

This compact shall be liberally construed so as to effectuate the purposes stated herein. The provisions of this compact shall be severable and if any phrase, clause, sentence, or provision of this compact is declared to be contrary to the constitution of any party state or of the United States or the applicability thereof to any government, agency, individual, or circumstance is held invalid, the compact shall not be affected thereby. If this compact shall be held contrary to the constitution of any party state thereto, the compact shall remain in full force and effect as to the remaining states and in full force and effect as to the state affected as to all severable matters. (2008-120, s. 1; 2009-15, s. 1.)

§ 113-300.7. Appointment of Compact Administrator; implementation; rules; amendments.

(a) The Chair of the Wildlife Resources Commission, in consultation with the Chair of the Marine Fisheries Commission and the Fisheries Director, shall appoint the Compact Administrator for North Carolina. The Compact

Administrator shall serve at the pleasure of the Chair of the Wildlife Resources Commission.

(b)  The Wildlife Resources Commission, the Secretary of Environment and Natural Resources, and the Division of Marine Fisheries may suspend or revoke the license, privilege, or right of any person to hunt, fish, trap, possess, or transport wildlife in this State to the extent that the license, privilege, or right has been suspended or revoked by another compact member under the provisions of this Article.

(c)  The Wildlife Resources Commission and the Marine Fisheries Commission shall adopt rules necessary to carry out the purposes of this Article.

(d)  Any proposed amendment to the Compact shall be submitted to the General Assembly as an amendment to G.S. 113-300.6. In order to be endorsed by the State of North Carolina as provided by subsection (b) of Article IX of the Compact, a proposed amendment to the Compact must be enacted into law.  (2008-120, s. 1; 2009-15, s. 2.)


§ 113-300.8.  Violations.

It is unlawful for a person whose license, privilege, or right to hunt, fish, trap, possess, or transport wildlife has been suspended or revoked under the provisions of this Article to exercise that right or privilege within this State or to purchase or possess a license granting that right or privilege. A person who hunts, fishes, traps, possesses, or transports wildlife in this State or who purchases or possesses a license to hunt, fish, trap, possess, or transport wildlife in this State in violation of a suspension or revocation under this Article is guilty of a Class 1 misdemeanor.  (2008-120, s. 1.)


Article 23.

Administrative Provisions; Regulatory Authority of Wildlife Resources Commission.

§ 113-301:  Repealed by Session Laws 1979, c. 830, s. 1.

§ 113-301.1. Wildlife Resources Commission obligated to make efforts to notify members of the public who may be affected by operative provisions of statutes and rules.

(a)     The Wildlife Resources Commission must prepare and distribute to license agents informational materials relating to hunting, fishing, trapping, and boating laws and rules administered by the Wildlife Resources Commission. The materials furnished an agent should be appropriate to the types of licenses the agent customarily handles, and in a quantity reasonably anticipated to be sufficient to meet the needs of licensees obtaining licenses from the agent.

(b)     In issuing new licenses and permits from the Raleigh office by mail, the Wildlife Resources Commission must generally inform the licensee or permittee of governing provisions of law and rules applicable to the type of license or permit secured. In issuing renewal licenses and permits by mail, the Wildlife Resources Commission must inform the licensee or permittee of any substantial changes in the law or rules that may affect the activities of the licensee or permittee.

(c)     After adopting rules that impose new restrictions upon the activities of members of the public who do not normally hold licenses or permits to engage in the activity in question, the Wildlife Resources Commission must take appropriate steps to publicize the new restrictions. These steps may include press releases to the media, informing local authorities, and other forms of communication that give promise of reaching the segment of the public affected.

(d)     After adopting new restrictions on hunting, fishing, trapping, or boating at a time other than when usual annual changes in the rules affecting those activities are adopted, the Wildlife Resources Commission must take appropriate steps to publicize the new restrictions in a manner designed to reach persons who may be affected.

(e)     Repealed by Session Laws 1987, c. 827, s. 9. (1979, c. 830, s. 1; 1979, 2nd Sess., c. 1285, s. 10; 1987, c. 827, s. 9; 2004-195, s. 1.1.)


§ 113-302. Prima facie evidence provisions.

(a)     Except as provided below, possession of game or game fish in any hotel, restaurant, cafe, market, or store, or by any produce dealer, constitutes prima facie evidence of possession for the purpose of sale. This subsection does not apply to:

(1)   Possession of propagated game birds or hatchery-reared trout that is in accordance with licensing requirements and wrapping or tagging provisions that may apply; or

(2)   Game or game fish brought in by patrons in accordance with G.S. 113-276(i).

(b)   The flashing or display of any artificial light between a half hour after sunset and a half hour before sunrise in any area which is frequented or inhabited by wild deer by any person who has accessible to him a firearm, crossbow, or other bow and arrow constitutes prima facie evidence of taking deer with the aid of an artificial light. This subsection does not apply to the headlights of any vehicle driven normally along any highway or other public or private roadway. (1965, c. 957, s. 2; 1979, c. 830, s. 1.)


§ 113-302.1. Inspection of licensed or commercial premises; authority to secure inspection warrants.

(a)   Protectors are authorized to enter and make a reasonable inspection at an appropriate time of day of any premises in which a person subject to administrative control under G.S. 113-276.2 conducts his operations to determine whether any wildlife on the premises is possessed in accordance with applicable laws and rules, required records are being kept, and other legal requirements are being observed. It is an appropriate time of day for inspection if the establishment is open for business or if a proprietor or employee is on the premises.

(b)   In cases not controlled by subsection (a), protectors who believe that wildlife may be on the premises of any public refrigeration storage plant, meat shop, store, produce market, hotel, restaurant, or other public food-storage or eating place may request permission to enter the nonpublic areas of the premises to make a reasonable inspection to determine whether any wildlife on the premises is possessed in accordance with applicable laws and rules. If the person in charge of the premises refuses the inspection request of a protector, he is authorized to procure and execute an administrative search warrant issued under the terms of Article 4A of Chapter 15 of the General Statutes or under any successor legislation.

(c) In cases controlled by subsection (a), an administrative search warrant may be secured in the protector's discretion or if case law requires it. Nothing in this section is intended to prevent a lawful search of premises, with or without a search warrant under Chapter 15A of the General Statutes, when the circumstances so justify. (1979, c. 830, s. 1; 1987, c. 827, s. 98.)

§ 113-303. Arrest, service of process and witness fees of protectors.

All arrest fees and other fees that may be charged in any bill of costs for service of process by protectors must be paid to the county in which the trial is held. No witness fee may be taxed in any bill of costs by virtue of the appearance of a protector as a witness in a criminal case within his enforcement jurisdiction. Acceptance by any protector of any arrest fee, witness fee, or any other fee to which he is not entitled is a Class 1 misdemeanor. (1965, c. 957, s. 2; 1993, c. 539, s. 866; 1994, Ex. Sess., c. 24, s. 14(c).)

§ 113-304. Reciprocal agreements by Wildlife Resources Commission.

The Wildlife Resources Commission is empowered to make reciprocal agreements with other jurisdictions respecting the matters governed in this Subchapter. Pursuant to such agreements the Wildlife Resources Commission may by rule modify provisions of this Subchapter in order to effectuate the purposes of such agreements, in the overall best interests of the conservation of wildlife resources. (1965, c. 957, s. 2; 1973, c. 1262, s. 18; 1987, c. 827, s. 98.)

§ 113-305. Cooperative agreements by Wildlife Resources Commission.

The Wildlife Resources Commission is empowered to enter into cooperative agreements with public and private agencies and individuals respecting the matters governed in this Subchapter. Pursuant to such agreements the Wildlife Resources Commission may expend funds, assign employees to additional duties within or without the State, assume additional responsibilities, and take other actions that may be required by virtue of such agreements, in the overall best interests of the conservation of wildlife resources. (1965, c. 957, s. 2; 1973, c. 1262, s. 18.)

§ 113-306. Administrative authority of Wildlife Resources Commission; disposition of license funds; delegation of powers; injunctive relief; emergency powers.

(a) In the overall best interests of the conservation of wildlife resources, the Wildlife Resources Commission may lease or purchase lands, equipment, and other property; accept gifts and grants on behalf of the State; establish wildlife refuges, management areas, and boating and fishing access areas, either alone or in cooperation with others; provide matching funds for entering into projects with some other governmental agency or with some scientific, educational, or charitable foundation or institution; condemn lands in accordance with the provisions of Chapter 40A of the General Statutes and other governing provisions of law; and sell, lease, or give away property acquired by it. Provided, that any private person selected to receive gifts or benefits by the Wildlife Resources Commission be selected:

(1) With regard to the overall public interest that may result; and

(2) From a defined class upon such a rational basis open to all within the class as to prevent constitutional infirmity with respect to requirements of equal protection of the laws or prohibitions against granting exclusive privileges or emoluments.

(b) Except as otherwise specifically provided by law, all money credited to, held by, or to be received by the Wildlife Resources Commission from the sale of licenses authorized by this Subchapter must be consolidated and placed in the Wildlife Resources Fund.

(c) The Wildlife Resources Commission may, within the terms of policies set by rule, delegate to the Executive Director all administrative powers granted to it.

(d) The Wildlife Resources Commission is hereby authorized and directed to develop a plan and policy of wildlife management for all lands owned by the State of North Carolina which are suitable for this purpose. The Division of State Property and Construction of the Department of Administration shall determine which lands are suitable for the purpose of wildlife management. Nothing in the wildlife management plan shall prohibit, restrict, or require the change in use of State property which is presently being used or will in the future be used to carry out the goals and objectives of the State agency utilizing such land. Each plan of wildlife management developed by the Wildlife Resources Commission shall consider the question of public hunting; and whenever and wherever possible and consistent with the primary land use of the controlling agency, public hunting shall be allowed under cooperative agreement with the Wildlife Resources Commission. Any dispute over the question of public hunting shall be resolved by the Division of State Property and Construction.

(e) Subject to any policy directives adopted by the members of the Wildlife Resources Commission, the Executive Director in his discretion may institute an action in the name of the Wildlife Resources Commission in the appropriate court for injunctive relief to prevent irreparable injury to wildlife resources or to prevent or regulate any activity within the jurisdiction of the Wildlife Resources Commission which constitutes a public nuisance or presents a threat to public health or safety.

(f) The Wildlife Resources Commission may adopt rules governing the exercise of emergency powers by the Executive Director when the Commission determines that such powers are necessary to respond to a wildlife disease that threatens irreparable injury to wildlife or the public. The rules shall provide that the Executive Director must consult with the Commission, the State Veterinarian, and the Governor prior to implementing the emergency powers. The rules shall also specify the method by which the public will be notified of the exercise of emergency powers. The exercise of emergency powers shall not extend for more than 90 days after the Commission's determination that a disease outbreak has occurred, unless a temporary rule is adopted by the Commission in accordance with G.S. 150B-21.1 to replace the emergency powers. If a temporary rule is adopted prior to the expiration of the 90 days, the Executive Director may continue to exercise emergency powers until either a permanent rule to replace the temporary rule becomes effective or the temporary rule expires as provided by G.S. 150B-21.1(d). The Commission's determination that a disease outbreak has occurred shall constitute a basis for adoption of a temporary rule. The emergency powers that may be authorized by rules adopted pursuant to this subsection include:

(1) Prohibiting activities that aid in the transmission or movement of the disease.

(2) Implementing activities to reduce infection opportunities.

(3) Implementing requirements to assist in the detection and isolation of the disease. (1965, c. 957, s. 2; 1973, c. 1262, s. 18; 1977, c. 759; 1979, c. 830, s. 1; 1981, c. 482, s. 3; 1987, c. 827, ss. 98, 106; 2007-401, s. 1.)

§ 113-307. Adoption of federal laws and regulations.

To the extent that the Wildlife Resources Commission is granted authority under this Chapter or under any other provision of law, including Chapter 75A of the General Statutes, over subject matter as to which there is concurrent federal jurisdiction, the Wildlife Resources Commission in its discretion may by reference in its rules adopt relevant provisions of federal law and regulations as State rules. To prevent confusion or conflict of jurisdiction in enforcement, the Wildlife Resources Commission may provide for an automatic incorporation by reference into its rules of future changes within any particular set of federal laws or regulations relating to some subject clearly within the jurisdiction of the Wildlife Resources Commission. (1965, c. 957, s. 2; 1973, c. 1262, s. 18; 1987, c. 827, s. 107.)

§ 113-307.1. Legislative assent to specific federal acts.

(a)     The consent of the General Assembly of North Carolina is hereby given to the making by the Congress of the United States, or under its authority, of all such rules and regulations as the federal government shall determine to be needful in respect to game animals, game and nongame birds, and fish on such lands in the western part of North Carolina as shall have been, or may hereafter be, purchased by the United States under the terms of the act of Congress of March 1, 1911, entitled "An act to enable any state to cooperate with any other state or states, or with the United States, for the protection of the watersheds of navigable streams, and to appoint a commission for the acquisition of lands for the purposes of conserving the navigability of navigable rivers" (36 Stat. 961), and acts of Congress supplementary thereto and amendatory thereof, and in or on the waters thereon.

Nothing in this subsection shall be construed as conveying the ownership of wildlife from the State of North Carolina or permit the trapping, hunting, or transportation of any game animals, game or nongame birds, or fish by any person, including any agency, department, or instrumentality of the United States or agents thereof, on the lands in North Carolina, as shall have been or may hereafter be purchased by the United States under the terms of any act of Congress, except in accordance with the provisions of this Subchapter and its implementing regulations. Provided, that the provisions of G.S. 113-39 apply with respect to licenses.

Any person, including employees or agents of any department or instrumentality of the United States, violating the provisions of this subsection is guilty of a Class 1 misdemeanor.

(b) The State of North Carolina hereby assents to the provisions of the act of Congress entitled "An act to provide that the United States shall aid the states in wildlife restoration projects, and for other purposes," approved September 2, 1937 (Public Law 415, 75th Congress), and the Wildlife Resources Commission is hereby authorized, empowered, and directed to perform such acts as may be necessary to the conduct and establishment of cooperative wildlife restoration projects, as defined in said act of Congress, in compliance with said act and rules and regulations promulgated by the Secretary of the Interior thereunder; and no funds accruing to the State of North Carolina from license fees paid by hunters shall be diverted for any other purpose than the protection and propagation of game and wildlife in North Carolina and administration of the laws enacted for such purposes, which laws are and shall be administered by the Wildlife Resources Commission.

(c) Assent is hereby given to the provisions of the act of Congress entitled "An act to provide that the United States shall aid the states in fish restoration and management projects, and for other purposes," approved August 9, 1950 (Public Law 681, 81st Congress), and the Wildlife Resources Commission is hereby authorized, empowered, and directed to perform such acts as may be necessary to the conduct and establishment of cooperative fish restoration projects, as defined in said act of Congress, in compliance with said act and rules and regulations promulgated by the Secretary of the Interior thereunder; and no funds accruing to the State of North Carolina from license fees paid by fishermen shall be directed for any other purpose than the administration of the Wildlife Resources Commission and for the protection, propagation, preservation, and investigation of fish and wildlife.

(d) If as a precondition to receiving funds under any cooperative program there must be a separation of license revenues received from certain classes of licensees and utilization of such revenues for limited purposes, the Wildlife Resources Commission is directed to make such arrangements for separate accounting within the Wildlife Resources Fund, or for separate funding, as may be necessary to insure the use of the revenues for the required purposes and eligibility for the cooperative funds. This subsection applies whether the cooperative program is with a public or private agency and whether the Wildlife Resources Commission acts alone on behalf of the State or in conjunction with some other State agency. (1915, c. 205; C.S., s. 2099; 1939, c. 79, ss. 1, 2;

1979, c. 830, s. 1; 1993, c. 539, s. 867; 1994, Ex. Sess., c. 24, s. 14(c); 2004-199, s. 3.)

Article 23A.

Promotion of Coastal Fisheries and Seafood Industry.

§ 113-308. Definitions.

The definitions as given in G.S. 113-128 shall apply to this Article, except that the following will additionally apply:

(1)     Agency: A group or an association which shall make applications and otherwise act for the fishing and seafood industry or a distinguishable part thereof. (1967, c. 890, s. 1.)

§ 113-309. Declaration of policy.

It is declared to be in the interest of the public welfare of North Carolina that those engaged in "coastal fisheries," as defined in G.S. 113-129, shall be permitted and encouraged to act jointly and cooperatively for the purposes of promoting the common good, welfare, and advancement of their industry. (1967, c. 890, s. 2.)

§ 113-310. Certain activities not to be deemed illegal or in restraint of trade.

No association, meeting or activity undertaken in pursuance of the provisions of this Article and intended to benefit all of the coastal fisheries or distinguishable part thereof hereinunder certified by the Marine Fisheries Commission shall be deemed or considered illegal or in restraint of trade. (1967, c. 890, s. 3; 1973, c. 1262, s. 28.)

§ 113-311. Referendum and assessment declared to be in public interest.

It is hereby declared to be in the interest of the public that the coastal fisheries or any distinguishable part thereof shall be permitted by referendum to be held among themselves as prescribed by this Article, to levy upon themselves an assessment on such respective catches, volume, landings, income, or production for the purposes of promoting the common good, welfare, and advancement of the fishing and seafood industry of North Carolina, in addition to any and all taxes, levies, and licenses in effect on June 22, 1967, or that may be enacted and levied or imposed subsequently. (1967, c. 890, s. 4.)

§ 113-312. Application to Marine Fisheries Commission for authority to conduct referendum.

Any agency fairly representative of any distinguishable part or all of the fishing and seafood industry may at any time make application in writing or petition to the Marine Fisheries Commission for certification and approval to conduct a referendum among the coastal fisheries or any distinguishable part thereof for the purpose of levying an assessment under the provisions of this Article, collecting, and utilizing the proceeds for the purposes stated in such referendum and as set forth in this Article. (1967, c. 890, s. 5; 1973, c. 1262, s. 28.)

§ 113-313. Action of Marine Fisheries Commission on application.

Upon receiving an application or petition as herein provided, the Marine Fisheries Commission shall at its next regular quarterly meeting consider such application as follows:

(1)     The Marine Fisheries Commission shall determine if the agency is in fact fairly representative of the coastal fisheries or distinguishable part thereof making application or petitioning for referendum and record in its minutes its determination.

(2)     The Marine Fisheries Commission shall determine if the application or petition is in conformity with the provisions and purposes of this Article and record in its minutes its determination.

(3)     If the Marine Fisheries Commission determines in the affirmative as to (1) and (2) above, it shall authorize and empower the agency to hold and

conduct a referendum on the question of whether or not members of the fishing and seafood industry, or the distinguishable part thereof, making application or petition, shall levy upon themselves an assessment under and subject to the conditions and provisions and for the purpose stated in this Article. (1967, c. 890, s. 6; 1973, c. 1262, s. 28.)

§ 113-314. Agency to determine time and place of referendum, amount and basis of assessment, etc.; notice of referendum.

The agency shall fix, determine, and publicly announce such referendum at least 30 days before the date set for such referendum, the date, hours, and polling places for voting in such referendum, the amount and basis of the assessment proposed to be collected, the means by which such assessment shall be collected if favorably voted upon, and the general purposes to which said amount so collected shall be applied. Such public notice shall be published at least once 20 days prior to the election in one or more newspapers having general circulation in the area where the vote is to be taken. (1967, c. 890, s. 7.)

§ 113-315. Maximum assessment.

No assessment levied on any commodity under the provisions of this Article shall exceed one percent (1%) of the average value of this commodity during the next three years for which published statistics by the State of North Carolina or the federal government are available next preceding the application or petition. (1967, c. 890, s. 8.)

§ 113-315.1. Arrangements for and management of referendum; expenses.

The arrangements for and management of any referendum conducted under the provisions of this Article shall be under the direction of the agency duly certified and authorized to conduct the same, and any and all expenses in connection herewith shall be borne by the agency. (1967, c. 890, s. 9.)

§ 113-315.2. Referendum may be by mail ballot or box ballot; who may vote.

Any referendum conducted under the provisions of this Article may be held by mail ballot or by box ballot as may be determined and publicly announced as herein provided by the agency before such referendum is called. A person licensed by the Marine Fisheries Commission to engage in business and commerce as may be directly affected by the paying of the assessment, or anyone who would be subject to paying such assessment should the question be voted in the affirmative, shall be eligible and may vote in such referendum. (1967, c. 890, s. 10; 1973, c. 1262, s. 86; 1977, c. 771, s. 4; 1987, c. 641, s. 6.)


§ 113-315.3. Preparation and distribution of ballots; conduct of referendum; canvass and declaration of results.

The duly certified agency shall prepare and distribute in advance of such referendum all necessary ballots for the purpose thereof, and shall under rules and regulations drawn up and promulgated by said agency, arrange for the necessary poll holders or officials for conducting the said referendum; and following said referendum and within 10 days thereafter the duly certified agency shall canvass and publicly declare the result of such referendum; except that in the event a mail ballot is used, a mail ballot shall be posted by registered mail on a prearranged date at least 30 days following announcement of same to each duly licensed voter by the agency, and a return, self-addressed envelope of suitable size and construction for containing the completed ballot with ample postage affixed shall be enclosed along with complete instructions on the voting procedure, these instructions stating that the ballot should be marked by the voter to indicate and show his preference, then inserted into the return envelope, sealed, and posted or returned within 10 days of the date of the original or first posting, and on a predesignated date and hour at least 15 days after the original mailing and at an open and public meeting, the return envelopes described above shall be opened, the ballots counted, tabulated, and the results publicly declared by the agency or its authorized representatives. (1967, c. 890, s. 11.)


§ 113-315.4. Levy and collection of assessment; use of proceeds and other funds.

If in such referendum called under the provisions of this Article two thirds or more of the voters eligible and voting vote in the affirmative and in favor of the levying and collection of such assessment proposed in such referendum, then such assessment shall be collected annually, or more often as predetermined by the agency, for the three years set forth in the call for such referendum, and the collection of such assessment shall be under such method, rules, and regulations as may be determined by the agency prior to the announcement of the referendum and included in the announcement of the referendum; said assessment so collected shall be paid into the treasury of the agency, to be used together with other funds, including donations and grants from individuals, firms, governmental agencies, or corporations, and from other fees, dues, or assessments, for the purpose set out in the referendum. (1967, c. 890, s. 12.)

§ 113-315.5. Alternative method for collection of assessment.

As an alternate method for the collection of assessments provided for in G.S. 113-315.4, upon the request or petition of the agency and action by the Marine Fisheries Commission as prescribed in G.S. 113-313, the Secretary shall notify, by letter, all persons or firms licensed by the Marine Fisheries Commission to engage in business and commerce as may be directly affected by the paying of the assessment, that on and after the date specified in the letter the assessment shall become due and payable, and shall be remitted by said persons or firms to the Secretary who shall thereupon pay the amount of the assessments to the agency. The books and records of all such persons and firms shall at all times during regular business hours be open for inspection by the Secretary or his duly authorized agents. (1967, c. 890, s. 13; 1973, c. 1262, ss. 28, 86; 1977, c. 356; c. 771, s. 4; 1987, c. 641, s. 6; 1995, c. 504, s. 6; c. 509, s. 57.)

§ 113-315.6. Subsequent referendum where assessment defeated.

In the event such referendum as herein provided for shall not be voted on affirmatively by two thirds or more of the voters eligible and voting, then the agency shall have full power and authority to call another referendum for the purposes herein set forth at any time after the next succeeding 12 months, on the question of an assessment for three years. (1967, c. 890, s. 14.)

§ 113-315.7. Subsequent referendum where assessment adopted.

In the event such referendum as herein provided for shall be voted on affirmatively by two thirds or more of the voters eligible and voting, then the agency shall in its discretion have full power and authority to call and conduct during the third year after the latest referendum another referendum for the purpose set forth herein for the next ensuing three years. (1967, c. 890, s. 15.)

§ 113-315.8. Refund of assessment; refusal to pay assessment.

Any persons or firm hereinunder assessed shall have the right to demand of and receive from the treasurer or disbursing office of the agency a refund of such assessment so collected, provided such demand for refund is made in writing within 30 days from the end of the assessment year which shall be determined by the agency. Should a person or firm hereinunder assessed refuse to pay and does not pay the assessment within 30 days of when it is due and payable, then in such event suit may be brought by the duly certified agency in a court of competent jurisdiction to enforce the collection of the said assessment. (1967, c. 890, s. 16; 1971, c. 642, s. 1.)

§ 113-315.9. Bond of financial officer; audit.

(a) Before collecting and receiving such assessments, such treasurer or financial officer shall give bond to the agency to run in favor of the agency in the amount of the estimated total of such assessments as will be collected, and from time to time the agency may alter the amount of such bond which, at all times, must be equal to the total financial assets of the agency, such bond to have as surety thereon a surety company licensed to do business in the State of North Carolina, and to be in the form and amount approved by the agency and to be filed with the chairman or executive head of such agency.

(b) The chairman or executive head of such agency shall cause an annual certified audit to be made of the financial records of the agency. Such audit shall include, among other things, total annual compensation of each employee of the agency and detailed expenses incurred and reimbursed for each employee of the agency. The chairman or executive head of such agency shall cause a copy of the certified audit to be submitted to the Department within 60 days of the end of the agency's fiscal year and shall cause a copy of the audit, or a summary thereof, to be published at least once in one or more newspapers having general circulation in the area where the assessments are made within 60 days of the end of the agency's fiscal year. If the chairman or executive head of the agency shall fail to carry out the provisions of this paragraph, he shall be guilty of a Class 1 misdemeanor. (1967, c. 890, s. 17; 1971, c. 642, s. 2; 1973, c. 1262, ss. 28, 86; 1977, c. 771, s. 4; 1989, c. 727, s. 115; 1993, c. 539, s. 868; 1994, Ex. Sess., c. 24, s. 14(c).)

§§ 113-315.10 through 113-315.14. Reserved for future codification purposes.


Article 23B.

Fishermen's Economic Development Program.

§ 113-315.15. Short title.

This Article shall be known as the Fishermen's Economic Development Act. (1973, c. 618, s. 1.)


§ 113-315.16. Legislative findings.

The legislature finds that the fishermen of North Carolina perform essential functions in providing wholesome food for the diets of the citizens of North Carolina, that they properly earn a livelihood by performing these essential functions, that they are entitled to the same or similar governmental services provided other segments of our society so as to become more proficient in the performance of these essential functions, and that the quality of life for North Carolinians is enhanced by the economic development of the fishing industry. (1973, c. 618, s. 1.)


§ 113-315.17. Definitions.

As used in this Article:

(1)   "Economic development" means: giving helpful and useful aid to improve the proficiency of the citizens, and the efficiency of the operations are

improved to the end that the economic well-being of fishermen is improved, the quality of life is enhanced and equality of opportunity is provided.

(2) "Fisherman" means: any person, firm, corporation, cooperative, partnership, or any legally constituted group, engaged in the harvesting, handling, processing, packaging, and marketing of fishery or seafood products from coastal fishing waters as defined by G.S. 113-129. (1973, c. 618, s. 1.)


§ 113-315.18. Fishermen's Economic Development Program.

The Secretary is hereby authorized to provide through his Department and the extension services of the University of North Carolina those services intended to promote the economic development of the fishermen, including but not limited to:

(1) Instituting business management services to promote better business management practices throughout the fishing and seafood industry, and to promote the better use of credit and other business management techniques.

(2) Providing counseling services to the fishermen at all levels and assisting them in meeting the federal and State environmental, safety and health requirements.

(3) Improving waterways, harbors, inlets, and generally the water transportation system of North Carolina so as to more efficiently and safely accommodate commercial and sport fishing craft, and to provide access to and from fishing grounds. (1973, c. 618, s. 1; c. 1262, s. 28; 1975, c. 19, s. 36; 1977, c. 771, s. 4; 1989, c. 727, s. 116.)


§ 113-315.19. Personnel needs.

To effectively carry out the duties and responsibilities set forth above, the Secretary may employ or contract with the extension services of the University of North Carolina to employ the following persons:

(1) A person to have responsibility for the successful execution of the program and to coordinate as deemed desirable with other agencies of the State and federal government,

(2) A business management specialist,

(3) An insurance and finance specialist,

(4) A specialist who could understand, interpret, and counsel on regulations and requirements,

(5) A specialist in waterways, and water transportation, and

(6) Such clerical personnel as necessary to carry out the provisions of this Article. (1973, c. 618, s. 1.)


§§ 113-315.20 through 113-315.24. Reserved for future codification purposes.


Article 23C.

North Carolina Marine Industrial Park Authority.

§ 113-315.25. Creation of Authority; membership; appointment; terms and vacancies; officers; meetings and quorum; compensation.

(a) There is hereby created the North Carolina Marine Industrial Park Authority. It shall be governed by a board composed of 11 members to be appointed as follows. The Board is hereby designated as the Authority.

(b) Nine members shall be appointed by the Governor.

The initial appointments by the Governor shall be made on or after the date of ratification, four terms to expire July 1, 1981; four terms to expire July 1, 1983; and one term to expire July 1, 1985. Thereafter, at the expiration of each stipulated term of office all appointments shall be for a term of four years. The members of the Authority shall be selected as follows: one member be appointed to the Authority for a term to expire July 1, 1983, who is a resident of a village or town where a Marine Industrial Park is located; one member be appointed to the Authority for a term to expire July 1, 1983, who is a resident of a county where a Marine Industrial Park is located; two members be appointed to the Authority for terms which expire July 1, 1981, from the area of the State where a Marine Industrial Park is located; five members (two terms expire July 1, 1981; two terms expire July 1, 1983; and one term expires July 1, 1985) be appointed to the Authority who are residents of the State at large and insofar as practicable shall represent all the other sections of the State. At the expiration of the terms for the representatives as stated above the Governor shall use his discretion on reappointments. However, there shall be no less than five members of the Authority from coastal counties and there should be at least one member on the Authority from each village or town in which the Marine Parks are located. Any vacancy occurring in the membership of the Authority shall be filled by the appointing authority for the unexpired term. The Governor shall have the authority to remove any member appointed by the Governor.

(c) Repealed by Session Laws 1981 (Regular Session, 1982), c. 1191, s. 36.

(d) The General Assembly shall appoint two persons, one upon the recommendation of the Speaker of the House of Representatives, and one upon the recommendation of the President Pro Tempore of the Senate. Appointments by the General Assembly shall be made in accordance with G.S. 120-121, and vacancies in those appointments shall be filled in accordance with G.S. 120-122. The terms of the initial appointees by the General Assembly shall expire on June 30, 1983. The terms of subsequent appointees by the General Assembly shall be two years.

(e) The Governor shall annually appoint from the members of the Authority the chairman and vice-chairman of the Authority. The Secretary of Commerce or his designee shall serve as secretary of the Authority.

(f) No person shall serve on the Authority for more than two complete consecutive terms.

(g) The Authority shall meet once in each 90 days at such regular meeting time as the Authority by rule may provide and at any place within the State as the Authority may provide, and shall also meet upon the call of its chairman or a majority of its members. A majority of its members shall constitute a quorum for the transaction of business. The members of the Authority shall not be entitled to compensation for their services, but shall receive per diem and necessary travel and subsistence expense in accordance with G.S. 138-5 and 138-6. (1979, c. 459, s. 1; 1981 (Reg. Sess., 1982), c. 1191, ss. 36, 37; 1989, c. 751, s. 8(12); 1991 Session Laws (1992 Regular Session), c. 959, s. 85(b); 1995, c. 490, s. 47; 2013-211, s. 1.)

§ 113-315.26. Personnel.

The Secretary of Commerce shall appoint any personnel as deemed necessary who shall serve at the pleasure of the Secretary of Commerce. The Secretary of Commerce shall have the power to appoint, employ and dismiss any employees deemed necessary to accomplish the purposes of this Article subject to the availability of funds. It is recommended that, to the fullest extent possible, the Secretary of Commerce consult with the Authority on matters of personnel. (1979, c. 459, s. 2; 1983, c. 717, s. 24; 1983 (Reg. Sess., 1984), c. 1034, s. 164; 1989, c. 751, s. 8(13); c. 752, s. 39(d); 1991 (Reg. Sess., 1992), c. 959, s. 24; 2013-211, s. 1.)

§ 113-315.27. Executive committee.

There shall be an executive committee consisting of the chairman of the Authority and two other members elected annually by the Authority. The executive committee shall be vested with authority to do all acts which are specifically authorized by the bylaws of the Authority. Members of the executive committee shall serve until their successors are elected. (1979, c. 459, s. 3.)

§ 113-315.28. Purposes of Authority.

Through the Authority created by this Article, the State of North Carolina may engage in promoting, developing, constructing, equipping, maintaining and operating one or more marine industrial parks within the State, or within the jurisdiction of the State, and works of internal improvements related to the purposes set forth in this section, including the acquisition or construction, maintenance and operation of watercraft and facilities located at the parks or essential for the proper operation of the parks. The Authority is created as an instrumentality of the State of North Carolina for the accomplishment of the following general purposes:

(1) To develop and improve the Wanchese Marine Industrial Park, and such other marine industrial parks, including inland ports and facilities, as may be deemed feasible for a more expeditious and efficient handling of marine commerce from and to any place or places in the State of North Carolina and other states and foreign countries;

(2) To acquire, construct, equip, maintain, develop and improve the port facilities at the parks and to maintain, develop, and improve the navigability of waterways in or adjacent to the parks and those waterways connecting the parks with the channels of commerce of the Atlantic Ocean;

(3) To foster and stimulate the growth of marine-related industries in the State of North Carolina;

(4) Repealed by Session Laws 2013-211, s. 1, effective June 26, 2013.

(5) To accept funds from any counties or cities containing a marine industrial park and to use the same in such manner, within the purposes of said Authority, as shall be stipulated by the funding county or city, and to act as agent or instrumentality of any funding counties or cities in any matter coming within the general purposes of said Authority;

(5a) To encourage and develop the general maritime and marine-related industries and activities at or in the vicinity of the marine industrial parks;

(6) And in general to do and perform any act or function which may tend to be useful toward the development and improvement of marine industrial parks in the State of North Carolina, and to increase the movement of waterborne marine commerce, foreign and domestic, to, through, and from the marine industrial parks.

The enumeration of the above purposes shall not limit or circumscribe the broad objective of developing to the utmost the marine industry possibilities of the State of North Carolina. (1979, c. 459, s. 4; 1993, c. 278, s. 1; 1998-212, s. 15.5(a); 2013-211, s. 1.)

§ 113-315.29. Powers of Authority.

In order to enable it to carry out the purposes of this Article, the Authority shall:

(1) Have the powers of a body corporate, including the power to sue and be sued, to make contracts, and to adopt and use a common seal and to alter the same as may be deemed expedient;

(2) Have the authority to make all necessary contracts and arrangements with other marine industrial park or port authorities of this and other states for the interchange of business, and for such other purposes as will facilitate and increase the marine industries;

(3) Be authorized and empowered to rent, lease, buy, own, acquire, mortgage, otherwise encumber, and dispose of such property, real or personal, as said Authority may deem proper to carry out the purposes and provisions of this Article, all or any of them;

(4) Be authorized and empowered to acquire, construct, maintain, equip and operate any wharves, docks, piers, quays, elevators, compresses, refrigeration storage plants, warehouses and other structures, and any and all facilities needful for the convenient use of the same in the aid of commerce, including the dredging of approaches to port facilities at the parks and improving the navigability of those waterways connecting the parks with the channels of commerce of the Atlantic Ocean;

(5) Be authorized and empowered to pay all necessary costs and expenses involved and incident to the formation and organization of the Authority, and incident to its administration and operation, and to pay all other costs and expenses reasonably necessary or expedient in carrying out and accomplishing the purposes of this Article;

(6) Be authorized and empowered to apply for and accept loans and grants of money from any federal agency or the State of North Carolina and its political subdivisions or from any public or private sources available for any and all of the purposes authorized in this Article, and to expend these funds in accordance with the directions and requirements of the granting or loaning authority, or imposed on the loans and grants by any federal agency, the State of North Carolina and its political subdivisions, or any public or private lender or donor, and to give such evidences of indebtedness as shall be required, provided, however, that no indebtedness of any kind incurred or created by the Authority

shall constitute an indebtedness of the State of North Carolina, or any of its political subdivisions, and no such indebtedness shall involve or be secured by the faith, credit or taxing power of the State of North Carolina, or any of its political subdivisions;

(7) Be authorized and empowered to act as agent for the United States of America, or any of its agencies, departments, corporations, or instrumentalities in any matter coming within the purposes or powers of the Authority;

(8) Have power to adopt, alter or repeal bylaws and rules governing the manner in which its business may be transacted and in which the power granted to it may be enjoyed, and may provide for the appointment of any committees as the Authority may deem necessary or expedient in facilitating its business;

(8a) Have the authority to assess and collect fees for its services or for the use of its facilities;

(9) Be authorized and empowered to do any and all other acts and things in this Article authorized or required to be done, whether or not included in the general powers in this section mentioned; and

(10) Be authorized and empowered to do any and all things necessary to accomplish the purposes of this Article. (1979, c. 459, s. 5; 1987, c. 827, s. 108; 1993, c. 323, s. 1; 2013-211, s. 1.)


§ 113-315.30. Approval of acquisition and disposition of real property.

Any transactions relating to the acquisition or disposition of real property or any estate or interest in real property, by the North Carolina State Marine Industrial Park Authority, shall be subject to prior review by the Governor and Council of State, and shall become effective only after the same has been approved by the Governor and Council of State. Upon the acquisition of real property or other estate or interest in real property, by the Authority, the fee title or other estate shall vest in and the instrument of conveyance shall name the "North Carolina Marine Industrial Park Authority" as grantee, lessee, or transferee. Upon the disposition of real property or any interest or estate therein, the instrument of conveyance or transfer shall be executed by the North Carolina Marine Industrial Park Authority. The approval of any transaction by the Governor and Council of State may be evidenced by a duly certified copy of excerpt of minutes of the meeting of the Governor and Council of State, attested by the private secretary to the Governor or the Governor, reciting such approval, affixed to the instrument of acquisition or transfer, and the certificate may be recorded as a part of the instrument of acquisition or transfer, and shall be conclusive evidence of review and approval of the subject transaction by the Governor and Council of State. The Governor, acting with the approval of the Council of State, may delegate the review and approval of such classes of lease, rental, easement, or right-of-way transactions as the Governor deems advisable, and the Governor may likewise delegate the review and approval of the severance of buildings and timber from the land. (1979, c. 459, s. 6; 2013-211, s. 1.)

§ 113-315.31. Issuance of bonds.

(a) As a means of raising the funds needed from time to time in the acquisition, construction, equipment, maintenance and operation of any facility, building, structure, or any other matter or thing which the Authority is authorized to acquire, construct, equip, maintain, or operate by this Article, all or any of them, the Authority is hereby authorized at one time or from time to time to issue with the approval of the Governor negotiable revenue bonds of the Authority. The principal and interest of revenue bonds shall be payable solely from the revenue to be derived from the operation of all or any part of its properties and facilities.

(b) A pledge of the net revenues derived from the operation of the properties and facilities, all or any of them, shall be made to secure the payment of the bonds issued to finance them as and when they mature.

(c) Revenue bonds issued under the provisions of this Article shall not be deemed to constitute a debt of the State of North Carolina or a pledge of the faith and credit of the State. The issuance of such revenue bonds shall not directly or indirectly or contingently obligate the State to levy or to pledge any form of taxation whatever or to make any appropriation for their payment.

(d) Such bonds and the income derived from them shall be exempt from all taxation within the State.

(e) Notwithstanding any other provisions of this Article, the State Treasurer shall have the exclusive power to issue bonds and notes authorized under the act upon request of the Authority and with the approval of the Governor after receiving the advice of the Local Government Commission. The State Treasurer in his sole discretion shall determine the interest rates, maturities, and other terms and conditions of the bonds and notes authorized by this Article. The North Carolina Marine Industrial Park Authority shall determine when a bond issue is indicated. The Authority shall cooperate with the State Treasurer in structuring any bond issue in general, and also in soliciting proposals from financial consultants, underwriters, and bond attorneys. (1979, c. 459, s. 7; 1983, c. 577, s. 2; 1985 (Reg. Sess., 1986), c. 955, ss. 13, 14; 2006-203, s. 28; 2013-211, s. 1.)


§ 113-315.32. Power of eminent domain.

For the acquiring of rights-of-way and property necessary for the construction of wharves, piers, ships, docks, quays, elevators, compresses, refrigerator storage plants, warehouses and other riparian and littoral terminals and structures and approaches thereto, including the navigation stabilization structures and transportation facilities needful for the convenient use of same, the Authority shall have the right and power to acquire the same by purchase, by negotiation, or by condemnation, and should it elect to exercise the right of eminent domain, condemnation proceedings shall be maintained by and in the name of the Authority, and it may proceed in the manner provided for the Board of Transportation by Article 9 of Chapter 136 of the General Statutes. The power of eminent domain shall not apply to property of persons, State agency or corporations already devoted to public use, other than lands subject to the power of eminent domain by the State of North Carolina in the reservation clauses of a deed recorded in the Dare County Registry at Book 79 Page 548. (1979, c. 459, s. 8; 1998-212, s. 15.5(b); 2013-211, s. 1.)


§ 113-315.33. Exchange of property; removal of buildings, etc.

The Authority may exchange any property or properties acquired under the authority of this Chapter for other property, or properties usable in carrying out the powers conferred by this Article, and also may remove from lands needed for its purposes and reconstruct on other locations, buildings, terminals, or other structures, upon the payment of just compensation, if in its judgment, it is necessary or expedient so to do in order to carry out any of its plans for marine industrial park development, under the authorization of this Article. (1979, c. 459, s. 9; 2013-211, s. 1.)

§ 113-315.34. Jurisdiction of the Authority; application of Chapter 20; appointment and authority of special police.

(a) The jurisdiction of the Authority in any of the parks shall extend to all properties owned by or under control of the Authority and shall also extend over the waters and shores within the parks and over that part of all tributary streams flowing into the parks in which the tide ebbs and flows, and shall extend to the outer edge of the outer bar situated at the approach to the port of any park.

(b) All the provisions of Chapter 20 of the General Statutes relating to the use of the highways of the State and the operation of motor vehicles thereon are hereby made applicable to the streets, alleys and driveways on the properties owned by or under the control of the North Carolina Marine Industrial Park Authority. Any person violating any of the provisions of said Chapter in or on such streets, alleys or driveways shall, upon conviction thereof, be punished as therein prescribed. Nothing herein contained shall be construed as in any way interfering with the ownership and control of such streets, alleys and driveways on the properties of said Authority as is now vested by law in the said Authority.

(c) The Authority shall post copies of rules concerning traffic and parking at appropriate places on property of the Authority. Violation of a rule concerning traffic or parking on property of the Authority is a Class 3 misdemeanor.

(d) The Secretary of Commerce is authorized to appoint such number of employees of the Authority as he may think proper as special policemen, who, when so appointed, shall have within the jurisdiction of the Authority all the powers of policemen of incorporated towns. Special policemen may arrest persons who violate State law or a rule adopted by the Authority. Employees appointed as such special policemen shall take the general oath of office prescribed by G.S. 11-11. (1979, c. 459, s. 10; 1987, c. 827, s. 109; 1989, c. 751, s. 8(14); 1991 (Reg. Sess., 1992), c. 959, s. 25; 1993, c. 539, s. 869; 1994, Ex. Sess., c. 24, s. 14(c); 2013-211, s. 1.)

§ 113-315.35. Audit.

The operations of the North Carolina Marine Industrial Park Authority shall be subject to the oversight of the State Auditor pursuant to Article 5A of Chapter 147 of the General Statutes. (1979, c. 459, s. 11; 1983, c. 913, s. 14; 2013-211, s. 1.)

§ 113-315.36. Building contracts.

(a) The following general laws, to the extent provided below, do not apply to the North Carolina Marine Industrial Park Authority:

(1) Repealed by Session Laws 1999-368, s. 1.

(2) Except for G.S. 143-128.2, Article 8 of Chapter 143 of the General Statutes does not apply to public building contracts of the Authority that require the estimated expenditure of public money in an amount less than two hundred fifty thousand dollars ($250,000). With respect to a contract that is exempted from certain provisions of Article 8 under this subdivision, the powers and duties set out in Article 8 shall be exercised by the Authority, and the Secretary of Administration and other State officers, employees, or agencies shall have no duties or responsibilities concerning the contract.

(3) G.S. 143-341(3) does not apply to plans and specifications for construction or renovation authorized by the Authority that require the estimated expenditure of public money in an amount less than two hundred fifty thousand dollars ($250,000).

(b) Notwithstanding the other provisions of this section, the services of the Department of Administration may be made available to the Authority, when requested by the Authority, with regard to matters governed by Article 8 of Chapter 143 of the General Statutes and G.S. 143-341(3). The Authority shall report quarterly to the Joint Legislative Commission on Governmental Operations on any building contract to which this exemption is applied. The quarterly report required by this subsection shall specifically include information regarding the Authority's compliance with the provisions of G.S. 143-128.2. (1979, c. 459, s. 12; 1997-331, s. 2; 1999-368, ss. 1, 2; 2001-496, s. 3.2; 2013-211, s. 1.)

§ 113-315.37. Liberal construction of Article.

It is intended that the provisions of this Article shall be liberally construed to accomplish the purposes provided for, or intended to be provided for, herein, and where strict construction would result in the defeat of the accomplishment of any of the acts authorized herein, and a liberal construction would permit or assist in the accomplishment thereof, the liberal construction shall be chosen. (1979, c. 459, s. 13.)

§ 113-315.38. Warehouses, wharves, etc., on property abutting navigable waters.

The powers, authority and jurisdiction granted to the North Carolina Marine Industrial Park Authority under this Article and Chapter shall not be construed so as to prevent other persons, firms and corporations, including municipalities, from owning, constructing, leasing, managing and operating warehouses, structures and other improvements on property they own, lease, or control abutting upon and adjacent to navigable waters and streams in this State, nor to prevent other persons, firms and corporations from constructing, owning, leasing and operating wharves, docks and piers associated with the warehouses, structures, and other improvements, nor to prevent other persons, firms and corporations from encumbering, leasing, selling, conveying or otherwise dealing with and disposing of the properties, facilities, lands and improvements after construction. (1979, c. 459, s. 14; 2013-211, s. 1.)

§ 113-315.39. Taxation.

The property of the Authority shall not be subject to any taxes or assessments. (1979, c. 459, s. 15; 2013-211, s. 1.)

Article 24.

Miscellaneous Transitional Provisions.

§ 113-316. General statement of purpose and effect of revisions of Subchapter IV made in 1965 and 1979.

To clarify the conservation laws of the State and the authority and jurisdiction of the Department and the North Carolina Wildlife Resources Commission: commercial fishing waters are renamed coastal fishing waters and the Department is given jurisdiction over and responsibility for the marine and estuarine resources in coastal fishing waters; the laws pertaining to commercial fishing operations and marine fishing and fisheries regulated by the Department are consolidated and revised generally and broadened to reflect the jurisdictional change respecting coastal fisheries; laws relating to the conservation of wildlife resources administered by the Wildlife Resources Commission are consolidated and revised; and the enforcement authority of marine fisheries inspectors and wildlife protectors is clarified, including the authority of wildlife protectors over boating and other activities other than conservation within the jurisdiction of the Wildlife Resources Commission. (1965, c. 957, s. 1; 1973, c. 1262, ss. 28, 86; 1977, c. 771, s. 4; 1979, c. 830, s. 1; 1989, c. 727, s. 117.)

§ 113-317. Repealed by Session Laws 1979, c. 830, s. 1.

§§ 113-318 through 113-320. Repealed by Session Laws 1973, c. 1262, s. 28.

§§ 113-321 through 113-322. Repealed by Session Laws 1979, c. 830, s. 1.

§§ 113-323 through 113-330: Reserved for future codification purposes.

Article 25.

Endangered and Threatened Wildlife and Wildlife Species of Special Concern.

§ 113-331. Definitions.

All of the definitions contained in Article 12 of this Chapter 113 shall apply in this Article except to the extent that they may be herein modified for the purposes of this Article 25. As used in this Article, unless the context requires otherwise:

(1) "Conserve" and "conservation" mean the use and application of all methods, procedures and biological information for the purpose of bringing

populations of native and once-native species of wildlife in balance with the optimum carrying capacity of their habitat, and maintaining such balance. These methods and procedures include all activities associated with scientific resource management such as research; census; law enforcement; habitat protection, acquisition, and enhancement; and restoration of species to unoccupied parts of historic range. With respect to endangered and threatened species, the terms mean the use of methods and procedures to bring the species to the point at which the measures provided are no longer necessary.

(2) "Endangered species" means any native or once-native species of wild animal whose continued existence as a viable component of the State's fauna is determined by the Wildlife Resources Commission to be in jeopardy or any species of wild animal determined to be an "endangered species" pursuant to the Endangered Species Act.

(3) "Endangered Species Act" means the Endangered Species Act of 1973, Public Law 93-205 (87 Stat. 884), as it may be subsequently amended.

(4) "Advisory Committee" means the North Carolina Nongame Wildlife Advisory Committee which is the advisory body of knowledgeable and representative citizens established by resolution of the Wildlife Resources Commission and charged to consider matters relating to nongame wildlife conservation and to advise the Commission in such matters.

(5) "Protected animal" means a species of wild animal designated by the Wildlife Resources Commission as endangered, threatened, or of special concern.

(6) "Protected animal list" means any one of the lists of North Carolina animal species that are endangered, threatened, or of special concern.

(7) "Scientific council" means the group of scientists identified and assembled by the Advisory Committee to review the scientific evidence and to evaluate the status of wildlife species that are candidates for inclusion on a protected animal list.

(8) "Special concern species" means any species of wild animal native or once-native to North Carolina which is determined by the Wildlife Resources Commission to require monitoring but which may be taken under regulations adopted under the provisions of this Article.

(9) "Threatened species" means any native or once-native species of wild animal which is likely to become an endangered species within the foreseeable future throughout all or a significant portion of its range, or one that is designated as a threatened species pursuant to the Endangered Species Act.

(10) "Wild animal" means any native or once-native nongame amphibian, bird, crustacean, fish, mammal, mollusk or reptile not otherwise legally classified by statute or regulation such as game and fur bearing animals, except those inhabiting and depending upon coastal fishing waters, marine and estuarine resources, marine mammals found in coastal fishing waters, sea turtles found in coastal fishing waters, and those declared to be pests under the Structural Pest Control Act of North Carolina of 1955 or the North Carolina Pesticide Law of 1971. Nothing in this definition is intended to abrogate G.S. 113-132(a) or (c), confer jurisdiction upon the Wildlife Resources Commission as to any subject exclusively regulated by any other agency, or to authorize the Wildlife Resources Commission by its regulations to supersede any valid provision of law or regulation administered by any other agency. (1987, c. 382, s. 1.)

§ 113-332. Declaration of policy.

The General Assembly finds that the recreation and aesthetic needs of the people, the interests of science, the quality of the environment, and the best interests of the State require that endangered and threatened species of wild animals and wild animals of special concern be protected and conserved, that their numbers should be enhanced and that conservation techniques be developed for them; however, nothing in this Article shall be construed to limit the rights of a landholder in the management of his lands for agriculture, forestry, development or any other lawful purpose without his consent. The North Carolina Zoological Park is not subject to the provisions of this Article. (1987, c. 382, s. 1.)

§ 113-333. Powers and duties of the Commission.

(a) In the administration of this Article, the Wildlife Resources Commission shall have the following powers and duties:

(1)     To adopt and publish an endangered species list, a threatened species list, and a list of species of special concern, as provided for in G.S. 113-334, identifying each entry by its scientific and common name.

(2)     To reconsider and revise the lists from time to time in response to public proposals or as the Commission deems necessary.

(3)     To coordinate development and implementation of conservation programs and plans for endangered and threatened species of wild animals and for species of special concern.

(4)     To adopt and implement conservation programs for endangered, threatened, and special concern species and to limit, regulate, or prevent the taking, collection, or sale of protected animals.

(5)     To conduct investigations to determine whether a wild animal should be on a protected animal list and to determine the requirements for conservation of protected wild animal species.

(6)     To adopt and implement rules to limit, regulate, or prohibit the taking, possession, collection, transportation, purchase or sale of those species of wild animals in the classes Amphibia and Reptilia that do not meet the criteria for listing pursuant to G.S. 113-334 if the Commission determines that the species requires conservation measures in order to prevent the addition of the species to the protected animal lists pursuant to G.S. 113-334. This subdivision does not authorize the Commission to prohibit the taking of any species of the classes Amphibia and Reptilia solely to protect persons, property, or habitat; to prohibit possession by any person of four or fewer individual reptiles; or to prohibit possession by any person of 24 or fewer individual amphibians.

(b)     Using the procedures set out in Article 2A of Chapter 150B of the General Statutes, the Wildlife Resources Commission shall develop a conservation plan for the recovery of protected wild animal species. In developing a conservation plan for a protected wild animal species, the Wildlife Resources Commission shall consider the range of conservation, protection, and management measures that may be applied to benefit the species and its habitat. The conservation plan shall include a comprehensive analysis of all factors that have been identified as causing the decline of the protected wild animal species and all measures that could be taken to restore the species. The analysis shall consider the costs of measures to protect and restore the species and the impact of those measures on the local economy, units of local government, and the use and development of private property. The analysis shall consider reasonably available options for minimizing the costs and adverse economic impacts of measures to protect and restore the species.

(c) In implementing a conservation plan under this Article, the Wildlife Resources Commission shall not adopt any rule that restricts the use or development of private property. If a conservation plan identifies a conservation, protection, or restoration measure the implementation of which is beyond the scope of the authority of the Wildlife Resources Commission, the Commission may petition the General Assembly, any agency that has regulatory authority to implement the measure, a unit of local government, or any other public or private entity and request the assistance of that agency or entity in implementing the measure.

(d) The Commission is authorized to develop a bat eviction and exclusion curriculum that may be taught by trade associations or wildlife conservation organizations for certification. The curriculum may incorporate the training that is provided as part of Wildlife Damage Control Agent certification in best management practices for removing and evicting bats from structures and in preventing bats from reentering structures. (1987, c. 382, s. 1; 1995, c. 392, s. 1; 2003-100, s. 1; 2009-219, s. 1.)


§ 113-334. Criteria and procedures for placing animals on protected animal lists.

(a) All native or resident wild animals which are on the federal lists of endangered or threatened species pursuant to the Endangered Species Act have the same status on the North Carolina protected animals lists.

(b) The Advisory Committee, after considering a report on the status of a candidate species from the Scientific Council, may by resolution propose to the Wildlife Resources Commission that a species of wild animal be added to or removed from a protected animal list.

(c) If the Commission, with the advice of the Advisory Committee, finds there is probably merit in the proposal, it shall examine relevant scientific and economic data and factual information necessary to determine:

(1) Whether any other state or federal agency or private entity is taking steps to protect the wild animal which is the subject of the proposal;

(2) Whether there is present or threatened destruction, modification, or curtailment of its habitat;

(3) If there is over-utilization for commercial, recreational, scientific, or educational purposes;

(4) Whether there is critical population depletion from disease, predation, or other mortality factors;

(5) Whether alternative regulatory mechanisms exist; and

(6) The existence of other man-made factors affecting continued viability of the animal in North Carolina.

(d) The Commission, with the advice of the Advisory Committee, shall tentatively determine whether any regulatory action is warranted with regard to the proposal and, if so, the specific regulatory action to be proposed by it. Notice of its proposed rulemaking shall be published in the North Carolina Register and the subsequent proceedings shall conform with the Administrative Procedure Act. (1987, c. 382, s. 1.)


§ 113-335. North Carolina Nongame Wildlife Advisory Committee.

The North Carolina Nongame Wildlife Advisory Committee is created subject to constitution, organization, and function as determined appropriate and advisable by resolution of the Wildlife Resources Commission. The Advisory Committee is to be comprised of knowledgeable and representative citizens of North Carolina whose responsibility shall be to advise the Commission on matters related to conservation of nongame wildlife including creation of protected animal lists and development of conservation programs for endangered, threatened, and special concern species.

Members of the Advisory Committee shall receive necessary travel and subsistence expenses while on official business of the Committee in accordance with G.S. 138-5 and G.S. 138-6, to be paid from the Nongame Account of the

Wildlife Resources Fund. (1987, c. 382; 1989 (Reg. Sess., 1990), c. 1066, s. 48.)

§ 113-336. Powers and duties of the Advisory Committee.

The Advisory Committee shall have the following powers and duties:

(1) To gather and provide information and data and advise the Wildlife Resources Commission with respect to all aspects of the biology and ecology of endangered, threatened, and special concern species;

(2) To investigate and make recommendations to the Commission as to the status of endangered, threatened, and special concern species;

(3) To identify and assemble experts from the disciplines of ornithology, mammalogy, herpetology, ichthyology, taxonomy, ecology and other fields as necessary to serve as the Scientific Council and to charge the Scientific Council to review the scientific evidence, to evaluate the status of candidate species, and to report back their findings with recommendations;

(4) To develop and present to the Commission management and conservation practices for preserving endangered, threatened, and special concern species;

(5) To recommend critical habitat areas for protection or acquisition;

(6) To advise the Commission on matters submitted to it by the Commission which involve technical zoological questions or the development of pertinent regulations, and to make any recommendations as deemed by the Advisory Committee to be worthy of the Commission's attention. (1987, c. 382, s. 1.)

§ 113-337. Unlawful acts; penalties.

(a) It is unlawful:

(1) To take, possess, transport, sell, barter, trade, exchange, export, or offer for sale, barter, trade, exchange or export, or give away for any purpose

including advertising or other promotional purpose any animal on a protected wild animal list, except as authorized according to the regulations of the Commission, including those promulgated pursuant to G.S. 113-333(1);

(2) To perform any act specifically prohibited by the regulations of the Commission promulgated pursuant to its authority under G.S. 113-333.

(b) Each person convicted of violating the provisions of this Article is guilty of a Class 1 misdemeanor. (1987, c. 382, s. 1; 1999-408, s. 10.)

§§ 113-338 through 113-350: Reserved for future codification purposes.

§ 113-351. Unified hunting and fishing licenses; subsistence license waiver.

(a) Definitions. - The definitions set out in G.S. 113-174 apply to this Article.

(b) General Provisions Governing Licenses and Waivers. - The general provisions governing licenses set out in G.S. 113-174.1 apply to licenses and waivers issued under this section.

(c) (Effective until August 1, 2014) Types of Unified Hunting and Fishing Licenses; Fees; Duration. - The Wildlife Resources Commission shall issue the following Unified Hunting and Fishing Licenses:

(1) Annual Resident Unified Sportsman/Coastal Recreational Fishing License. - $55.00. This license is valid for a period of one year from the date of issuance. This license shall be issued only to an individual who is a resident of the State. This license authorizes the licensee to take all wild animals and wild birds, including waterfowl, by all lawful methods in all open seasons, including the use of game lands; to fish with hook and line for all fish in all inland fishing waters and joint fishing waters, including public mountain trout waters; and to engage in recreational fishing in coastal fishing waters.

(2) Annual Resident Unified Inland/Coastal Recreational Fishing License. - $35.00. This license is valid for a period of one year from the date of issuance. This license shall be issued only to an individual who is a resident of the State. This license authorizes the licensee to fish with hook and line for all fish in all

inland fishing waters and joint fishing waters, including public mountain trout waters, and to engage in recreational fishing in coastal fishing waters.

(3) Lifetime Unified Sportsman/Coastal Recreational Fishing Licenses. - Except as provided in sub-subdivision f. of this subdivision, a license issued under this subdivision is valid for the lifetime of the licensee. A license issued under this subdivision authorizes the licensee to take all wild animals and wild birds, including waterfowl, by all lawful methods in all open seasons, including the use of game lands; to fish with hook and line for all fish in all inland fishing waters and joint fishing waters, including public mountain trout waters; and to engage in recreational fishing in coastal fishing waters.

a. Infant Lifetime Unified Sportsman/Coastal Recreational Fishing License. - $275.00. This license shall be issued only to an individual who is younger than one year of age.

b. Youth Lifetime Unified Sportsman/Coastal Recreational Fishing License. - $450.00. This license shall be issued only to an individual who is one year of age or older but younger than 12 years of age.

c. Resident Adult Lifetime Unified Sportsman/Coastal Recreational Fishing License. - $675.00. This license shall be issued only to an individual who is 12 years of age or older but younger than 65 years of age and who is a resident of the State.

d. Nonresident Adult Lifetime Unified Sportsman/Coastal Recreational Fishing License. - $1,350. This license shall be issued only to an individual who is 12 years of age or older and who is not a resident of the State.

e. Resident Age 65 Lifetime Unified Sportsman/Coastal Recreational Fishing License. - $30.00. This license shall be issued only to an individual who is 65 years of age or older and who is a resident of the State.

f. Resident Disabled Veteran Lifetime Unified Sportsman/Coastal Recreational Fishing License. - $110.00. This license shall be issued only to an individual who is a resident of the State and who is a fifty percent (50%) or more disabled veteran as determined by the United States Department of Veterans Affairs. This license remains valid for the lifetime of the licensee so long as the licensee remains fifty percent (50%) or more disabled.

g. Resident Totally Disabled Lifetime Unified Sportsman/Coastal Recreational Fishing License. - $110.00. This license shall be issued only to an individual who is a resident of the State and who is totally and permanently disabled as determined by the Social Security Administration.

(4) Lifetime Unified Inland/Coastal Recreational Fishing Licenses. - Except as provided in sub-subdivisions b. and c. of this subdivision, a license issued under this subdivision is valid for the lifetime of the licensee. A license issued under this subdivision authorizes the licensee to fish with hook and line for all fish in all inland fishing waters and joint fishing waters, including public mountain trout waters, and to engage in recreational fishing in coastal fishing waters.

a. Resident Lifetime Unified Inland/Coastal Recreational Fishing License. - $450.00.

b. Resident Legally Blind Lifetime Unified Inland/Coastal Recreational Fishing License. - No charge. This license shall be issued only to an individual who is a resident of the State and who has been certified by the Department of Health and Human Services as an individual whose vision with glasses is insufficient for use in ordinary occupations for which sight is essential. This license remains valid for the lifetime of the licensee so long as the licensee remains legally blind.

c. Resident Adult Care Home Lifetime Unified Inland/Coastal Recreational Fishing License. - No charge. This license shall be issued only to an individual who is a resident of the State and who resides in an adult care home as defined in G.S. 131D-2.1 or G.S. 131E-101(1). This license remains valid for the lifetime of the licensee so long as the licensee remains a resident of an adult care home.

(c) (Effective August 1, 2014) Types of Unified Hunting and Fishing Licenses; Fees; Duration. - The Wildlife Resources Commission shall issue the following Unified Hunting and Fishing Licenses:

(1) Annual Resident Unified Sportsman/Coastal Recreational Fishing License. - $65.00. This license is valid for a period of one year from the date of issuance. This license shall be issued only to an individual who is a resident of the State. This license authorizes the licensee to take all wild animals and wild birds, including waterfowl, by all lawful methods in all open seasons, including the use of game lands; to fish with hook and line for all fish in all inland fishing

waters and joint fishing waters, including public mountain trout waters; and to engage in recreational fishing in coastal fishing waters.

(2)    Annual Resident Unified Inland/Coastal Recreational Fishing License. - $40.00. This license is valid for a period of one year from the date of issuance. This license shall be issued only to an individual who is a resident of the State. This license authorizes the licensee to fish with hook and line for all fish in all inland fishing waters and joint fishing waters, including public mountain trout waters, and to engage in recreational fishing in coastal fishing waters.

(3)    Lifetime Unified Sportsman/Coastal Recreational Fishing Licenses. - Except as provided in sub-subdivision f. of this subdivision, a license issued under this subdivision is valid for the lifetime of the licensee. A license issued under this subdivision authorizes the licensee to take all wild animals and wild birds, including waterfowl, by all lawful methods in all open seasons, including the use of game lands; to fish with hook and line for all fish in all inland fishing waters and joint fishing waters, including public mountain trout waters; and to engage in recreational fishing in coastal fishing waters.

a.    Infant Lifetime Unified Sportsman/Coastal Recreational Fishing License. - $275.00. This license shall be issued only to an individual who is younger than one year of age.

b.    Youth Lifetime Unified Sportsman/Coastal Recreational Fishing License. - $450.00. This license shall be issued only to an individual who is one year of age or older but younger than 12 years of age.

c.    Resident Adult Lifetime Unified Sportsman/Coastal Recreational Fishing License. - $675.00. This license shall be issued only to an individual who is 12 years of age or older but younger than 70 years of age and who is a resident of the State.

d.    Nonresident Adult Lifetime Unified Sportsman/Coastal Recreational Fishing License. - $1,550. This license shall be issued only to an individual who is 12 years of age or older and who is not a resident of the State.

e.    Resident Age 70 Lifetime Unified Sportsman/Coastal Recreational Fishing License. - $30.00. This license shall be issued only to an individual who is 70 years of age or older and who is a resident of the State.

f. Resident Disabled Veteran Lifetime Unified Sportsman/Coastal Recreational Fishing License. - $110.00. This license shall be issued only to an individual who is a resident of the State and who is a fifty percent (50%) or more disabled veteran as determined by the United States Department of Veterans Affairs or as established by rules of the Wildlife Resources Commission. This license remains valid for the lifetime of the licensee so long as the licensee remains fifty percent (50%) or more disabled.

g. Resident Totally Disabled Lifetime Unified Sportsman/Coastal Recreational Fishing License. - $110.00. This license shall be issued only to an individual who is a resident of the State and who is totally and permanently disabled as determined by the Social Security Administration or as established by rules of the Wildlife Resources Commission.

(4) Lifetime Unified Inland/Coastal Recreational Fishing Licenses. - Except as provided in sub-subdivisions b. and c. of this subdivision, a license issued under this subdivision is valid for the lifetime of the licensee. A license issued under this subdivision authorizes the licensee to fish with hook and line for all fish in all inland fishing waters and joint fishing waters, including public mountain trout waters, and to engage in recreational fishing in coastal fishing waters.

a. Resident Lifetime Unified Inland/Coastal Recreational Fishing License. - $450.00.

b. Resident Legally Blind Lifetime Unified Inland/Coastal Recreational Fishing License. - No charge. This license shall be issued only to an individual who is a resident of the State and who has been certified by the Department of Health and Human Services as an individual whose vision with glasses is insufficient for use in ordinary occupations for which sight is essential. This license remains valid for the lifetime of the licensee so long as the licensee remains legally blind.

c. Resident Adult Care Home Lifetime Unified Inland/Coastal Recreational Fishing License. - No charge. This license shall be issued only to an individual who is a resident of the State and who resides in an adult care home as defined in G.S. 131D-2.1 or G.S. 131E-101(1). This license remains valid for the lifetime of the licensee so long as the licensee remains a resident of an adult care home.

(d) Resident Subsistence Unified Inland/Coastal Recreational Fishing License Waiver. - A county department of social services shall issue a Resident

Subsistence Unified Inland/Coastal Recreational Fishing License Waiver to an individual who receives benefits from Medicaid, Food and Nutrition Services, or Work First Family Assistance through the county department of social services and who requests a waiver. This waiver shall be issued at no charge. This waiver is valid for a period of one year from the date of issuance. This waiver shall be issued only to an individual who is a resident of the State. This waiver authorizes the waiver holder to fish with hook and line for all fish in all inland fishing waters and joint fishing waters, except for public mountain trout waters, and to engage in recreational fishing in coastal fishing waters. County departments of social services shall supply the Wildlife Resources Commission with the name, mailing address, and telephone number of each individual who receives a waiver. (2005-455, s. 1.16; 2006-79, s. 2; 2006-255, s. 10; 2007-97, s. 14; 2009-462, s. 4(e); 2013-283, s. 10.)

§§ 113-352 through 113-377: Reserved for future codification purposes.

Article 26.

Marine Fisheries Compact and Commission.

§§ 113-377.1 through 113-377.7: Transferred to §§ 113-252 through 113-258 by Session Laws 1965, c. 957.

SUBCHAPTER IVA. REPEALS.

Article 26A.

Repeal of Acts.

§ 113-377.8. Repeal of certain public, public-local, special and private acts.

The following public, public-local, special and private acts are hereby repealed: Chapter 36 of the Public Laws of 1901; Chapter 113 of the Public Laws of 1901;

Chapter 260 of the Public Laws of 1901; Chapter 308 of the Public Laws of 1901; Chapter 326 of the Public Laws of 1901; Chapter 370 of the Public Laws of 1901; Chapter 431 of the Public Laws of 1901; Chapter 435 of the Public Laws of 1901; Chapter 475 of the Public Laws of 1901; Chapter 589 of the Public Laws of 1901; Chapter 673 of the Public Laws of 1901; Chapter 702 of the Public Laws of 1901; Chapter 771 of the Public Laws of 1901; Chapter 131 of the Public Laws of 1903; Chapter 414 of the Public Laws of 1903; Chapter 520 of the Public Laws of 1903; Chapter 631 of the Public Laws of 1903; Chapter 650 of the Public Laws of 1903; Chapter 658 of the Public Laws of 1903; Chapter 668 of the Public Laws of 1903; Chapter 732 of the Public Laws of 1903; Chapter 752 of the Public Laws of 1903; Chapter 86 of the Public Laws of 1905; Chapter 265 of the Public Laws of 1905; Chapter 283 of the Public Laws of 1905; Chapter 351 of the Public Laws of 1905; Chapter 363 of the Public Laws of 1905; Chapter 500 of the Public Laws of 1905; Chapter 560 of the Public Laws of 1905; Chapter 386 of the Public Laws of 1907; Chapter 572 of the Public Laws of 1907; Chapter 690 of the Public Laws of 1907; Chapter 811 of the Public Laws of 1907; Chapter 977 of the Public Laws of 1907; Chapter 426 of the Public Laws of 1909; Chapter 466 of the Public Laws of 1909; Chapter 585 of the Public Laws of 1909; Chapter 755 of the Public Laws of 1909; Chapter 871 of the Public Laws of 1909; Chapter 525 of the Public-Local Laws of 1911; Chapter 547 of the Public-Local Laws of 1911; Chapter 572 of the Public-Local Laws of 1913; Chapter 587 of the Public-Local Laws of 1913; Chapter 402 of the Private Laws of 1913; Chapter 58 of the Public-Local Laws, Extra Session of 1913; Chapter 211 of the Public-Local Laws, Extra Session of 1913; Chapter 30 of the Public Laws of 1915; Chapter 180 of the Public Laws of 1915; Chapter 610 of the Public-Local Laws of 1915; Chapter 599 of the Public-Local Laws of 1917; Chapter 202 of the Public-Local Laws, Extra Session 1920; Chapter 114 of the Public-Local Laws of 1921; Chapter 384 of the Public-Local Laws of 1921; Chapter 432 of the Public-Local Laws of 1921; Chapter 439 of the Public-Local Laws of 1921; Chapter 157 of the Public-Local Laws, Extra Session of 1921; Chapter 130 of the Public-Local Laws of 1923; Chapter 352 of the Public-Local Laws of 1923; Chapter 533 of the Public-Local Laws of 1923; Chapter 548 of the Public-Local Laws of 1923; Chapter 461 of the Public-Local Laws of 1925; Chapter 623 of the Public-Local Laws of 1925; Chapter 228 of the Public-Local Laws of 1927; Chapter 208 of the Public-Local Laws of 1929; Chapter 42 of the Public Laws of 1933; Chapter 51 of the Public Laws of 1933; Chapter 241 of the Public-Local Laws of 1933; Chapter 575 of the Public-Local Laws of 1933; Chapter 365 of the Public-Local Laws of 1935; Chapter 368 of the Public-Local Laws of 1935; Chapter 509 of the Public-Local Laws of 1935; Chapter 513 of the Public-Local Laws of 1935; Chapter 352 of the Public Laws of 1937; Chapter 266 of the Public-Local Laws of 1937; Chapter 632 of the

Public-Local Laws of 1937; Chapter 265 of the Public Laws of 1939; Chapter 138 of the Public-Local Laws of 1939; Chapter 179 of the Public-Local Laws of 1939; Chapter 335 of the Public-Local Laws of 1941; Chapter 221 of the Special Laws of 1947; Chapter 485 of the Special Laws of 1947; Chapter 1017 of the Special Laws of 1947; Chapter 1031 of the Special Laws of 1949.

Provided that any public, public-local, special or private law herein repealed may be covered by a regulation of the Board of Conservation and Development to effectuate the same privileges or protection therein provided upon the petition of either the representative or senator from that county or district filed within six months from the date of ratification. (1951, c. 1045, s. 2.)

SUBCHAPTER V. OIL AND GAS CONSERVATION.

Article 27.

Oil and Gas Conservation.

Part 1. General Provisions.

§ 113-378. Persons drilling for oil or gas to register and furnish bond.

Any person, firm or corporation before making any drilling exploration in this State for oil or natural gas shall register with the Department of Environment and Natural Resources. To provide for such registration, the drilling operator must furnish the name and address of such person, firm or corporation, and the location of the proposed drilling operations, and file with the Department a bond running to the State of North Carolina in an amount totaling the sum of (i) five thousand dollars ($5,000) plus (ii) one dollar ($1.00) per linear foot proposed to be drilled for the well. Any well opened by the drilling operator shall be plugged upon abandonment in accordance with the rules of the Department. (1945, c. 765, s. 2; 1971, c. 813, s. 1; 1973, c. 1262, s. 86; 1977, c. 771, s. 4; 1987, c. 827, s. 110; 1989, c. 727, s. 118; 1997-443, s. 11A.119(a); 2011-276, s. 1; 2013-365, s. 5(a).)

§ 113-379. Filing log of drilling and development of each well.

Upon the completion or shutting down of any abandoned well, the drilling operator shall file with the Department or other State agency, or with any division thereof hereinafter created for the regulation of drilling for oil or natural gas, a complete log of the drilling and development of each well. (1945, c. 765, s. 3; 1973, c. 1262, s. 86; 1977, c. 771, s. 4; 1989, c. 727, s. 119.)

§ 113-380. Violation a misdemeanor.

Except as otherwise provided, any person, firm or officer of a corporation violating any of the provisions of this Article shall upon conviction thereof be guilty of a Class 1 misdemeanor. (1945, c. 765, s. 4; 1971, c. 813, s. 2; 1993, c. 539, s. 870; 1994, Ex. Sess., c. 24, s. 14(c); 2012-143, s. 2(a).)

Part 2. The Oil and Gas Conservation Act.

§ 113-381. Title.

This law shall be designated and known as the Oil and Gas Conservation Act. (1945, c. 702, s. 1.)

§ 113-382. Declaration of policy.

In recognition of imminent evils that can occur in the production and use and waste of natural oil and/or gas in the absence of equal or correlative rights of owners of crude oil or natural gas in a common source of supply to produce and use the same, and in the absence of adequate measures for the protection of the environment, this law is enacted for the protection of public interests against such evils by prohibiting waste and compelling ratable production and authorizing regulations for the protection of the environment. (1945, c. 702, s. 2; 1971, c. 813, ss. 3, 4.)

§§ 113-383 through 113-386. Repealed by Session Laws 1973, c. 1262, s. 86.

§ 113-387. Production of crude oil and gas regulated; tax assessments.

All common sources of supply of crude oil discovered after January 1, 1945, if so found necessary by the Department, shall have the production of oil therefrom controlled or regulated in accordance with the provisions of this law, and the Department is hereby authorized to assess from time to time against each barrel of oil produced and saved a tax not to exceed five mills on each barrel. All moneys so collected shall be used solely to pay the expenses and other costs in connection with the administration of this law.

All common sources of supply of natural gas discovered after January 1, 1945, if so found necessary by the Department, shall have the production of gas therefrom controlled or regulated in accordance with the provisions of this law, and the Department is hereby authorized to assess from time to time against each 1000 cubic feet of gas produced and saved from a gas well a tax not to exceed one-half mill on each 1000 cubic feet of gas. All moneys so collected shall be used solely to pay the expenses and other costs in connection with the administration of this law. (1945, c. 702, s. 7; 1973, c. 1262, s. 86.)


§ 113-388. Collection of assessments.

Any person purchasing oil or gas in this State at the well, under any contract or agreement requiring payment for such production to the respective owners thereof, in respect of which production any sums assessed under the provisions of G.S. 113-387 are payable to the Department, is hereby authorized, empowered and required to deduct from any sums so payable to any such person the amount due the Department by virtue of any such assessment and remit that sum to the Department.

Further, any person taking oil or gas from any well in this State for use or resale, in respect of which production any sums assessed under the provisions of G.S. 113-387 are payable to the Department, shall remit any sums so due to the Department in accordance with those rules of the Department which may be adopted in regard thereto. (1945, c. 702, s. 8; 1973, c. 1262, s. 86; 1987, c. 827, s. 110.)


§ 113-389. Definitions.

Unless the context otherwise requires, the words defined in this section shall have the following meaning when found in this law:

(1) "Base fluid" shall mean the continuous phase fluid type, such as water, used in a hydraulic fracturing treatment.

(1a) "Commission" shall mean the North Carolina Mining and Energy Commission.

(1b) "Department" shall mean the Department of Environment and Natural Resources.

(1c) "Division" shall mean the Division of Energy, Mineral, and Land Resources of the Department of Environment and Natural Resources.

(2) "Field" shall mean the general area which is underlaid or appears to be underlaid by at least one pool; and "field" shall include the underground reservoir or reservoirs containing crude petroleum oil or natural gas, or both. The words "field" and "pool" mean the same thing when only one underground reservoir is involved; "field," unlike "pool," may relate to two or more pools.

(3) "Gas" shall mean all natural gas, including casing-head gas, and all other hydrocarbons not defined as oil in subdivision (7).

(3a) "Hydraulic fracturing additive" shall mean any chemical substance or combination of substances, including any chemical or proppants, which is intentionally added to a base fluid for purposes of preparing a hydraulic fracturing fluid or treatment of a well.

(3b) "Hydraulic fracturing fluid" shall mean the fluid, including the applicable base fluid and all hydraulic fracturing additives, used to perform a hydraulic fracturing treatment.

(3c) "Hydraulic fracturing treatment" shall mean all stages of the treatment of a well by the application of hydraulic fracturing fluid under pressure that is expressly designed to initiate or propagate fractures in a target geologic formation to enhance production of oil and gas.

(4) "Illegal gas" shall mean gas which has been produced within the State of North Carolina from any well during any time that well has produced in excess of the amount allowed by any rule, regulation or order of the

Department, as distinguished from gas produced within the State of North Carolina from a well not producing in excess of the amount so allowed, which is "legal gas."

(5) "Illegal oil" shall mean oil which has been produced within the State of North Carolina from any well during any time that that well has produced in excess of the amount allowed by rule, regulation or order of the Department, as distinguished from oil produced within the State of North Carolina from a well not producing in excess of the amount so allowed, which is "legal oil."

(6) "Illegal product" shall mean any product of oil or gas, any part of which was processed or derived, in whole or in part, from illegal oil or illegal gas or from any product thereof, as distinguished from "legal product," which is a product processed or derived to no extent from illegal oil or illegal gas.

(6a) "Lessee" shall mean the person entitled under an oil and gas lease to drill and operate wells.

(6b) "Lessor" shall mean the owner of subsurface oil or gas resources who has executed a lease and who is entitled to the payment of a royalty on production.

(7) "Oil" shall mean crude petroleum oil, and other hydrocarbons, regardless of gravity, which are produced at the well in liquid form by ordinary production methods, and which are not the result of condensation of gas after it leaves the reservoir.

(7a) "Oil and gas developer or operator" or "developer or operator" shall mean a person who acquires a lease for the purpose of conducting exploration for or extracting oil or gas.

(7b) "Oil and gas operations" or "activities" shall mean the exploration for or drilling of an oil and gas well that requires entry upon surface estate and the production operations directly related to the exploration or drilling.

(8) "Owner" shall mean the person who has the right to drill into and to produce from any pool, and to appropriate the production either for himself or for himself and others.

(9) "Person" shall mean any natural person, corporation, association, partnership, receiver, trustee, guardian, executor, administrator, fiduciary or representative of any kind.

(10) "Pool" shall mean an underground reservoir containing a common accumulation of crude petroleum oil or natural gas or both. Each zone of a general structure which is completely separated from the other zone in the structure is covered by the term "pool" as used herein.

(11) "Producer" shall mean the owner of a well or wells capable of producing oil or gas, or both.

(12) "Product" means any commodity made from oil or gas and shall include refined crude oil, crude tops, topped crude, processed crude petroleum, residue from crude petroleum, cracking stock, uncracked fuel oil, fuel oil, treated crude oil, residuum, gas oil, casing-head gasoline, natural gas gasoline, naphtha, distillate, gasoline, kerosene, benzine, wash oil, waste oil, blended gasoline, lubricating oil, blends or mixtures of oil with one or more liquid products or by-products derived from oil or gas, and blends or mixtures of two or more liquid products or by-products derived from oil or gas, whether hereinabove enumerated or not.

(12a) "Proppant" shall mean sand or any natural or man-made material that is used in a hydraulic fracturing treatment to prop open the artificially created or enhanced fractures once the treatment is completed.

(12b) "Surface owner" means the person who holds record title to or has a purchaser's interest in the surface of real property.

(13) "Tender" shall mean a permit or certificate of clearance for the transportation of oil, gas or products, approved and issued or registered under the authority of the Department.

(14) "Waste" in addition to its ordinary meaning, shall mean "physical waste" as that term is generally understood in the oil and gas industry. It shall include:

a. The inefficient, excessive or improper use or dissipation of reservoir energy; and the locating, spacing, drilling, equipping, operating or producing of any oil or gas well or wells in a manner which results, or tends to result, in reducing inefficiently the quantity of oil or gas ultimately to be recovered from any pool in this State.

b. The inefficient storing of oil, and the locating, spacing, drilling, equipping, operating or producing of any oil or gas well or wells in a manner causing, or tending to cause, unnecessary or excessive surface loss or destruction of oil or gas.

c. Abuse of the correlative rights and opportunities of each owner of oil and gas in a common reservoir due to nonuniform, disproportionate, and unratable withdrawals causing undue drainage between tracts of land.

d. Producing oil or gas in such manner as to cause unnecessary water channelling or coning.

e. The operation of any oil well or wells with an inefficient gas-oil ratio.

f. The drowning with water of any stratum or part thereof capable of producing oil or gas.

g. Underground waste however caused and whether or not defined.

h. The creation of unnecessary fire hazards.

i. The escape into the open air, from a well producing both oil and gas, of gas in excess of the amount which is necessary in the efficient drilling or operation of the well.

j. Permitting gas produced from a gas well to escape into the air.

(15) "Water supply" shall mean any groundwater or surface water intended or used for human consumption; household purposes; or farm, livestock, or garden purposes. (1945, c. 702, s. 9; 1973, c. 1262, s. 86; 1977, c. 771, s. 4; 1989, c. 727, s. 218(59); 1997-443, s. 11A.119(a); 2011-276, s. 3(a); 2012-143, s. 2(b).)


§ 113-390. Waste prohibited.

Waste of oil or gas as defined in this law is hereby prohibited. (1945, c. 702, s. 10.)

§ 113-391. Jurisdiction and authority; rules and orders.

(a) The Mining and Energy Commission, created by G.S. 143B-293.1, in conjunction with rule-making authority specifically reserved to the Environmental Management Commission under subsection (a3) of this section, shall establish a modern regulatory program for the management of oil and gas exploration and development in the State and the use of horizontal drilling and hydraulic fracturing treatments for that purpose. The program shall be designed to protect public health and safety; protect public and private property; protect and conserve the State's air, water, and other natural resources; promote economic development and expand employment opportunities; and provide for the productive and efficient development of the State's oil and gas resources. To establish the program, the Commission shall adopt rules for all of the following purposes:

(1) Regulation of pre-drilling exploration activities, including seismic and other geophysical and stratigraphic surveys and testing.

(2) Regulation of drilling, operation, casing, plugging, completion, and abandonment of wells.

(3) Prevention of pollution of water supplies by oil, gas, or other fluids used in oil and gas exploration and development.

(4) Protection of the quality of the water, air, soil, or any other environmental resource against injury or damage or impairment.

(5) Regulation of horizontal drilling and hydraulic fracturing treatments for the purpose of oil and gas exploration. Such rules shall, at a minimum, include standards or requirements related to the following:

a. Information and data to be submitted in association with applications for permits to conduct oil and gas exploration and development activities using horizontal drilling and hydraulic fracturing treatments, which may include submission of hydrogeological investigations and identification of mechanisms to prevent and diagnose sources of groundwater contamination in the area of drilling sites. In formulating these requirements, the Commission shall consider (i) how North Carolina's geology differs from other states where oil and gas exploration and development activities using horizontal drilling and hydraulic fracturing treatments are common and (ii) the routes of possible groundwater contamination resulting from these activities and the potential role of vertical geological structures such as dikes and faults as conduits for groundwater contamination.

b. Collection of baseline data, including groundwater, surface water, and air quality in areas where oil and gas exploration and development activities are proposed. With regard to rules applicable to baseline data for groundwater and surface water, the Commission shall adopt rules that, at a minimum, establish standards to satisfy the pre-drilling testing requirement established under G.S. 113-421(a), including contaminants for which an operator or developer must test and necessary qualifications for persons conducting such tests.

c. Appropriate construction standards for oil and gas wells, which shall address the additional pressures of horizontal drilling and hydraulic fracturing treatments. These rules, at a minimum, shall include standards for casing and cementing sufficient to handle highly pressurized injection of hydraulic fracturing fluids into a well for purposes of fracturing bedrock and extraction of gas, and construction standards for other gas production infrastructure, such as storage pits and tanks.

d. Appropriate siting standards for wells and other gas production infrastructure, such as storage pits and tanks, including appropriate setback requirements and identification of areas, such as floodplains, where oil and gas exploration and production activities should be prohibited. Siting standards adopted shall be consistent with any applicable water quality standards adopted by the Environmental Management Commission or by local governments pursuant to water quality statutes, including standards for development in water supply watersheds.

e. Limits on water use, including, but not limited to, a requirement that oil and gas operators prepare and have a water and wastewater management plan approved by the Department, which, among other things, limits water withdrawals during times of drought and periods of low flows. Rules adopted shall be (i) developed in light of water supply in the areas of proposed activity, competing water uses in those areas, and expected environmental impacts from such water withdrawals and (ii) consistent with statutes, and rules adopted by the Environmental Management Commission pursuant to those statutes, which govern water quality and management of water resources, including, but not limited to, statutes and rules applicable to water withdrawal registration, interbasin transfer requirements, and water quality standards related to wastewater discharges.

f. Management of wastes produced in connection with oil and gas exploration and development and use of horizontal drilling and hydraulic fracturing treatments for that purpose. Such rules shall address storage, transportation, and disposal of wastes that may contain radioactive materials or wastes that may be toxic or have other hazardous wastes' characteristics that are not otherwise regulated as a hazardous waste by the federal Resource Conservation and Recovery Act (RCRA), such as top-hole water, brines, drilling fluids, additives, drilling muds, stimulation fluids, well servicing fluids, oil, production fluids, and drill cuttings from the drilling, alteration, production, plugging, or other activity associated with oil and gas wells. Wastes generated in connection with oil and gas exploration and development and use of horizontal drilling and hydraulic fracturing treatments for that purpose that constitute hazardous waste under RCRA shall be subject to rules adopted by the Commission for Public Health to implement RCRA requirements in the State.

g. Prohibitions on use of certain chemicals and constituents in hydraulic fracturing fluids, particularly diesel fuel.

h. Disclosure of chemicals and constituents used in oil and gas exploration, drilling, and production, including hydraulic fracturing fluids, to State regulatory agencies and to local government emergency response officials, and, with the exception of those items constituting trade secrets, as defined in G.S. 66-152(3), and that are designated as confidential or as a trade secret under G.S. 132-1.2, requirements for disclosure of those chemicals and constituents to the public.

i. Installation of appropriate safety devices and development of protocols for response to well blowouts, chemical spills, and other emergencies, including requirements for approved emergency response plans and certified personnel to implement these plans as needed.

j. Measures to mitigate impacts on infrastructure, including damage to roads by truck traffic and heavy equipment, in areas where oil and gas exploration and development activities that use horizontal drilling and hydraulic fracturing technologies are proposed to occur.

k. Notice, record keeping, and reporting.

l. Proper well closure, site reclamation, post-closure monitoring, and financial assurance. Rules for financial assurance shall require that an oil or gas developer or operator establish financial assurance that will ensure that sufficient funds are available for well closure, post-closure maintenance and monitoring, any corrective action that the Department may require, and to satisfy any potential liability for sudden and nonsudden accidental occurrences, and subsequent costs incurred by the Department in response to an incident involving a drilling operation, even if the developer or operator becomes insolvent or ceases to reside, be incorporated, do business, or maintain assets in the State.

(6) To require surveys upon application of any owner who has reason to believe that a well has been unlawfully drilled by another person into land of the owner without permission. In the event such surveys are required, the costs thereof shall be borne by the owner making the request.

(7) To require the making of reports showing the location of oil and gas wells and the filing of logs and drilling records.

(8) To prevent "blowouts," "caving," and "seepage," as such terms are generally understood in the oil and gas industry.

(9) To identify the ownership of all oil or gas wells, producing leases, refineries, tanks, plants, structures, and all storage and transportation equipment and facilities.

(10) To regulate the "shooting," perforating, and chemical treatment of wells.

(11) To regulate secondary recovery methods, including the introduction of gas, air, water, or other substances into producing formations.

(12) To regulate the spacing of wells and to establish drilling units.

(13) To regulate and, if necessary in its judgment for the protection of unique environmental values, to prohibit the location of wells in the interest of protecting the quality of the water, air, soil, or any other environmental resource against injury, damage, or impairment.

(13a) Criteria to set the amount of a bond required pursuant to G.S. 113-421(a3), including, at a minimum, the number of wells proposed at a site, the pre-drilling condition of the property, the amount of acreage that would be impacted by the proposed oil and gas activities, and other factors designed to enable establishment of bonds on a site-by-site basis.

(14) Any other matter the Commission deems necessary for implementation of a modern regulatory program for the management of oil and gas exploration and development in the State and the use of horizontal drilling and hydraulic fracturing for that purpose.

(a1) The regulatory program required to be established and the rules required to be adopted pursuant to subsection (a) of this section shall not include a program or rules for the regulation of oil and gas exploration and development in the waters of the Atlantic Ocean and the coastal sounds as defined in G.S. 113A-103.

(a2) In addition to the matters for which the Commission is required to adopt rules pursuant to subsection (a) of this section, the Commission may adopt rules as it deems necessary for any of the following purposes:

(1) To require the operation of wells with efficient gas-oil ratios and to fix such ratios.

(2) To limit and prorate the production of oil or gas, or both, from any pool or field for the prevention of waste as defined in this Article and rules adopted thereunder.

(3) To require, either generally or in or from particular areas, certificates of clearance or tenders in connection with the transportation of oil or gas.

(4) To prevent, so far as is practicable, reasonably avoidable drainage from each developed unit which is not equalized by counter-drainage.

(a3) The Environmental Management Commission shall adopt rules, after consideration of recommendations from the Mining and Energy Commission, for all of the following purposes:

(1) Stormwater control for sites on which oil and gas exploration and development activities are conducted.

(2) Regulation of toxic air emissions from drilling operations. In formulating appropriate standards, the Department shall assess emissions from oil and gas exploration and development activities that use horizontal drilling and hydraulic fracturing technologies, including emissions from associated truck traffic, in order to (i) determine the adequacy of the State's current air toxics program to protect landowners who lease their property to drilling operations and (ii)

determine the impact on ozone levels in the area in order to determine measures needed to maintain compliance with federal ozone standards.

(a4) The Department shall administer and enforce the provisions of this Article, and rules adopted thereunder, and all other laws relating to the conservation of oil and gas, except for jurisdiction and authority reserved to the Department of Labor and the Mining and Energy Commission, as otherwise provided. The Commission and the Department may issue orders as may be necessary from time to time in the proper administration and enforcement of this Article and rules adopted thereunder.

(b) The Commission and the Department, as appropriate, shall have the authority and it shall be their duty to make such inquiries as may be proper to implement the provisions of this Article. In the exercise of such power the Commission and the Department, as appropriate, shall have the authority to collect data; to make investigations and inspections; to examine properties, leases, papers, books and records; to examine, check, test and gauge oil and gas wells, tanks, refineries, and means of transportation; to hold hearings; and to provide for the keeping of records and the making of reports; and to take such action as may be reasonably necessary to enforce this law.

(b1) In the exercise of their respective authority over oil and gas exploration and development activities, the Commission and the Department, as applicable, shall have access to all data, records, and information related to such activities, including, but not limited to, seismic surveys, stratigraphic testing, geologic cores, proposed well bore trajectories, hydraulic fracturing fluid chemicals and constituents, drilling mud chemistry, and geophysical borehole logs. With the exception of information designated as a trade secret, as defined in G.S. 66-152(3), and that is designated as confidential or as a trade secret under G.S. 132-1.2, the Department shall make any information it receives available to the public. The State Geologist shall serve as the custodian of all data, information, and records received by the Department pursuant to this subsection and shall ensure that the information is maintained securely as provided in G.S. 132-7.

(c) Repealed by Session Laws 2012-143, s. 2(c), effective August 1, 2012.

(d) The Department of Labor shall develop, adopt, and enforce rules establishing health and safety standards for workers engaged in oil and gas operations in the State, including operations in which hydraulic fracturing treatments are used for that purpose.

(e)     The Department shall submit an annual report on its activities conducted pursuant to this Article and rules adopted thereunder to the Environmental Review Commission, the Joint Legislative Commission on Energy Policy, the Senate and House of Representatives Appropriations Subcommittees on Natural and Economic Resources, and the Fiscal Research Division of the General Assembly on or before October 1 of each year. (1945, c. 702, s. 11; 1971, c. 813, ss. 5, 6; 1973, c. 1262, s. 86; 1987, c. 827, s. 111; 1989, c. 727, s. 120; 2012-143, s. 2(c); 2013-365, s. 5(b).)


§ 113-392. Protecting pool owners; drilling units in pools; location of wells; shares in pools.

(a)     Whether or not the total production from a pool be limited or prorated, no rule or order of the Commission shall be such in terms or effect:

(1)     That it shall be necessary at any time for the producer from, or the owner of, a tract of land in the pool, in order that he may obtain such tract's just and equitable share of the production of such pool, as such share is set forth in this section, to drill and operate any well or wells on such tract in addition to such well or wells as can produce without waste such share, or

(2)     As to occasion net drainage from a tract unless there be drilled and operated upon such tract a well or wells in addition to such well or wells thereon as can produce without waste such tract's just and equitable share, as set forth in this section, of the production of such pool.

(b)     For the prevention of waste and to avoid the augmenting and accumulation of risks arising from the drilling of an excessive number of wells, the Commission shall, after a hearing, establish a drilling unit or units for each pool. The Commission may establish drainage units of uniform size for the entire pool or may, if the facts so justify, divide into zones any pool, establish a drainage unit for each zone, which unit may differ in size from that established in any other zone; and the Commission may from time to time, if the facts so justify, change the size of the unit established for the entire pool or for any zone or zones, or part thereof, establishing new zones and units if the facts justify their establishment.

(c)     Each well permitted to be drilled upon any drilling unit shall be drilled approximately in the center thereof, with such exception as may reasonably be necessary where it is shown, after notice and upon hearing, and the Commission finds that the unit is partly outside the pool or, for some other reason, a well approximately in the center of the unit would be nonproductive or where topographical conditions are such as to make the drilling approximately in the center of the unit unduly burdensome. Whenever an exception is granted, the Commission shall take such action as will offset any advantage which the person securing the exception may have over producers by reason of the drilling of the well as an exception, and so that drainage from developed units to the tract with respect to which the exception is granted will be prevented or minimized and the producer of the well drilled as an exception will be allowed to produce no more than his just and equitable share of the oil and gas in the pool, as such share is set forth in this section.

(d) Subject to the reasonable requirements for prevention of waste, a producer's just and equitable share of the oil and gas in the pool (also sometimes referred to as a tract's just and equitable share) is that part of the authorized production for the pool (whether it be the total which could be produced without any restriction on the amount of production, or whether it be an amount less than that which the pool could produce if no restriction on the amount were imposed) which is substantially in the proportion that the quantity of recoverable oil and gas in the developed area of his tract in the pool bears to the recoverable oil and gas in the total developed area of the pool, insofar as these amounts can be ascertained practically; and to that end, the rules, permits and orders of the Commission shall be such as will prevent or minimize reasonably avoidable net drainage from each developed unit (that is, drainage which is not equalized by counter-drainage), and will give to each producer the opportunity to use his just and equitable share of the reservoir energy. (1945, c. 702, s. 12; 1973, c. 1262, s. 86; 1987, c. 827, s. 112; 2012-143, s. 2(d).)


§ 113-393. Development of lands as drilling unit by agreement or order of Commission.

(a) Integration of Interests and Shares in Drilling Unit. - When two or more separately owned tracts of land are embraced within an established drilling unit, the owners thereof may agree validly to integrate their interests and to develop their lands as a drilling unit. Where, however, such owners have not agreed to integrate their interests, the Commission shall, for the prevention of waste or to avoid drilling of unnecessary wells, require such owners to do so and to develop their lands as a drilling unit. All orders requiring such integration shall be made after notice and hearing, and shall be upon terms and conditions that are just and reasonable, and will afford to the owner of each tract the opportunity to recover or receive his just and equitable share of the oil and gas in the pool without unnecessary expense, and will prevent or minimize reasonably avoidable drainage from each developed unit which is not equalized by counter-drainage. The portion of the production allocated to the owner of each tract included in a drilling unit formed by an integration order shall, when produced, be considered as if it had been produced from such tract by a well drilled thereon.

In the event such integration is required, and provided also that after due notice to all the owners of tracts within such drilling unit of the creation of such drilling unit, and provided further that the Commission has received no protest thereto, or request for hearing thereon, whether or not 10 days have elapsed after notice has been given of the creation of the drilling unit, the operator designated by the Commission to develop and operate the integrated unit shall have the right to charge to each other interested owner the actual expenditures required for such purpose not in excess of what are reasonable, including a reasonable charge for supervision, and the operator shall have the right to receive the first production from the well drilled by him thereon, which otherwise would be delivered or paid to the other parties jointly interested in the drilling of the well, so that the amount due by each of them for his shares of the expense of drilling, equipping, and operating the well may be paid to the operator of the well out of production; with the value of the production calculated at the market price in the field at the time such production is received by the operator or placed to his credit. After being reimbursed for the actual expenditures for drilling and equipping and operating expenses incurred during the drilling operations and until the operator is reimbursed, the operator shall thereafter pay to the owner of each tract within the pool his ratable share of the production calculated at the market price in the field at the time of such production less the reasonable expense of operating the well. In the event of any dispute relative to such costs, the Commission shall determine the proper costs.

(b)     When Each Owner May Drill. - Should the owners of separate tracts embraced within a drilling unit fail to agree upon the integration of the tracts and the drilling of a well on the unit, and should it be established that the Commission is without authority to require integration as provided for in subsection (a) of this section, then, subject to all other applicable provisions of this law, the owner of each tract embraced within the drilling unit may drill on his tract, but the allowable production from each tract shall be such proportion of the allowable for the full drilling unit as the area of such separately owned tract bears to the full drilling unit.

(c) Cooperative Development Not in Restraint of Trade. - Agreements made in the interests of conservation of oil or gas, or both, or for the prevention of waste, between and among owners or operators, or both, owning separate holdings in the same oil or gas pool, or in any area that appears from geological or other data to be underlaid by a common accumulation of oil or gas, or both, or between and among such owners or operators, or both, and royalty owners therein, of a pool or area, or any part thereof, as a unit for establishing and carrying out a plan for the cooperative development and operation thereof, when such agreements are approved by the Commission, are hereby authorized and shall not be held or construed to violate any of the statutes of this State relating to trusts, monopolies, or contracts and combinations in restraining of trade.

(d) Variation from Vertical. - Whenever the Department fixes the location of any well or wells on the surface, the point at which the maximum penetration of such wells into the producing formation is reached shall not unreasonably vary from the vertical drawn from the center of the hole at the surface, provided, that the Commission shall prescribe rules and the Department shall prescribe orders governing the reasonableness of such variation. This subsection shall not apply to wells drilled for the purpose of exploration or development of natural gas through use of horizontal drilling in conjunction with hydraulic fracturing treatments. (1945, c. 702, s. 13; 1973, c. 1262, s. 86; 1987, c. 827, s. 112; 2012-143, s. 3(a).)

§ 113-394. Limitations on production; allocating and prorating "allowables."

(a) The Commission may limit the total amount of oil, including condensate, which may be produced in the State by fixing an amount which shall be designated "allowable" for the State. The Commission may then allocate or distribute the "allowable" for the State among the pools on a reasonable basis and in such manner as to avoid undue discrimination, and so that waste will be prevented. In allocating the "allowable" for the State, and in fixing "allowables" for pools producing oil or hydrocarbons forming condensate, or both oil and such hydrocarbons, the Commission may take into account the producing conditions and other relevant facts with respect to such pools, including the separate needs for oil, gas and condensate, and may formulate rules setting forth standards or a program for the distribution of the "allowable" for the State, and distribute the "allowable" for the State in accordance with such standards or program, and where conditions in one pool or area are substantially similar to those in another pool or area, then the same standards or programs shall be applied to such pools and areas so that as far as practicable a uniform program will be followed; provided, however, the Commission shall allow the production of a sufficient amount of natural gas from any pool to supply adequately the reasonable market demand for such gas for light and fuel purposes if such production can be obtained without waste, and the condensate "allowable" for such pool shall not be less than the total amount of condensate produced or obtained in connection with the production of the gas "allowable" for light and fuel purposes, and provided further that, if the amount allocated to pool as its share of the "allowable" for the State is in excess of the amount which the pool should produce to prevent waste, then the Commission shall fix the "allowable" for the pool so that waste will be prevented.

In allocating "allowables" to pools, the Commission shall not be bound by nominations or desires of purchasers to purchase oil from particular fields or areas, and the Commission shall allocate the "allowable" for the State in such manner as will prevent undue discrimination against any pool or area in favor of another or others which would result from selective buying or nominating by purchasers of oil, as such term "selective buying or nominating" is understood in the oil business.

(b) Repealed by Session Laws 2013-365, s. 4, effective July 29, 2013.

(c) Whenever the Commission limits the total amount of oil or gas which may be produced in any pool in this State to an amount less than that which the pool could produce if no restrictions were imposed (which limitation may be imposed either incidental to, or without, a limitation of the total amount of oil or gas which may be produced in the State), the Commission shall prorate or distribute the "allowable" production among the producers in the pool on a reasonable basis, and so that each producer will have the opportunity to produce or receive his just and equitable share, as such share is set forth in subsection G.S. 113-392(d), subject to the reasonable necessities for the prevention of waste.

(d) Whenever the Commission limits the total amount of gas which may be produced from a pool, the Commission shall then allocate or distribute the allowable production among the developed areas in the pool on a reasonable basis, so that each producer will have the opportunity to produce his just and equitable share, as such share is set forth in subsection G.S. 113-392(d), whether the restriction for the pool as a whole is accomplished by order or by the automatic operation of the prohibitory provisions of this law. As far as applicable, the provisions of subsection (a) of this section shall be followed in allocating any "allowable" of gas for the State.

(e)     After the effective date of any rule or order of the Commission fixing the "allowable" production of oil or gas, or both, or condensate, no person shall produce from any well, lease, or property more than the "allowable" production which is fixed, nor shall such amount be produced in a different manner than that which may be authorized. (1945, c. 702, s. 14; 1973, c. 1262, s. 86; 1975, c. 19, ss. 37, 38; 1987, c. 827, s. 112; 2012-143, s. 2(e); 2013-365, s. 4.)


§ 113-395. Permits, fees, and notice required for oil and gas activities.

(a)     Before any well, in search of oil or gas, shall be drilled, the person desiring to drill the same shall submit an application for a permit to the Department upon such form as the Department may prescribe and shall pay a fee of three thousand dollars ($3,000) for each well. The drilling of any well is prohibited unless the Department has issued a permit for the activity.

(b)     Any person desiring to use hydraulic fracturing treatments in conjunction with oil and gas operations or activities shall submit an application for a permit to the Department upon such form as the Department may prescribe. The use of hydraulic fracturing treatments is prohibited unless the Department has issued a permit for the activity.

(c)     Each abandoned well and each dry hole shall be plugged promptly in the manner and within the time required by rules prescribed by the Department, and the owner of such well shall give notice, upon such form as the Department may prescribe, of the abandonment of each dry hole and of the owner's intention to abandon, and shall pay a fee of four hundred fifty dollars ($450.00). No well shall be abandoned until such notice has been given and such fee has been paid. (1945, c. 702, s. 15; 1973, c. 1262, s. 86; 1987, c. 827, s. 113; 2011-276, s. 2; 2012-143, s. 3(c).)


§ 113-396. Wells to be kept under control.

In order to protect further the natural gas fields and oil fields in this State, it is hereby declared to be unlawful for any person to permit negligently any gas or oil well to go wild or to get out of control. The owner of any such well shall, after 24 hours' written notice by the Department given to him or to the person in possession of such well, make reasonable effort to control such well.

In the event of the failure of the owner of such well within 24 hours after service of the notice above provided for, to control the same, if such can be done within the period, or to begin in good faith upon service of such notice, operations to control such well, or upon failure to prosecute diligently such operations, then the Department shall have the right to take charge of the work of controlling such well, and it shall have the right to proceed, through its own agents or by contract with a responsible contractor, to control the well or otherwise to prevent the escape or loss of gas or oil from such well all at the reasonable expense of the owner of the well. In order to secure to the Department the payment of the reasonable cost and expense of controlling or plugging such well, the Department shall retain the possession of the same and shall be entitled to receive and retain the rents, revenues and income therefrom until the costs and expenses incurred by the Department shall be repaid. When all such costs and expenses have been repaid, the Department shall restore possession of such well to the owner; provided, that in the event the income received by the Department shall not be sufficient to reimburse the Department as provided for in this section, the Department shall have a lien or privilege upon all of the property of the owner of such well, except such as is exempt by law, and the Department shall proceed to enforce such lien or privilege by suit brought in any court of competent jurisdiction, the same as any other civil action, and the judgment so obtained shall be executed in the same manner now provided by law for execution of judgments. Any excess over the amount due the Department which the property seized and sold may bring, after payment of court costs, shall be paid over to the owner of such well. (1945, c. 702, s. 16; 1973, c. 1262, s. 86.)


§ 113-397. Hearing in emergency.

If an emergency situation, as defined by the Department, arises under this Article, the Department may conduct a hearing to determine the appropriate course of action after giving any notice it considers practicable. Chapter 150B of the General Statutes does not apply to a hearing under this section. The rules of evidence apply in a hearing under this section. (1945, c. 702, s. 17; 1973, c. 1262, s. 86; 1987, c. 827, s. 114.)

§ 113-398. Procedure and powers in hearings by Department.

In the exercise and enforcement of its jurisdiction, the said Department is authorized to summon witnesses, administer oaths, make ancillary orders and require the production of records and books for the purpose of examination at any hearing or investigation conducted by it. In connection with the exercise and enforcement of its jurisdiction, the Department shall also have the right and authority to certify as for contempt, to the court of any county having jurisdiction, violations by any person of any of the provisions of this Article or of the rules or orders of the Department, and if it be found by said court that such person has knowingly and willfully violated same, then such person shall be punished as for contempt in the same manner and to the same extent and with like effect as if said contempt had been of an order, judgment or decree of the court to which said certification is made. (1945, c. 702, s. 18; 1973, c. 1262, s. 86; 1987, c. 827, s. 115.)

§ 113-399. Suits by Department.

The Department may bring an action in any court of competent jurisdiction in the State to enforce, by injunction or another remedy, an order issued or rule adopted by the Department under this Article. The court may enter any judgment or order necessary to enforce an order issued or rule adopted by the Department under this Article. (1945, c. 702, s. 19; 1973, c. 1262, s. 86; 1987, c. 827, s. 116.)

§ 113-400. Assessing costs of hearings.

The said Department is hereby authorized and directed to tax and assess against the parties involved in any hearing the costs incurred therein. (1945, c. 702, s. 20; 1973, c. 1262, s. 86.)

§ 113-401. Party to hearings; review.

The term "party" as used in this Article shall include any person, firm, corporation or association. In proceedings for review of an order or decision of said Department, the Department shall have all rights and privileges granted by this Article to any other party to such proceedings. (1945, c. 702, s. 21; 1973, c. 1262, s. 86.)

§ 113-402. Administrative review.

A party who is dissatisfied with a decision or order of the Department under this Article may obtain administrative review of the decision by filing a petition for a contested case hearing under G.S. 150B-23 within 10 days after the decision or order is made. (1945, c. 702, s. 22; 1973, c. 1262, s. 86; 1987, c. 827, s. 117.)

§ 113-403. Judicial review.

Article 4 of Chapter 150B of the General Statutes governs judicial review of a decision or order made under this Article. (1945, c. 702, s. 23; 1973, c. 1262, s. 86; 1987, c. 827, s. 118.)

§§ 113-404 through 113-405: Repealed by Session Laws 1987, c. 827, s. 119.

§ 113-406. Effect of pendency of judicial review; stay of proceedings.

The filing or pendency of the application for judicial review provided for in this Article shall not in itself stay or suspend the operation of any order or decision of the Department, but, during the pendency of such proceeding the court, in its discretion, may stay or suspend, in whole or in part, the operation of the order or decision of the Department. No order so staying or suspending an order or decision of the Department shall be made by any court of this State otherwise than on five days' notice and, after a hearing, and if a stay or suspension is allowed the order granting the same shall contain a specific finding, based upon evidence submitted to the court and identified by reference thereto, that great or irreparable damage would otherwise result to the petitioner and specifying the nature of the damage. (1945, c. 702, s. 26; 1973, c. 1262, s. 86; 1987, c. 827, s. 120.)


§ 113-407. Stay bond.

In case the order or decision of the Department is stayed or suspended, the order or judgment of the court shall not become effective until a bond shall have been executed and filed with and approved by the court, payable to the Department, sufficient in amount and security to secure the prompt payment, by the party petitioning for the stay, of all damages caused by the delay in the enforcement of the order or decision of the Department. (1945, c. 702, s. 27; 1973, c. 1262, s. 86.)


§ 113-408. Enjoining violation of laws and rules; service of process; application for drilling well to include residence address of applicant.

Whenever it shall appear that any person is violating, or threatening to violate, any statute of this State with respect to the conservation of oil or gas, or both, or any provision of this law, or any rule or order made thereunder by any act done in the operation of any well producing oil or gas, or by omitting any act required to be done thereunder, the Department, through the Attorney General, may bring suit against such person in the superior court in the county in which the well in question is located, to restrain such person or persons from continuing such violation or from carrying out the threat of violation. In such suit the Department may obtain injunctions, prohibitory and mandatory, including temporary restraining orders and temporary injunctions, as the facts may warrant, including, when appropriate, an injunction restraining any person from moving or disposing of illegal oil, illegal gas or illegal product, and any or all such commodities may be ordered to be impounded or placed under the control of an agent appointed by the court if, in the judgment of the court, such action is advisable.

If any such defendant cannot be personally served with summons in that county, personal jurisdiction of that defendant in such suit may be obtained by service made on any employee or agent of that defendant working on or about the oil or gas well involved in such suit, and by the Department mailing a copy of the complaint in the action to the defendant at the address of the defendant then recorded with the director of production and conservation.

Each application for the drilling of a well in search of oil or gas in this State shall include the address of the residence of the applicant or each applicant, which address shall be the address of each person involved in accordance with the records of the director of production and conservation, until such address is changed on the records of the Department after written request. (1945, c. 702, s. 28; 1973, c. 1262, s. 86; 1987, c. 827, s. 121.)


§ 113-409. Punishment for making false entries, etc.

Any person who, for the purpose of evading this law, or of evading any rule or order made thereunder, shall intentionally make or cause to be made any false entry or statement of fact in any report required to be made by this law or by any rule or order made hereunder; or who, for such purpose, shall make or cause to be made any false entry in any account, record, or memorandum kept by any person in connection with the provisions of this law or of any rule or order made thereunder; or who, for such purpose, shall omit to make, or cause to be omitted, full, true and correct entries in such accounts, records, or memoranda, of all facts and transactions pertaining to the interest or activities in the petroleum industry of such person as may be required by the Department under authority given in this law or by any rule or order made hereunder; or who, for such purpose shall remove out of the jurisdiction of the State, or who shall mutilate, alter, or by any other means falsify, any book, record, or other paper, pertaining to the transactions regulated by this law, or by any rule or order made hereunder, shall be deemed guilty of a Class 2 misdemeanor. (1945, c. 702, s. 29; 1973, c. 1262, s. 86; 1987, c. 827, s. 122; 1993, c. 539, s. 871; 1994, Ex. Sess., c. 24, s. 14(c).)


§ 113-410. Penalties for other violations.

(a)     Any person who fails to secure a permit prior to drilling a well or using hydraulic fracturing treatments, or who knowingly and willfully violates any provision of this Article, or any rule or order of the Commission or the Department made hereunder, shall, in the event a penalty for such violation is not otherwise provided for herein, be subject to a penalty of not to exceed twenty-five thousand dollars ($25,000) a day for each and every day of such violation, and for each and every act of violation, such penalty to be recovered in a suit in the superior court of the county where the defendant resides, or in the county of the residence of any defendant if there be more than one defendant, or in the superior court of the county where the violation took place. The place of suit shall be selected by the Department, and such suit, by direction of the Department, shall be instituted and conducted in the name of the Department by the Attorney General. The payment of any penalty as provided for herein shall not have the effect of changing illegal oil into legal oil, illegal gas into legal gas, or illegal product into legal product, nor shall such payment have the effect of authorizing the sale or purchase or acquisition, or the transportation, refining, processing, or handling in any other way, of such illegal oil, illegal gas or illegal product, but, to the contrary, penalty shall be imposed for each prohibited transaction relating to such illegal oil, illegal gas or illegal product.

(b)     Any person knowingly and willfully aiding or abetting any other person in the violation of any statute of this State relating to the conservation of oil or gas, or the violation of any provisions of this law, or any rule or order made thereunder, shall be subject to the same penalties as prescribed in subsection (a) of this section for the violation by such other person.

(c)     In determining the amount of a penalty under this section, the Department shall consider all of the following factors:

(1)     The degree and extent of harm to the natural resources of the State, to the public health, or to private property resulting from the violation.

(2)     The duration and gravity of the violation.

(3)     The effect on ground or surface water quantity or quality or on air quality.

(4)     The cost of rectifying the damage.

(5)     The amount of money the violator saved by noncompliance.

(6)     Whether the violation was committed willfully or intentionally.

(7)     The prior record of the violator in complying or failing to comply with this Article or a rule adopted pursuant to this Article.

(8) The cost to the State of the enforcement procedures.

(d) If any civil penalty has not been paid within 60 days after notice of assessment has been served on the violator or within 30 days after service of the final decision by the administrative law judge in accordance with G.S. 150B-34, a final decision by the Committee on Civil Penalty Remissions established under G.S. 143B-293.6, or a court order, whichever is later, the Secretary or the Secretary's designee shall request the Attorney General to institute a civil action in the superior court of any county in which the violator resides or has his or its principal place of business to recover the amount of the civil penalty.

(e) The clear proceeds of penalties provided for in this section shall be remitted to the Civil Penalty and Forfeiture Fund in accordance with G.S. 115C-457.2. (1945, c. 702, s. 30; 1973, c. 1262, s. 86; 1987, c. 827, s. 122; 1998-215, s. 50; 2012-143, s. 2(f).)

§ 113-411. Dealing in or handling of illegal oil, gas or product prohibited.

(a) The sale, purchase or acquisition, or the transportation, refining, processing or handling in any other way of illegal oil, illegal gas or illegal product is hereby prohibited. All persons purchasing any petroleum product must first be licensed to do so by the Department.

(b) Unless and until the Department provides for certificates of clearance or tenders, or some other method, so that any person may have an opportunity to determine whether any contemplated transaction of sale, purchase or acquisition, or transportation, refining, processing or handling in any other way, involves illegal oil, illegal gas or illegal product, no penalty shall be imposed for the sale, purchase or acquisition, or the transportation, refining, processing or handling in any other way of illegal oil, illegal gas or illegal product, except under circumstances hereinafter stated. Penalties shall be imposed for the commission of each transaction prohibited in this section when the person committing the same knows that illegal oil, illegal gas or illegal product is involved in such transaction, or when such person could have known or determined such fact by the exercise of reasonable diligence or from facts within his knowledge. However, regardless of lack of actual notice or knowledge, penalties as provided in this law shall apply to any sale, purchase or acquisition, and to the transportation, refining, processing or handling in any other way, of illegal oil, illegal gas or illegal product, where administrative provision is made for identifying the character of the commodity as to its legality. It shall likewise be a violation for which penalties shall be imposed for any person to sell, purchase or acquire, or to transport, refine, process or handle in any other way any oil, gas or any product without complying with any rule or order of the Department relating thereto. (1945, c. 702, s. 31; 1973, c. 1262, s. 86; 1987, c. 827, s. 122.)

§ 113-412. Seizure and sale of contraband oil, gas and product.

Apart from, and in addition to, any other remedy or procedure which may be available to the Department, or any penalty which may be sought against or imposed upon any person with respect to violations relating to illegal oil, illegal gas, or illegal product, all illegal oil, illegal gas and illegal product shall, except under such circumstances as are stated herein, be contraband and shall be seized and sold. Such sale shall not take place unless the court shall find, in the proceeding provided for in this paragraph, that the commodity involved is contraband. Whenever the Department believes that illegal oil, illegal gas or illegal product is subject to seizure and sale, as provided herein, it shall, through the Attorney General, have issued a warrant of attachment and bring a civil action in rem for that purpose in the superior court of the county where the commodity is found, or the action may be maintained in connection with any suit or cross bill for injunction or for penalty relating to any prohibited transaction involving such illegal oil, illegal gas or illegal product. Any interested person who may show himself to be adversely affected by any such seizure and sale shall have the right to intervene in such suit to protect his rights.

The action referred to above shall be strictly in rem and shall proceed in the name of the State as plaintiff against the illegal oil, illegal gas or illegal product mentioned in the complaint, as defendant, and no bond or bonds shall be required of the plaintiff in connection therewith. Upon the filing of the complaint, the clerk of the court shall issue a summons directed to the sheriff of the county, or to such other officer or person as the court may authorize to serve process, requiring him to summon any and all persons (without undertaking to name them) who may be interested in the illegal oil, illegal gas, or illegal product mentioned in the complaint to appear and answer within 30 days after the issuance and service of such summons. The summons shall contain the style and number of the suit and a very brief statement of the nature of the cause of action. It shall be served by posting one copy thereof at the courthouse door of the county where the commodity involved in the suit is alleged to be located and by posting another copy thereof near the place where the commodity is alleged to be located. Copy of such summons shall be posted at least five days before the return day stated therein, and the posting of such copy shall constitute constructive possession of such commodity by the State. A copy of the summons shall also be published once each week for four weeks in some newspaper published in the county where the suit is pending and having a bona fide circulation therein. No judgment shall be pronounced by any court condemning such commodity as contraband until after the lapse of five days from the last publication of said summons. Proof of service of said summons, and the manner thereof, shall be as provided by general law.

Where it appears by a verified pleading on the part of the plaintiff, or by affidavit, or affidavits, or by oral testimony, that grounds for the seizure and sale exist, the clerk, in addition to the summons or warning order, shall issue a warrant of attachment, which shall be signed by the clerk and bear the seal of the court. Such warrant of attachment shall specifically describe the illegal oil, illegal gas or illegal product, so that the same may be identified with reasonable certainty. It shall direct the sheriff to whom it is addressed to take into his custody, actual or constructive, the illegal oil, illegal gas or illegal product, described therein, and to hold the same subject to the orders of the court. Said warrant of attachment shall be executed as a writ of attachment is executed. No bond shall be required before the issuance of such warrant of attachment, and the sheriff shall be responsible upon his official bond for the proper execution thereof.

In a proper case, the court may direct the sheriff to deliver the custody of any illegal oil, illegal gas or illegal product seized by him under a warrant of attachment, to a commissioner to be appointed by the court, which commissioner shall act as the agent of the court and shall give bond with such approved surety as the court may direct, conditioned that he will faithfully conserve such illegal oil, illegal gas or illegal product, as may come into his custody and possession in accordance with the orders of the court; provided, that the court may in its discretion appoint any member of the Department or any agent of the Department as such commissioner of the court.

Sales of illegal oil, illegal gas or illegal product seized under the authority of this law, and notices of such sales, shall be in accordance with the laws of this State relating to the sale and disposition of attached property; provided, however, that where the property is in custody of a commissioner of the court, the sale shall be held by said commissioner and not by the sheriff. For his services hereunder, such commissioner shall receive a reasonable fee to be paid out of the proceeds of the sale or sales to be fixed by the court ordering such sale.

The court may order that the commodity be sold in specified lots or portions, and at specified intervals, instead of being sold at one time. Title to the amount sold shall pass as of the date of the law which is found by the court to make the commodity contraband. The judgment shall provide for the clear proceeds of the sales to be remitted to the Civil Penalty and Forfeiture Fund in accordance with G.S. 115C-457.2. The amount sold shall be treated as legal oil, legal gas or legal product, as the case may be, in the hands of the purchaser, but the purchaser and the commodity shall be subject to all applicable laws, rules, and orders with respect to further sale or purchase or acquisition, and with respect to the transportation, refining, processing, or handling in any other way, of the commodity purchased.

Nothing in this section shall deny or abridge any cause of action a royalty owner, or a lienholder, or any other claimant, may have, because of the forfeiture of the illegal oil, illegal gas, or illegal product, against the person whose act resulted in such forfeiture. No illegal oil, illegal gas or illegal product shall be sold for less than the average market value at the time of sale of similar products of like grade and character. (1945, c. 702, s. 32; 1973, c. 1262, s. 86; 1987, c. 827, s. 123; 1998-215, s. 51.)


§ 113-413: Repealed by Session Laws 1987, c. 827, s. 124.


§ 113-414. Filing list of renewed leases in office of register of deeds.

On December 31 of each year, or within 10 days thereafter, every person, firm or corporation holding petroleum leases shall file in the office of the register of deeds of the county within which the land covered by such leases is located, a list showing the leases which have been renewed for the ensuing year. (1945, c. 702, s. 34.)


§ 113-415. Conflicting laws.

No provision of this Article shall be construed to repeal, amend, abridge or otherwise affect: (i) the authority and responsibility vested in the Environmental Management Commission by Article 7 of Chapter 87 of the General Statutes, pertaining to the location, construction, repair, operation and abandonment of wells, or the authority and responsibility vested in the Environmental Management Commission related to the control of water and air pollution as provided in Articles 21 and 21A of Chapter 143 of the General Statutes; or (ii) the authority or responsibility vested in the Department and the Commission for Public Health by Article 10 of Chapter 130A of the General Statutes pertaining to public water-supply requirements, or the authority and responsibility vested in the Commission for Public Health related to the management of solid and hazardous waste as provided in Article 9 of Chapter 130A of the General Statutes. (1971, c. 813, s. 7; 1973, c. 476, s. 128; c. 1262, s. 23; 1989, c. 727, s. 121; 2007-182, s. 2; 2012-143, s. 2(g).)

§§ 113-416 through 113-419. Repealed by Session Laws 1959, c. 779, s. 3.

Part 3. Landowner Protection.

§ 113-420. Notice and entry to property.

(a) Notice Required for Activities That Do Not Disturb Surface of Property. - If an oil or gas developer or operator is not the surface owner of the property on which oil and gas operations are to occur, before entering the property for oil or gas operations that do not disturb the surface, including inspections, staking, surveys, measurements, and general evaluation of proposed routes and sites for oil or gas drilling operations, the developer or operator shall give written notice to the surface owner at least 14 days before the desired date of entry to the property. Notice shall be given by certified mail, return receipt requested. The requirements of this subsection may not be waived by agreement of the parties. The notice, at a minimum, shall include all of the following:

(1) The identity of person(s) requesting entry upon the property.

(2) The purpose for entry on the property.

(3) The dates, times, and location on which entry to the property will occur, including the estimated number of entries.

(b) Notice Required for Land-Disturbing Activities. - If an oil or gas developer or operator is not the surface owner of the property on which oil or gas operations are to occur, before entering the property for oil or gas operations that disturb the surface, the developer or operator shall give written notice to the surface owner at least 30 days before the desired date of entry to the property. Notice shall be given by certified mail, return receipt requested. The notice, at a minimum, shall include all of the following:

(1) A description of the exploration or development plan, including, but not limited to (i) the proposed locations of any roads, drill pads, pipeline routes, and other alterations to the surface estate and (ii) the proposed date on or after which the proposed alterations will begin.

(2) An offer of the oil and gas developer or operator to consult with the surface owner to review and discuss the location of the proposed alterations.

(3) The name, address, telephone number, and title of a contact person employed by or representing the oil or gas developer or operator who the surface owner may contact following the receipt of notice concerning the location of the proposed alterations.

(b1) Persons Entering Land; Identification Required; Presumption of Proper Protection While on Surface Owners' Property. - Persons who enter land on behalf of an oil or gas developer or operator for oil and gas operations shall carry on their person identification sufficient to identify themselves and their employer or principal and shall present the identification to the surface owner upon request. Entry upon land by such a person creates a rebuttable presumption that the surface owner properly protected the person against personal injury or property damage while the person was on the land.

(c) Venue. - If the oil or gas developer or operator fails to give notice or otherwise comply with the provisions of this section, the surface owner may seek appropriate relief in the superior court for the county in which the oil or gas well is located and may receive actual damages. (2011-276, s. 3(b); 2012-143, s. 4(a).)

§ 113-421. Presumptive liability for water contamination; compensation for other damages; responsibility for reclamation.

(a) Presumptive Liability for Water Contamination. - It shall be presumed that an oil or gas developer or operator is responsible for contamination of all water supplies that are within 5,000 feet of a wellhead that is part of the oil or gas developer's or operator's activities unless the presumption is rebutted by a defense established as set forth in subsection (a1) of this subsection. If a contaminated water supply is located within 5,000 feet of a wellhead, in addition to any other remedy available at law or in equity, including payment of compensation for damage to a water supply, the developer or operator shall provide a replacement water supply to the surface owner and other persons using the water supply at the time the oil or gas developer's activities were commenced on the property, which water supply shall be adequate in quality and quantity for those persons' use.

(a1) [Rebuttal of Presumption. -] In order to rebut a presumption arising pursuant to subsection (a) of this section, an oil or gas developer or operator shall have the burden of proving by a preponderance of the evidence any of the following:

(1) The contamination existed prior to the commencement of the drilling activities of the oil or gas developer or operator, as evidenced by a pre-drilling test of the water supply in question conducted in conformance with G.S. 113-423(f).

(2) The surface owner or owner of the water supply in question refused the oil or gas developer or operator access to conduct a pre-drilling test of the water supply conducted in conformance with G.S. 113-423(f).

(3) The water supply in question is not within 5,000 feet of a wellhead that is part of the oil or gas developer's or operator's activities.

(4) The contamination occurred as the result of a cause other than activities of the developer or operator.

(a2) Compensation for Other Damages Required. - The oil or gas developer or operator shall be obligated to pay the surface owner compensation for all of the following:

(1) Any damage to a water supply in use prior to the commencement of the activities of the developer or operator which is due to those activities.

(2) The cost of repair of personal property of the surface owner, which personal property is damaged due to activities of the developer or operator, up to the value of replacement by personal property of like age, wear, and quality.

(3) Damage to any livestock, crops, or timber determined according to the market value of the resources destroyed, damaged, or prevented from reaching market due to the oil or gas developer's or operator's activities.

(a3) Reclamation of Surface Property Required. - An oil or gas developer or operator shall reclaim all surface areas affected by its operations no later than two years following completion of the operations. If the developer or operator is not the surface owner of the property, prior to commencement of activities on the property, the oil or gas developer or operator shall provide a bond running to the surface owner sufficient to cover reclamation of the surface owner's property. Upon registration with the Department pursuant to G.S. 113-378, a developer shall request that the Mining and Energy Commission set the amount of the bond required by this subsection. As part of its request, the developer shall provide supporting documentation, including information about the proposed oil and gas activities to be conducted, the site on which they are to occur, and any additional information required by the Commission. The Commission shall set the amount of the bond in accordance with the criteria adopted by the Commission pursuant to G.S. 113-391(a)(13a) and notify the developer and surface owner of the amount within 30 days of setting the amount of a bond. A surface owner or developer may appeal the amount of a bond set pursuant to this subsection to the Commission within 60 days after receipt of notice from the Commission of the amount required. After evaluation of the appeal and issuance of written findings, the Commission may order that the amount of the bond be modified. Parties aggrieved by a decision of the Commission pursuant to this subsection may appeal the decision as provided under Article 4 of Chapter 150B of the General Statutes within 30 days of the date of the decision.

(a4) Remediation Required. - Nothing in this Article shall be construed to obviate or affect the obligation of a developer or operator to comply with any other requirement under law to remediate contamination caused by its activities.

(a5) Replacement Water Supply Required. - If a water supply belonging to the surface owner or third parties is contaminated due to the activities of the developer or operator, in addition to any other remedy available at law or in equity, the developer or operator shall provide a replacement water supply to persons using the water supply at the time the oil or gas developer's activities were commenced on the property, which water supply shall be adequate in quality and quantity for those persons' use.

(b) Time Frame for Compensation. - When compensation is required, the surface owner shall have the option of accepting a one-time payment or annual payments for a period of time not less than 10 years.

(c) Venue. - The surface owner has the right to seek damages pursuant to this section in the superior court for the county in which the oil or gas well is located. The superior court for the county in which the oil or gas well is located has jurisdiction over all proceedings brought pursuant to this section. If the surface owner or the surface owner's assignee is the prevailing party in an action to recover unpaid royalties or other damages owed due to activities of the developer or operator, the court shall award any court costs and reasonable attorneys' fees to the surface owner or the surface owner's assignee.

(d) [Certain Limits Void. -] Conditions precedent, notice provisions, or arbitration clauses included in lease documents that have the effect of limiting access to the superior court in the county in which the oil or gas well is located are void and unenforceable. (2011-276, s. 3(b); 2012-143, s. 4(b); 2013-365, s. 5(c).)

§ 113-422. Indemnification.

An oil or gas developer or operator shall indemnify and hold harmless a surface owner against any claims related to the developer's or operator's activities on the surface owner's property, including, but not limited to, (i) claims of injury or death to any person; (ii) damage to impacted infrastructure or water supplies; (iii) damage to a third party's real or personal property; and (iv) violations of any federal, State, or local law, rule, regulation, or ordinance, including those for protection of the environment. (2011-276, s. 3(b); 2012-143, s. 4(c).)

§ 113-423. Required lease terms.

(a) Required Information to be Provided to Potential Lessors and Surface Owners. - Prior to executing a lease for oil and gas rights or any other conveyance of any kind separating rights to oil or gas from the freehold estate of surface property, an oil or gas developer or operator, or any agent thereof, shall provide the lessor with a copy of this Part and a publication produced by the Consumer Protection Division of the North Carolina Department of Justice entitled "Oil & Gas Leases: Landowners' Rights." If the lessor is not the surface owner of the property, the oil or gas developer or operator shall also provide the surface owner with a copy of this Part and the publication prior to execution of a lease for oil and gas rights.

(b)     Maximum Duration. - Any lease of oil or gas rights or any other conveyance of any kind separating rights to oil or gas from the freehold estate of surface property shall expire at the end of 10 years from the date the lease is executed, unless, at the end of the 10-year period, oil or gas is being produced for commercial purposes from the land to which the lease applies. If, at any time after the 10-year period, commercial production of oil or gas is terminated for a period of six months or more, all rights to the oil or gas shall revert to the surface owner of the property to which the lease pertains. No assignment or agreement to waive the provisions of this subsection shall be valid or enforceable. As used in this subsection, the term "production" includes the actual production of oil or gas by a lessee, or when activities are being conducted by the lessee for injection, withdrawal, storage, or disposal of water, gas, or other fluids, or when rentals or royalties are being paid by the lessee. No force majeure clause shall operate to extend a lease beyond the time frames set forth in this subsection.

(c)     Minimum Royalty Payments. - Any lease of oil or gas rights or any other conveyance of any kind separating rights to oil or gas from the freehold estate of surface property shall provide that the lessor shall receive a royalty payment of not less than twelve and one-half percent (12.5%) of the proceeds of sale of all oil or gas produced from the lessor's just and equitable share of the oil and gas in the pool, which sum shall not be diminished by pre-production or post-production costs, fees, or other charges assessed by the oil or gas developer or operator against the property owner. Royalty payments shall commence no later than six months after the date of first sale of product from the drilling operations subject to the lease and thereafter no later than 60 days after the end of the calendar quarter within which subsequent production is sold. At the time each royalty payment is made, the oil or gas developer or operator shall provide documentation to the lessor on the time period for which the royalty payment is made, the quantity of product sold within that period, and the price received, at a minimum. If royalty payments have not been made within the required time frames, the lessor shall be entitled to interest on the unpaid royalties commencing on the payment due date at the rate of twelve and one-half percent

(12.5%) per annum on the unpaid amounts. Upon written request, the lessor shall be entitled to inspect and copy records of the oil or gas developer or operator related to production and royalty payments associated with the lease.

(d) Bonus Payments. - Any bonus payments, or other initial payments, due under a lease of oil or gas rights or any other conveyance of any kind separating rights to oil or gas from the freehold estate of surface property shall be paid by the lessee to the lessor within 60 days of execution of a lease. If a bonus payment or other initial payment has not been made within the required time frame, the lessor shall be entitled to interest on the unpaid amount commencing on the payment due date at the rate of ten percent (10%) per annum on the unpaid amount.

(e) Agreements for Use of Other Resources; Associated Payments. - Any lease of oil or gas rights or any other conveyance of any kind separating rights to oil or gas from the freehold estate of surface property shall clearly state whether the oil or gas developer or operator shall use groundwater or surface water supplies located on the property and, if so, shall clearly state the estimated amount of water to be withdrawn from the supplies on the property, and shall require permission of the surface owner therefore. At a minimum, water used by the developer or operator shall not restrict the supply of water for domestic uses by the surface owner. The lease shall provide for full compensation to the surface owner for water used from the property by the developer or operator in an amount not less than the fair market value of the water consumed based on water sales in the area at the time of use.

(f) Pre-Drilling Testing of Water Supplies. - Any lease of oil or gas rights or any other conveyance of any kind separating rights to oil or gas from the freehold estate of surface property shall include a clause that requires the oil or gas developer or operator to conduct a test of all water supplies within 5,000 feet from a wellhead that is part of the oil or gas developer's or operator's activities at least 30 days prior to initial drilling activities and at least two follow-up tests within a 24-month period after production has commenced. The Department shall identify the location of all water supplies, including wells, on a property on which drilling operations are proposed to occur. A surface owner may elect to have the Department sample wells located on their property, in lieu of sampling conducted by the oil or gas developer or operator, in which case the developer or operator shall reimburse the Department for the reasonable costs involved in testing of the wells in question. Nothing in this subsection shall be construed to preclude or impair the right of any surface owner to refuse pre-drilling testing of wells located on their property.

(g) Recordation of Leases. - Any lease of oil or gas rights or any other conveyance of any kind separating rights to oil or gas from the freehold estate of surface property, including assignments of such leases, shall be recorded within 30 days of execution in the register of deeds office in the county that the land that is subject to the lease is located.

(h) Notice of Assignment Required. - Written notice of assignment of any lease of oil or gas rights or any other conveyance of any kind separating rights to oil or gas from the freehold estate of surface property shall be provided to the lessor within 30 days of such assignment. If the surface owner of the property is not the lessor, written notice of assignment of any lease of oil or gas rights shall also be given to the surface owner of the property to which the lease pertains within 30 days of such assignment.

(i) Lender Approval of Lease. - Any lease for oil or gas rights or any other conveyance of any kind separating rights to oil or gas from the freehold estate of surface property with a surface owner shall include a conspicuous boldface disclosure concerning notification to lenders, which shall be initialed by the surface owner, and state the following:

NOTICE TO LENDER(S) PRIOR TO EXECUTION OF LEASE:

Surface owners are advised to secure written approval from any lender who holds a mortgage or deed of trust on any portion of the surface property involved in the lease prior to execution of the lease and obtain written confirmation that execution of the lease will not violate any provision associated with any applicable mortgage or deed of trust, which could potentially result in foreclosure.

I have read and understood the                    _____

terms of this provision.                           Surface Owner's Initials

(j) Seven-Day Right of Rescission. - Any lease of oil or gas rights or any other conveyance of any kind separating rights to oil or gas from the freehold estate of surface property shall be subject to a seven-day right of rescission in which the lessor or lessee may cancel the lease. A bold and conspicuous notice of this right of rescission shall be included in all such leases. In order to cancel the lease, the lessor or lessee shall notify the other party in writing within seven business days of execution of the lease, and the lessor shall return any sums paid by the lessee to the lessor under the terms of the lease. (2011-276, s. 3(b); 2012-143, s. 4(d); 2012-201, s. 12(d).)

§ 113-423.1. Surface activities.

(a) Agreements on Rights and Obligations of Parties. - The developer or operator and the surface owner may enter into a mutually acceptable agreement that sets forth the rights and obligations of the parties with respect to the surface activities conducted by the developer or operator.

(b) Minimization of Intrusion Required. - An oil or gas developer or operator shall conduct oil and gas operations in a manner that accommodates the surface owner by minimizing intrusion upon and damage to the surface of the land. As used in this subsection, "minimizing intrusion upon and damage to the surface" means selecting alternative locations for wells, roads, pipelines, or production facilities, or employing alternative means of operation that prevent, reduce, or mitigate the impacts of the oil and gas operations on the surface, where such alternatives are technologically sound, economically practicable, and reasonably available to the operator. The standard of conduct set forth in this subsection shall not be construed to (i) prevent an operator from entering upon and using that amount of the surface as is reasonable and necessary to explore for, develop, and produce oil and gas and (ii) abrogate or impair a contractual provision binding on the parties that expressly provides for the use of the surface for the conduct of oil and gas operations or that releases the operator from liability for the use of the surface. Failure of an oil or gas developer or operator to comply with the requirements of this subsection shall give rise to a cause of action by the surface owner. Upon a determination by the trier of fact that such failure has occurred, a surface owner may seek compensatory damages and equitable relief. In any litigation or arbitration based upon this subsection, the surface owner shall present evidence that the developer's or operator's use of the surface materially interfered with the surface owner's use of the surface of the land. After such showing, the developer or operator shall bear the burden of proof of showing that it minimized intrusion upon and damage to the surface of the land in accordance with the provisions of this subsection. If a developer or operator makes that showing, the surface owner may present rebuttal evidence. A developer or operator may assert, as an affirmative defense, that it has conducted oil or gas operations in accordance with a regulatory requirement, contractual obligation, or land-use plan provision that is specifically applicable to the alleged intrusion or damage. Nothing in this subsection shall do any of the following:

(1)     Preclude or impair any person from obtaining any and all other remedies allowed by law.

(2)     Prevent a developer or operator and a surface owner from addressing the use of the surface for oil and gas operations in a lease, surface use agreement, or other written contract.

(3)     Establish, alter, impair, or negate the authority of local governments to regulate land use related to oil and gas operations.  (2012-143, s. 4(e).)


§ 113-424:  Repealed by Session Laws 2012-143, s. 4(f), effective July 2, 2012.


§ 113-425.  Registry of landmen required.

(a)     Establishment of Registry. - The Department of Environment and Natural Resources, in consultation with the Consumer Protection Division of the North Carolina Department of Justice, shall establish and maintain a registry of landmen operating in this State. As used in this section, "landman" means a person that, in the course and scope of the person's business, does any of the following:

(1)     Acquires or manages oil or gas interests.

(2)     Performs title or contract functions related to the exploration, exploitation, or disposition of oil or gas interests.

(3)     Negotiates for the acquisition or divestiture of oil or gas rights, including the acquisition or divestiture of land or oil or gas rights for a pipeline.

(4)     Negotiates business agreements that provide for the exploration for or development of oil or gas.

(b)     Registration Required. - A person may not act, offer to act, or hold oneself out as a landman in this State unless the person is registered with the

Department in accordance with this section. To apply for registration as a landman, a person shall submit an application to the Department on a form to be provided by the Department, which shall include, at a minimum, all of the following information:

(1) The name of the applicant or, if the applicant is not an individual, the names and addresses of all principals of the applicant.

(2) The business address, telephone number, and electronic mail address of the applicant.

(3) The social security number of the applicant or, if the applicant is not an individual, the federal employer identification number of the applicant.

(4) A list of all states and other jurisdictions in which the applicant holds or has held a similar registration or license.

(5) A list of all states and other jurisdictions in which the applicant has had a similar registration or license suspended or revoked.

(6) A statement whether any pending judgments or tax liens exist against the applicant.

(c) The Department may deny registration to an applicant, reprimand a registrant, suspend or revoke a registration, or impose a civil penalty on a registrant if the Department determines that the applicant or registrant does any of the following:

(1) Fraudulently or deceptively obtains, or attempts to obtain, a registration.

(2) Uses or attempts to use an expired, suspended, or revoked registration.

(3) Falsely represents oneself as a registered landman.

(4) Engages in any other fraud, deception, misrepresentation, or knowing omission of material facts related to oil or gas interests.

(5) Had a similar registration or license denied, suspended, or revoked in another state or jurisdiction.

(6) Otherwise violates this section.

(d) An applicant may challenge a denial, suspension, or revocation of a registration or a reprimand issued pursuant to subsection (c) of this section, as provided in Chapter 150B of the General Statutes.

(e) The Department shall adopt rules as necessary to implement the provisions of this section. (2012-143, s. 4(g).)

§ 113-426. Publication of information for landowners.

In order to effect the pre-lease publication distribution requirement as set forth in G.S. 113-423(a), and to otherwise inform the public, the Consumer Protection Division of the North Carolina Department of Justice, in consultation with the North Carolina Real Estate Commission, shall develop and make available a publication entitled "Oil & Gas Leases: Landowners' Rights" to provide general information on consumer protection issues and landowner rights, including information on leases of oil or gas rights, applicable to exploration and extraction of gas or oil. The Division and the Commission shall update the publication as necessary. (2012-143, s. 4(h).)

§ 113-427. Additional remedies.

The remedies provided by this Part are not exclusive and do not preclude any other remedies that may be allowed by law. (2012-143, s. 4(i).)

Chapter 113A.

Pollution Control and Environment.

Article 1.

Environmental Policy Act.

§ 113A-1. Title.

This Article shall be known as the North Carolina Environmental Policy Act of 1971. (1971, c. 1203, s. 1; 1991, c. 431, s. 1.)

§ 113A-2. Purposes.

The purposes of this Article are: to declare a State policy which will encourage the wise, productive, and beneficial use of the natural resources of the State without damage to the environment, maintain a healthy and pleasant environment, and preserve the natural beauty of the State; to encourage an educational program which will create a public awareness of our environment and its related programs; to require agencies of the State to consider and report upon environmental aspects and consequences of their actions involving the expenditure of public moneys or use of public land; and to provide means to implement these purposes. (1971, c. 1203, s. 2; 1991 (Reg. Sess., 1992), c. 945, s. 1.)

§ 113A-3. Declaration of State environmental policy.

The General Assembly of North Carolina, recognizing the profound influence of man's activity on the natural environment, and desiring, in its role as trustee for future generations, to assure that an environment of high quality will be maintained for the health and well-being of all, declares that it shall be the continuing policy of the State of North Carolina to conserve and protect its natural resources and to create and maintain conditions under which man and nature can exist in productive harmony. Further, it shall be the policy of the State to seek, for all of its citizens, safe, healthful, productive and aesthetically pleasing surroundings; to attain the widest range of beneficial uses of the environment without degradation, risk to health or safety; and to preserve the important historic and cultural elements of our common inheritance. (1971, c. 1203, s. 3.)

§ 113A-4. Cooperation of agencies; reports; availability of information.

The General Assembly authorizes and directs that, to the fullest extent possible:

(1) The policies, rules, and public laws of this State shall be interpreted and administered in accordance with the policies set forth in this Article; and

(2) Every State agency shall include in every recommendation or report on any action involving expenditure of public moneys or use of public land for projects and programs significantly affecting the quality of the environment of this State, a detailed statement by the responsible official setting forth the following:

a. The environmental impact of the proposed action;

b. Any significant adverse environmental effects which cannot be avoided should the proposal be implemented;

c. Mitigation measures proposed to minimize the impact;

d. Alternatives to the proposed action;

e. The relationship between the short-term uses of the environment involved in the proposed action and the maintenance and enhancement of long-term productivity; and

f. Any irreversible and irretrievable environmental changes which would be involved in the proposed action should it be implemented.

(2a) Prior to making any detailed statement, the responsible official shall consult with and obtain the comments of any agency which has either jurisdiction by law or special expertise with respect to any environmental impact involved. Any unit of local government or other interested party that may be adversely affected by the proposed action may submit written comment. The responsible official shall consider written comment from units of local government and interested parties that is received within the established comment period. Copies of such detailed statement and such comments shall be made available to the Governor, to such agency or agencies as he may designate, and to the appropriate multi-county regional agency as certified by the Secretary of Administration, shall be placed in the public file of the agency and shall accompany the proposal through the existing agency review processes. A copy of such detailed statement shall be made available to the public and to counties, municipalities, institutions and individuals, upon request.

(3) The Governor, and any State agency charged with duties under this Article, may call upon any of the public institutions of higher education of this State for assistance in developing plans and procedures under this Article and in meeting the requirements of this Article, including without limitation any of the

following units of the University of North Carolina: the Water Resources Research Institute, the Institute for Environmental Studies, the Triangle Universities Consortium on Air Pollution, and the School of Government at the University of North Carolina at Chapel Hill. (1971, c. 1203, s. 4; 1987, c. 827, s. 125; 1991, c. 431, s. 2; 1991 (Reg. Sess., 1992), c. 945, s. 2; 2006-264, s. 29(g).)

§ 113A-5. Review of agency actions involving major adverse changes or conflicts.

Whenever, in the judgment of the responsible State official, the information obtained in preparing the statement indicates that a major adverse change in the environment, or conflicts concerning alternative uses of available natural resources, would result from a specific program, project or action, and that an appropriate alternative cannot be developed, such information shall be presented to the Governor for review and final decision by him or by such agency as he may designate, in the exercise of the powers of the Governor. (1971, c. 1203, s. 5.)

§ 113A-6. Conformity of administrative procedures to State environmental policy.

All agencies of the State shall periodically review their statutory authority, administrative rules, and current policies and procedures for the purpose of determining whether there are any deficiencies or inconsistencies therein which prohibit or hinder full compliance with the purposes and provisions of this Article and shall propose to the Governor such measures as may be necessary to bring their authority, rules, policies and procedures into conformity with the intent, purposes and procedures set forth in this Article. (1971, c. 1203, s. 6; 1987, c. 827, s. 126.)

§ 113A-7. Other statutory obligations of agencies.

Nothing in this Article shall in any way affect nor detract from specific statutory obligations of any State agency

(1)     To comply with criteria or standards of environmental quality or to perform other statutory obligations imposed upon it,

(2)     To coordinate or consult with any other State agency or federal agency, or

(3)     To act, or refrain from acting contingent upon the recommendations or certification of any other State agency or federal agency. (1971, c. 1203, s. 7.)


§ 113A-8.  Major development projects.

(a)     The governing bodies of all cities, counties, and towns acting individually, or collectively, may by ordinance require any special-purpose unit of government or private developer of a major development project to submit detailed statements, as defined in G.S. 113A-4(2), of the impact of such projects for consideration by those governing bodies in matters within their jurisdiction. Any such ordinance may not be designed to apply to only a particular major development project, and shall be applied consistently.

(b)     Any ordinance adopted pursuant to this section shall exempt those major development projects for which a detailed statement of the environmental impact of the project or a functionally equivalent permitting process is required by federal or State law, regulation, or rule.

(c)     Any ordinance adopted pursuant to this section shall establish minimum criteria to be used in determining whether a statement of environmental impact is required.  A detailed statement of environmental impact may not be required for a project that does not exceed the minimum criteria and any exceptions to the minimum criteria established by the ordinance. (1971, c. 1203, s. 8; 1991, c. 431, s. 3.)


§ 113A-8.1.  Surface water transfers.

An environmental assessment shall be prepared for any transfer for which a petition is filed in accordance with G.S. 143-215.22L. The determination of whether an environmental impact statement is needed with regard to the proposed transfer shall be made in accordance with the provisions of this Article. (1998-168, s. 6; 2007-484, s. 43.7C; 2007-518, s. 4.)

§ 113A-9. Definitions.

As used in this Article, unless the context indicates otherwise, the term:

(1)     "Environmental assessment" (EA) means a document prepared by a State agency to evaluate whether the probable impacts of a proposed action require the preparation of an environmental impact statement under this Article.

(2)     "Environmental document" means an environmental assessment, an environmental impact statement, or a finding of no significant impact.

(3)     "Environmental impact statement" (EIS) means the detailed statement described in G.S. 113A-4(2).

(4)     "Finding of no significant impact" (FONSI) means a document prepared by a State agency that lists the probable environmental impacts of a proposed action, concludes that a proposed action will not result in a significant adverse effect on the environment, states the specific reason or reasons for such conclusion, and states that an environmental impact statement is not required under this Article.

(5)     "Major development project" shall include but is not limited to shopping centers, subdivisions and other housing developments, and industrial and commercial projects, but shall not include any projects of less than two contiguous acres in extent.

(6)     "Minimum criteria" means a rule that designates a particular action or class of actions for which the preparation of environmental documents is not required.

(7)     "Public land" means all land and interests therein, title of which is vested in the State of North Carolina, in any State agency, or in the State for the use of any State agency or political subdivision of the State, and includes all vacant and unappropriated land, swampland, submerged land, land acquired by the State by virtue of being sold for taxes, escheated land, and acquired land.

(8) "Special-purpose unit of government" includes any special district or public authority.

(9) "State agency" includes every department, agency, institution, public authority, board, commission, bureau, division, council, member of Council of State, or officer of the State government of the State of North Carolina, but does not include local governmental units or bodies such as cities, towns, other municipal corporations or political subdivisions of the State, county or city boards of education, other local special-purpose public districts, units or bodies of any kind, or private corporations created by act of the General Assembly, except in those instances where programs, projects and actions of local governmental units or bodies are subject to review, approval or licensing by State agencies in accordance with existing statutory authority, in which case local governmental units or bodies shall supply information which may be required by such State agencies for preparation of any environmental statement required by this Article.

(10) "State official" means the Director, Commissioner, Secretary, Administrator or Chairman of the State agency having primary statutory authority for specific programs, projects or actions subject to this Article, or his authorized representative.

(11) "Use of public land" means activity that results in changes in the natural cover or topography that includes:

a. The grant of a lease, easement, or permit authorizing private use of public land; or

b. The use of privately owned land for any project or program if the State or any agency of the State has agreed to purchase the property or to exchange the property for public land. (1971, c. 1203, s. 9; 1991 (Reg. Sess., 1992), c. 945, s. 3.)

§ 113A-10. Provisions supplemental.

The policies, obligations and provisions of this Article are supplementary to those set forth in existing authorizations of and statutory provisions applicable to State agencies and local governments. In those instances where a State agency is required to prepare an environmental document or to comment on an environmental document under provisions of federal law, the environmental document or comment shall meet the provisions of this Article. (1971, c. 1203, s. 10; 1991 (Reg. Sess., 1992), c. 945, s. 4.)

§ 113A-11. Adoption of rules.

(a) The Department of Administration shall adopt rules to implement this Article.

(b) Each State agency may adopt rules that establish minimum criteria. An agency may include a particular action or class of actions in its minimum criteria only if the agency makes a specific finding that the action or class of actions has no significant impact on the environment. Rules establishing minimum criteria shall be consistent with rules adopted by the Department of Administration. In addition to all other rule-making requirements, rules establishing minimum criteria are subject to approval by the Secretary of Administration. (1991 (Reg. Sess., 1992), c. 899, s. 1; c. 945, s. 7(b).)

§ 113A-12. Environmental document not required in certain cases.

No environmental document shall be required in connection with:

(1) The construction, maintenance, or removal of an electric power line, water line, sewage line, stormwater drainage line, telephone line, telegraph line, cable television line, data transmission line, or natural gas line within or across the right-of-way of any street or highway.

(2) An action approved under a general permit issued under G.S. 113A-118.1, 143-215.1(b)(3), or 143-215.108(c)(8).

(3) A lease or easement granted by a State agency for:

a. The use of an existing building or facility.

b. Placement of a wastewater line on or under submerged lands pursuant to a permit granted under G.S. 143-215.1.

c. A shellfish cultivation lease granted under G.S. 113-202.

(4) The construction of a driveway connection to a public roadway.

(5) A project for which public monies are expended if the expenditure is solely for the payment of incentives pursuant to an agreement that makes the incentive payments contingent on prior completion of the project or activity, or completion on a specified timetable, and a specified level of job creation or new capital investment.

(6) A major development as defined in G.S. 113A-118 that receives a permit issued under Article 7 of Chapter 113A of the General Statutes. (1991 (Reg. Sess., 1992), c. 945, ss. 5, 7(a); c. 1030, s. 51.15; 2010-186, s. 1; 2010-188, s. 1; 2011-398, s. 59(a).)

§ 113A-13. Administrative and judicial review.

The preparation of an environmental document required under this Article is intended to assist the responsible agency in determining the appropriate decision on the proposed action. An environmental document required under this Article is a necessary part of an application or other request for agency action. Administrative and judicial review of an environmental document is incidental to, and may only be undertaken in connection with, review of the agency action. No other review of an environmental document is allowed. (1991 (Reg. Sess., 1992), c. 945, ss. 5, 7(a).)

§§ 113A-14 through 113A-20. Reserved for future codification purposes.

Article 2.

Interstate Environmental Compact.

§ 113A-21. Title.

This Article shall be known and cited as "The Interstate Environmental Compact Act of 1971." (1971, c. 805, s. 1.)

§ 113A-22. Purpose.

The General Assembly of North Carolina recognizes and declares:

(1)     The concern for the purity and life-giving qualities of our environment is of primary interest to every citizen of North Carolina and to all Americans.

(2)     The quality of our environment depends upon the management of the air, water, and land resources upon which our lives depend.

(3)     The ultimate responsibility for the health, safety, and welfare of the citizens of North Carolina rests upon the State government.

(4)     The environment of every state is affected with local, state, regional, and national interests since ecological systems cross state boundaries.

(5)     The discharge of this responsibility of environmental protection can be enhanced by acting in concert and cooperation with other states and with the federal government. (1971, c. 805, s. 2.)


§ 113A-23. Compact provisions.

The Interstate Environmental Compact is hereby enacted into law and entered into with all other jurisdictions legally joining herein in the form substantially as follows:


Article 1. Findings, Purposes and Reservations of Power.


(1)     Findings. - Signatory states hereby find and declare:

(a)     The environment of every state is affected with local, state, regional, and national interests and its protection, under appropriate arrangements for intergovernmental cooperation, are public purposes of the respective signatories.

(b)     Certain environmental pollution problems transcend state boundaries and thereby become common to adjacent states requiring cooperative efforts.

(c)     The environment of each state is subject to the effective control of the signatories, and coordinated, cooperative or joint exercise of control measures is in their common interests.

(2)     Purposes. - The purposes of the signatories in enacting this Compact are:

(a)     To assist and participate in the national environment protection programs as set forth in federal legislation; to promote intergovernmental cooperation for multi-state action relating to environmental protection through interstate agreements; and to encourage cooperative and coordinated environmental protection by the signatories and the federal government;

(b)     To preserve and utilize the functions, powers, and duties of existing state agencies of government to the maximum extent possible consistent with the purposes of the Compact.

(3)     Powers of the United States. - (a) Nothing contained in this Compact shall impair, affect or extend the constitutional authority of the United States. (b) The signatories hereby recognize the power and right of the Congress of the United States at any time by any statute expressly enacted for that purpose to revise the terms and conditions of its content.

(4)     Powers of the States. - Nothing contained in this Compact shall impair or extend the constitutional authority of any signatory state, nor shall the police powers of any signatory state be affected.

Article 2. Short Title, Definitions, Purposes and Limitations.

(1)     Short Title. - This Compact shall be known and may be cited as the Interstate Environmental Compact.

(2) Definitions. - For the purpose of this Compact and of any supplemental or concurring legislation enacted pursuant or in relation hereto, except as may be otherwise required by the context:

(a) "State" shall mean any one of the 50 states of the United States of America, the Commonwealth of Puerto Rico and the Territory of the Virgin Islands, but shall not include the District of Columbia.

(b) "Interstate environment pollution" shall mean any pollution of a stream or body of water crossing or marking a state boundary, interstate air quality control region designated by an appropriate federal agency or solid waste collection and disposal district or program involving the jurisdiction or territories of more than one state.

(c) "Government" shall mean the governments of the United States and the signatory states.

(d) "Federal government" shall mean the government of the United States of America and any appropriate department, instrumentality, agency, commission, bureau, division, branch or other unit thereof, as the case may be, but shall not include the District of Columbia.

(e) "Signator" shall mean any state which enters into this Compact and is a party thereto.

Article 3. Intergovernmental Cooperation.

(1) Agreements with the Federal Government and other Agencies. - Signatory states are hereby authorized jointly to participate in cooperative or joint undertakings for the protection of the interstate environment with the federal government or with any intergovernmental or interstate agencies.

Article 4. Supplementary Agreements, Jurisdiction and Enforcement.

(1) Signatories may enter into agreements for the purpose of controlling interstate environmental problems in accordance with applicable federal legislation and under terms and conditions as deemed appropriate by the agreeing states under paragraph (6) and paragraph (8) of this Article 4.

(2) Recognition of Existing Nonenvironmental Intergovernmental Arrangements. - The signatories agree that existing federal-state, interstate or intergovernmental arrangements which are not primarily directed to environmental protection purposes as defined herein are not affected by this Compact.

(3) Recognition of Existing Intergovernmental Agreements Directed to Environmental Objectives. - All existing interstate compacts directly relating to environmental protection are hereby expressly recognized and nothing in this Compact shall be construed to diminish or supersede the powers and functions of such existing intergovernmental agreements and the organizations created by them.

(4) Modification of Existing Commissions and Compacts. - Recognition herein of multi-state commissions and compacts shall not be construed to limit directly or indirectly the creation of additional multi-state organizations or interstate compacts, nor to prevent termination, modification, extension, or supplementation of such multi-state organizations and interstate compacts recognized herein by the federal government or states party thereto.

(5) Recognition of Future Multi-State Commissions and Interstate Compacts. - Nothing in this Compact shall be construed to prevent signatories from entering into multi-state organizations or other interstate compacts which do not conflict with their obligations under this Compact.

(6) Supplementary Agreements. - Any two or more signatories may enter into supplementary agreements for joint, coordinated or mutual environmental management activities relating to interstate pollution problems common to the territories of such states and for the establishment of common or joint regulations, management, services, agencies or facilities for such purposes or may designate an appropriate agency to act as their joint agency in regard thereto. No supplementary agreement shall be valid to the extent that it conflicts with the purposes of this Compact and the creation of a joint agency by supplementary agreement shall not affect the privileges, powers, responsibilities or duties under this Compact of signatories participating therein as embodied in this Compact.

(7)  Execution of Supplementary Agreements and Effective Date. - The Governor is authorized to enter into supplementary agreements for the State and his official signature shall render the agreement immediately binding upon the State; provided that:

(a)  The legislature of any signatory entering into such a supplementary agreement shall at any subsequent legislative session by concurrent resolution bring the supplementary agreement before it and by appropriate legislative action approve, reverse, modify, or condition the agreement of that state.

(b)  Nothing in this agreement shall be construed to limit the right of Congress by act of law expressly enacted for that purpose to disapprove or condition such a supplementary agreement.

(8)  Special Supplementary Agreements. - Signatories may enter into special supplementary agreements with the District of Columbia or foreign nations for the same purposes and with the same powers as under paragraph (6), Article 4, upon the conditions that such nonsignatory party accept the general obligations of signatories under this Compact. Provided, that such special supplementary agreements shall become effective only after being consented to by the Congress.

(9)  Jurisdiction of Signatories Reserved. - Nothing in this Compact or in any supplementary agreement thereunder shall be construed to restrict, relinquish or be in derogation of, any power or authority constitutionally possessed by any signatory within its jurisdiction.

(10)  Complementary Legislation by Signatories. - Signatories may enact such additional legislation as may be deemed appropriate to enable its officers and governmental agencies to accomplish effectively the purposes of this Compact and supplementary agreements recognized or entered into under the terms of this Article.

(11)  Legal Rights of Signatories. - Nothing in this Compact shall impair the exercise by any signatory of its legal rights or remedies established by the United States Constitution or any other laws of this nation.

Article 5. Construction, Amendment, and Effective Date.

(1) Construction. - It is the intent of the signatories that no provision of this Compact or supplementary agreement entered into hereunder shall be construed as invalidating any provision of law of any signatory and that nothing in this Compact shall be construed to modify or qualify the authority of any signatory to enact or enforce environmental protection legislation within its jurisdiction.

(2) Severability. - The provisions of this Compact or of agreements hereunder shall be severable and if any phrase, clause, sentence or provisions of this Compact, or such an agreement is declared to be contrary to the constitutionality of the remainder of this Compact or of any agreement and the applicability thereof to any participating jurisdiction, agency, person or circumstance shall not be affected thereby and shall remain in full force and effect as to the remaining participating jurisdictions and in full force and effect as to the signatory affected as to all severable matters. It is the intent of the signatories that the provisions of this Compact shall be reasonably and liberally construed in the context of its purposes.

(3) Amendments. - Amendments to this Compact may be initiated by legislative action of any signatory and become effective when concurred in by all signatories and approved by Congress.

(4) Effective Date. - This Compact shall become binding on a state when enacted by it into law and such state shall thereafter become a signatory and party hereto with any and all states legally joining herein. (1971, c. 805, s. 3.)

§§ 113A-24 through 113A-29. Reserved for future codification purposes.

Article 3.

Natural and Scenic Rivers System.

§ 113A-30. Short title.

This Article shall be known and may be cited as the "Natural and Scenic Rivers Act of 1971." (1971, c. 1167, s. 2.)

§ 113A-31. Declaration of policy.

The General Assembly finds that certain rivers of North Carolina possess outstanding natural, scenic, educational, geological, recreational, historic, fish and wildlife, scientific and cultural values of great present and future benefit to the people. The General Assembly further finds as policy the necessity for a rational balance between the conduct of man and the preservation of the natural beauty along the many rivers of the State. This policy includes retaining the natural and scenic conditions in some of the State's valuable rivers by maintaining them in a free-flowing state and to protect their water quality and adjacent lands by retaining these natural and scenic conditions. It is further declared that the preservation of certain rivers or segments of rivers in their natural and scenic condition constitutes a beneficial public purpose. (1971, c. 1167, s. 2.)

§ 113A-32. Declaration of purpose.

The purpose of this Article is to implement the policy as set out in G.S. 113A-31 by instituting a North Carolina natural and scenic rivers system, and by prescribing methods for inclusion of components to the system from time to time. (1971, c. 1167, s. 2.)

§ 113A-33. Definitions.

As used in this Article, unless the context requires otherwise:

(1)     "Department" means the Department of Environment and Natural Resources.

(2)     "Free-flowing," as applied to any river or section of a river, means existing or flowing in natural condition without substantial impoundment, diversion, straightening, rip-rapping, or other modification of the waterway. The existence of low dams, diversion works, and other minor structures at the time any river is proposed for inclusion in the North Carolina natural and scenic rivers system shall not automatically bar its consideration for such inclusion: Provided, that this shall not be construed to authorize, intend, or encourage future construction of such structures within components of the system.

(3) "River" means a flowing body of water or estuary or a section, portion, or tributary thereof, including rivers, streams, creeks, runs, kills, rills, and small lakes.

(4) "Road" means public or private highway, hard-surface road, dirt road, or railroad.

(5) "Scenic easement" means a perpetual easement in land which (i) is held for the benefit of the people of North Carolina, (ii) is specifically enforceable by its holder or beneficiary, and (iii) limits or obligates the holder of the servient estate, his heirs, and assigns with respect to their use and management of the land and activities conducted thereon. The object of such limitations and obligations is the maintenance or enhancement of the natural beauty of the land in question or of the areas affected by it.

(6) "Secretary" means the Secretary of Environment and Natural Resources. (1971, c. 1167, s. 2; 1973, c. 1262, s. 86; 1977, c. 771, s. 4; 1989, c. 727, s. 122; 1989 (Reg. Sess., 1990), c. 1004, s. 19(b); 1997-443, s. 11A.119(a).)

§ 113A-34. Types of scenic rivers.

The following types of rivers are eligible for inclusion in the North Carolina natural and scenic rivers system:

Class I. Natural river areas. Those free-flowing rivers or segments of rivers and adjacent lands existing in a natural condition. Those rivers or segments of rivers that are free of man-made impoundments and generally inaccessible except by trail, with the lands within the boundaries essentially primitive and the waters essentially unpolluted. These represent vestiges of primitive America.

Class II. Scenic river areas. Those rivers or segments of rivers that are largely free of impoundments, with the lands within the boundaries largely primitive and largely undeveloped, but accessible in places by roads.

Class III. Recreational river areas. Those rivers or segments of rivers that offer outstanding recreation and scenic values and that are largely free of impoundments. They may have some development along their shorelines and have more extensive public access than natural or scenic river segments. Recreational river segments may also link two or more natural and/or scenic river segments to provide a contiguous designated river area. No provision of this section shall interfere with flood control measures; provided that recreational river users can continue to travel the river. (1971, c. 1167, s. 2; 1989, c. 752, s. 156(a).)

§ 113A-35. Criteria for system.

For the inclusion of any river or segment of river in the natural and scenic river system, the following criteria must be present:

(1)　River segment length - must be no less than one mile.

(2)　Boundaries - of the system shall be the visual horizon or such distance from each shoreline as may be determined to be necessary by the Secretary, but shall not be less than 20 feet.

(3)　Water quality - shall not be less than that required for Class "C" waters as established by the North Carolina Environmental Management Commission.

(4)　Water flow - shall be sufficient to assure a continuous flow and shall not be subjected to withdrawal or regulation to the extent of substantially altering the natural ecology of the stream.

(5)　Public access - shall be limited, but may be permitted to the extent deemed proper by the Secretary, and in keeping with the property interest acquired by the Department and the purpose of this Article. (1971, c. 1167, s. 2; 1973, c. 1262, ss. 23, 86; 1989, c. 654, s. 1.)

§ 113A-35.1. Components of system; management plan; acquisition of land and easements; inclusion in national system.

(a)　That segment of the south fork of the New River extending from its confluence with Dog Creek in Ashe County downstream through Ashe and Alleghany Counties to its confluence with the north fork of the New River and the main fork of the New River in Ashe and Alleghany Counties downstream to the Virginia State line shall be a scenic river area and shall be included in the North Carolina Natural and Scenic Rivers System.

The Department shall prepare and implement a management plan for this river section. This management plan shall recognize and provide for the protection of the existing undeveloped scenic and pastoral features of the river. Furthermore, it shall specifically provide for continued use of the lands adjacent to the river for normal agricultural activities, including, but not limited to, cultivation of crops, raising of cattle, growing of trees and other practices necessary to these agricultural pursuits.

For purposes of implementing this section and the management plan, the Department may acquire lands or interests in lands, provide for protection of scenic values as described in G.S. 113A-38, and provide for public access. Easements obtained for the purpose of implementing this section and the management plan shall not abridge the water rights being exercised on May 26, 1975.

Should the Governor seek inclusion of this river segment in the National System of Wild and Scenic Rivers by action of the Secretary of Interior, such inclusion shall be at no cost to the federal government, as prescribed in the National Wild and Scenic Rivers Act, and therefore shall be under the terms described in this section of the North Carolina Wild and Scenic Rivers Act and in the management plan developed pursuant thereto.

(b) Repealed by Session Laws 2012-200, s. 24, effective August 1, 2012. (1973, c. 879; 1975, c. 404; 1977, c. 555; c. 771, s. 4; 1985, c. 129, s. 3; 1987, c. 827, s. 127; 1989, c. 654, s. 2; c. 765; 1999-147, s. 1; 2012-200, s. 24.)

§ 113A-35.2. Additional components.

That segment of the Linville River beginning at the State Highway 183 bridge over the Linville River and extending approximately 13 miles downstream to the boundary between the United States Forest Service lands and lands of Duke Power Company (latitude 35° 50' 20") shall be a natural river area and shall be included in the North Carolina Natural and Scenic River System.

That segment of the Horsepasture River in Transylvania County extending downstream from Bohaynee Road (N.C. 281) to Lake Jocassee shall be a natural river and shall be included in the North Carolina Natural and Scenic Rivers System.

That segment of the Lumber River extending from county road 1412 in Scotland County downstream to the North Carolina-South Carolina state line, a distance of approximately 102 river miles, shall be included in the Natural and Scenic Rivers System and classified as follows: from county road 1412 in Scotland County downstream to the junction of the Lumber River and Back Swamp shall be classified as scenic; from the junction of the Lumber River and Back Swamp downstream to the junction of the Lumber River and Jacob Branch and the river within the Fair Bluff town limits shall be classified as recreational; and from the junction of the Lumber River and Jacob Branch downstream to the North Carolina-South Carolina state line, excepting the Fair Bluff town limits, shall be classified as natural. (1975, c. 698; 1985, c. 344, s. 1; 1989, c. 752, s. 156(b).)

§ 113A-36. Administrative agency; federal grants; additions to the system; regulations.

(a) The Department is the agency of the State of North Carolina with the duties and responsibilities to administer and control the North Carolina natural and scenic rivers system.

(b) The Department shall be the agency of the State with the authority to accept federal grants of assistance in planning, developing (which would include the acquisition of land or an interest in land), and administering the natural and scenic rivers system.

(c) The Secretary of the Department shall study and from time to time submit to the Governor and to the General Assembly proposals for the additions to the system of rivers and segments of rivers which, in his judgment, fall within one or more of the categories set out in G.S. 113A-34. Each proposal shall specify the category of the proposed addition and shall be accompanied by a detailed report of the facts which, in the Secretary's judgment, makes the area a worthy addition to the system.

Before submitting any proposal to the Governor or the General Assembly for the addition to the system of a river or segment of a river, the Secretary or his authorized representative, shall hold a public hearing in the county or counties where said river or segment of river is situated. Notice of such public hearing shall be given by publishing a notice once each week for two consecutive weeks in a newspaper having general circulation in the county where said hearing is to be held, the second of said notices appearing not less than 10 days before said hearing. Any person attending said hearing shall be given an opportunity to be heard. Notwithstanding the provisions of the foregoing, no public hearing shall be required with respect to a river bounded solely by the property of one owner, who consents in writing to the addition of such river to the system.

The Department shall also conduct an investigation on the feasibility of the inclusion of a river or a segment of river within the system and file a written report with the Governor when submitting a proposal.

The Department shall also, before submitting such a proposal to the Governor or the General Assembly, notify in writing the owner, lessee, or tenant of any lands adjoining said river or segment of river of its intention to make such proposal. In the event the Department, after due diligence, is unable to determine the owner or lessee of any such land, the Department may publish a notice for four successive weeks in a newspaper having general circulation in the county where the land is situated of its intention to make a proposal to the Governor or General Assembly for the addition of a river or segment of river to the system.

(c1)   Upon receipt of a request in the form of a resolution from the commissioners of the county or counties in which a river segment is located and upon studying the segment and determining that it meets the criteria set forth in G.S. 113A-35, the Secretary may designate the segment a potential component of the natural and scenic rivers system. The designation as a potential component shall be transmitted to the Governor and all appropriate State agencies. Any segment so designated is subject to the provisions of this Article applicable to designated rivers, except for acquisition by condemnation or otherwise, and to any rules adopted pursuant to this Article. The Secretary shall make a full report and, if appropriate, a proposal for an addition to the natural and scenic rivers system to the General Assembly within 90 days after the convening of the next session following issuance of the designation, and the General Assembly shall determine whether to designate the segment as a component of the natural and scenic rivers system. If the next session of the General Assembly fails to take affirmative action on the designation, the designation as a potential component shall expire.

(d)   The Department may adopt rules to implement this Article. (1971, c. 1167, s. 2; 1973, c. 911; c. 1262, ss. 28, 86; 1977, c. 771, s. 4; 1985, c. 129, s. 1; 1987, c. 827, ss. 125, 128; 1989, c. 727, s. 123.)

§ 113A-37. Raising the status of an area.

Whenever in the judgment of the Secretary of the Department a scenic river segment has been sufficiently restored and enhanced in its natural scenic and recreational qualities, such segment may be reclassified with the approval of the Department, to a natural river area status and thereafter administered accordingly. (1971, c. 1167, s. 2; 1973, c. 1262, ss. 28, 86.)

§ 113A-38. Land acquisition.

(a) The Department of Administration is authorized to acquire for the Department, within the boundaries of a river or segment of river as set out in G.S. 113A-35 on behalf of the State of North Carolina, lands in fee title or a lesser interest in land, preferably "scenic easements." Acquisition of land or interest therein may be by donation, purchase with donated or appropriated funds, exchange or otherwise.

(b) The Department of Administration in acquiring real property or a property interest therein as set out in this Article shall have and may exercise the power of eminent domain in accordance with Article 3 of Chapter 40A of the General Statutes. (1971, c. 1167, s. 2; 1973, c. 1262, s. 86; 1977, c. 771, s. 4; 1987, c. 827, ss. 127, 129.)

§ 113A-39. Claim and allowance of charitable deduction for contribution or gift of easement.

The contribution or donation of a "scenic easement," right-of-way or any other easement or interest in land to the State of North Carolina, as provided in this Article, shall be deemed a contribution to the State of North Carolina within the provisions of G.S. 105-130.9 and section 170(c)(1) of the Internal Revenue Code. The value of the contribution or donation shall be the fair market value of the easement or other interest in land when the contribution or donation is made. (1971, c. 1167, s. 2; 1991, c. 45, s. 23.)

§ 113A-40. Component as part of State park, wildlife refuge, etc.

Any component of the State natural and scenic rivers system that is or shall become a part of any State park, wildlife refuge, or state-owned area shall be subject to the provisions of this Article and the Articles under which the other areas may be administered, and in the case of conflict between the provisions of these Articles the more restrictive provisions shall apply. (1971, c. 1167, s. 2.)


§ 113A-41. Component as part of national wild and scenic river system.

Nothing in this Article shall preclude a river or segment of a river from becoming part of the national wild and scenic river system. The Secretary of the Department is directed to encourage and assist any federal studies for the inclusion of North Carolina rivers in the national system. The Secretary may enter into cooperative agreements for joint federal-state administration of a North Carolina river or segment of river: Provided, that such agreements relating to water and land use are not less restrictive than the requirements of this Article. (1971, c. 1167, s. 2; 1973, c. 1262, s. 86.)


§ 113A-42. Violations.

(a) Civil Action. - Whoever violates, fails, neglects or refuses to obey any provision of this Article or rule or order of the Secretary may be compelled to comply with or obey the same by injunction, mandamus, or other appropriate remedy.

(b) Penalties. - Whoever violates, fails, neglects or refuses to obey any provision of this Article or rule or order of the Secretary is guilty of a Class 3 misdemeanor and may be punished only by a fine of not more than fifty dollars ($50.00) for each violation, and each day such person shall fail to comply, where feasible, after having been officially notified by the Department shall constitute a separate offense subject to the foregoing penalty. (1971, c. 1167, s. 2; 1973, c. 1262, s. 86; 1977, c. 771, s. 4; 1987, c. 827, s. 125; 1989, c. 727, s. 124; 1993, c. 539, s. 872; 1994, Ex. Sess., c. 24, s. 14(c).)


§ 113A-43. Authorization of advances.

The Department of Administration is hereby authorized to advance from land-purchase appropriations necessary amounts for the purchase of land in those cases where reimbursement will be later effected by the Bureau of Outdoor Recreation of the United States Department of the Interior. (1971, c. 1167, s. 2.)


§ 113A-44. Restrictions on project works on natural or scenic river.

The State Utilities Commission may not permit the construction of any dam, water conduit, reservoir, powerhouse transmission line, or any other project works on or directly affecting any river that is designated as a component or potential component of the State Natural and Scenic Rivers System. No department or agency of the State may assist by loan, grant, license, permit, or otherwise in the construction of any water resources project that would have a direct and adverse effect on any river that is designated as a component or potential component of the State Natural and Scenic Rivers System. This section shall not, however, preclude licensing of or assistance to a development below or above a designated or potential component. No department or agency of the State may recommend authorization of any water resources project that would have a direct and adverse effect on any river that is designated as a component or potential component of the State Natural and Scenic Rivers System, or request appropriations to begin construction of any such project, regardless of when authorized, without advising the Secretary in writing of its intention to do so at least 60 days in advance. Such department or agency making such recommendation or request shall submit a written impact statement to the General Assembly to accompany the recommendation or request specifically describing how construction of the project would be in conflict with the purposes of this act and how it would affect the component or potential component. (1985, c. 129, s. 2.)


§§ 113A-45 through 113A-49. Reserved for future codification purposes.


Article 4.

Sedimentation Pollution Control Act of 1973.

§ 113A-50. Short title.

This Article shall be known as and may be cited as the "Sedimentation Pollution Control Act of 1973." (1973, c. 392, s. 1.)

§ 113A-51. Preamble.

The sedimentation of streams, lakes and other waters of this State constitutes a major pollution problem. Sedimentation occurs from the erosion or depositing of soil and other materials into the waters, principally from construction sites and road maintenance. The continued development of this State will result in an intensification of pollution through sedimentation unless timely and appropriate action is taken. Control of erosion and sedimentation is deemed vital to the public interest and necessary to the public health and welfare, and expenditures of funds for erosion and sedimentation control programs shall be deemed for a public purpose. It is the purpose of this Article to provide for the creation, administration, and enforcement of a program and for the adoption of minimal mandatory standards which will permit development of this State to continue with the least detrimental effects from pollution by sedimentation. In recognition of the desirability of early coordination of sedimentation control planning, it is the intention of the General Assembly that preconstruction conferences be held among the affected parties, subject to the availability of staff. (1973, c. 392, s. 2; 1975, c. 647, s. 3.)

§ 113A-52. Definitions.

As used in this Article, unless the context otherwise requires:

(1) Repealed by Session Laws 1973, c. 1417, s. 1.

(1a) "Affiliate" has the same meaning as in 17 Code of Federal Regulations § 240.12(b)-2 (1 June 1993 Edition), which defines "affiliate" as a person that directly, or indirectly through one or more intermediaries, controls, is controlled by, or is under common control of another person.

(2) "Commission" means the North Carolina Sedimentation Control Commission.

(3) "Department" means the North Carolina Department of Environment and Natural Resources.

(4) "District" means any Soil and Water Conservation District created pursuant to Chapter 139, North Carolina General Statutes.

(5) "Erosion" means the wearing away of land surface by the action of wind, water, gravity, or any combination thereof.

(6) "Land-disturbing activity" means any use of the land by any person in residential, industrial, educational, institutional or commercial development, highway and road construction and maintenance that results in a change in the natural cover or topography and that may cause or contribute to sedimentation.

(7) "Local government" means any county, incorporated village, town, or city, or any combination of counties, incorporated villages, towns, and cities, acting through a joint program pursuant to the provisions of this Article.

(7a) "Parent" has the same meaning as in 17 Code of Federal Regulations § 240.12(b)-2 (1 June 1993 Edition), which defines "parent" as an affiliate that directly, or indirectly through one or more intermediaries, controls another person.

(8) "Person" means any individual, partnership, firm, association, joint venture, public or private corporation, trust, estate, commission, board, public or private institution, utility, cooperative, interstate body, or other legal entity.

(9) "Secretary" means the Secretary of Environment and Natural Resources.

(10) "Sediment" means solid particulate matter, both mineral and organic, that has been or is being transported by water, air, gravity, or ice from its site of origin.

(10a) "Subsidiary" has the same meaning as in 17 Code of Federal Regulations § 240.12(b)-2 (1 June 1993 Edition), which defines "subsidiary" as an affiliate that is directly, or indirectly through one or more intermediaries, controlled by another person.

(10b) "Tract" means all contiguous land and bodies of water being disturbed or to be disturbed as a unit, regardless of ownership.

(11) "Working days" means days exclusive of Saturday and Sunday during which weather conditions or soil conditions permit land-disturbing activity to be undertaken. (1973, c. 392, s. 3; c. 1417, s. 1; 1975, c. 647, s. 1; 1977, c. 771, s. 4; 1989, c. 179, s. 1; c. 727, s. 218(60); 1989 (Reg. Sess., 1990), c. 1004, s. 19(b); 1991, c. 275, s. 1; 1993 (Reg. Sess., 1994), c. 776, s. 1; 1997-443, s. 11A.119(a).)

§ 113A-52.01. Applicability of this Article.
This Article shall not apply to the following land-disturbing activities:

(1) Activities, including the breeding and grazing of livestock, undertaken on agricultural land for the production of plants and animals useful to man, including, but not limited to:

a. Forages and sod crops, grains and feed crops, tobacco, cotton, and peanuts.

b. Dairy animals and dairy products.

c. Poultry and poultry products.

d. Livestock, including beef cattle, llamas, sheep, swine, horses, ponies, mules, and goats.

e. Bees and apiary products.

f. Fur producing animals.

(2) Activities undertaken on forestland for the production and harvesting of timber and timber products and conducted in accordance with best management practices set out in Forest Practice Guidelines Related to Water Quality, as adopted by the Department.

(3) Activities for which a permit is required under the Mining Act of 1971, Article 7 of Chapter 74 of the General Statutes.

(4)     For the duration of an emergency, activities essential to protect human life. (1993 (Reg. Sess., 1994), c. 776, s. 2; 1997-84, s. 1.)


§ 113A-52.1. Forest Practice Guidelines.

(a)     The Department shall adopt Forest Practice Guidelines Related to Water Quality (best management practices). The adoption of Forest Practices Guidelines Related to Water Quality under this section is subject to the provisions of Chapter 150B of the General Statutes.

(b)     If land-disturbing activity undertaken on forestland for the production and harvesting of timber and timber products is not conducted in accordance with Forest Practice Guidelines Related to Water Quality, the provisions of this Article shall apply to such activity and any related land-disturbing activity on the tract.

(c)     The Secretary shall establish a Technical Advisory Committee to assist in the development and periodic review of Forest Practice Guidelines Related to Water Quality. The Technical Advisory Committee shall consist of one member from the forest products industry, one member who is a consulting forester, one member who is a private landowner knowledgeable in forestry, one member from the United States Forest Service, one member from the academic community who is knowledgeable in forestry, one member who is knowledgeable in erosion and sedimentation control, one member who is knowledgeable in wildlife management, one member who is knowledgeable in marine fisheries management, one member who is knowledgeable in water quality, and one member from the conservation community. (1989, c. 179, s. 2.)


§ 113A-53. Repealed by Session Laws 1973, c. 1262, s. 41.


§ 113A-54. Powers and duties of the Commission.

(a)     The Commission shall, in cooperation with the Secretary of Transportation and other appropriate State and federal agencies, develop, promulgate, publicize, and administer a comprehensive State erosion and sedimentation control program.

(b)     The Commission shall develop and adopt and shall revise as necessary from time to time, rules and regulations for the control of erosion and sedimentation resulting from land-disturbing activities. The Commission shall adopt or revise its rules and regulations in accordance with Chapter 150B of the General Statutes.

(c)     The rules and regulations adopted pursuant to G.S. 113A-54(b) for carrying out the erosion and sedimentation control program shall:

(1)     Be based upon relevant physical and developmental information concerning the watershed and drainage basins of the State, including, but not limited to, data relating to land use, soils, hydrology, geology, grading, ground cover, size of land area being disturbed, proximate water bodies and their characteristics, transportation, and public facilities and services;

(2)     Include such survey of lands and waters as may be deemed appropriate by the Commission or required by any applicable laws to identify those areas, including multijurisdictional and watershed areas, with critical erosion and sedimentation problems; and

(3)     Contain conservation standards for various types of soils and land uses, which standards shall include criteria and alternative techniques and methods for the control of erosion and sedimentation resulting from land-disturbing activities.

(d)     In implementing the erosion and sedimentation control program, the Commission shall:

(1)     Assist and encourage local governments in developing erosion and sedimentation control programs and, as a part of this assistance, the Commission shall develop a model local erosion and sedimentation control ordinance. The Commission shall approve, approve as modified, or disapprove local programs submitted to it pursuant to G.S. 113A-60.

(2)     Assist and encourage other State agencies in developing erosion and sedimentation control programs to be administered in their jurisdictions. The Commission shall approve, approve as modified, or disapprove programs submitted pursuant to G.S. 113A-56 and from time to time shall review these

programs for compliance with rules adopted by the Commission and for adequate enforcement.

(3) Develop recommended methods of control of sedimentation and prepare and make available for distribution publications and other materials dealing with sedimentation control techniques appropriate for use by persons engaged in land-disturbing activities, general educational materials on erosion and sedimentation control, and instructional materials for persons involved in the enforcement of this Article and erosion and sedimentation control rules, ordinances, regulations, and plans.

(4) Require submission of erosion and sedimentation control plans by those responsible for initiating land-disturbing activities for approval prior to commencement of the activities.

(e) To assist it in developing the erosion and sedimentation control program required by this Article, the Commission is authorized to appoint an advisory committee consisting of technical experts in the fields of water resources, soil science, engineering, and landscape architecture.

(f) Repealed by Session Laws 1987, c. 827, s. 10, effective August 13, 1987. (1973, c. 392, s. 5; c. 1331, s. 3; c. 1417, s. 6; 1975, 2nd Sess., c. 983, s. 74; 1977, c. 464, s. 35; 1979, c. 922, s. 2; 1983 (Reg. Sess., 1984), c. 1014, ss. 1, 2; 1987, c. 827, s. 10; 1987 (Reg. Sess., 1988), c. 1000, s. 3; 1989, c. 676, s. 1; 1993 (Reg. Sess., 1994), c. 776, s. 3; 2002-165, ss. 2.2, 2.3.)


§ 113A-54.1. Approval of erosion control plans.

(a) A draft erosion and sedimentation control plan must contain the applicant's address and, if the applicant is not a resident of North Carolina, designate a North Carolina agent for the purpose of receiving notice from the Commission or the Secretary of compliance or noncompliance with the plan, this Article, or any rules adopted pursuant to this Article. Except as provided in subsection (a1) of this section, if the applicant is not the owner of the land to be disturbed, the draft erosion and sedimentation control plan must include the owner's written consent for the applicant to submit a draft erosion and sedimentation control plan and to conduct the anticipated land-disturbing activity. The Commission shall approve, approve with modifications, or disapprove a draft erosion and sedimentation control plan for those land-disturbing activities for which prior plan approval is required within 30 days of receipt. The Commission shall condition approval of a draft erosion and sedimentation control plan upon the applicant's compliance with federal and State water quality laws, regulations, and rules. Failure to approve, approve with modifications, or disapprove a completed draft erosion and sedimentation control plan within 30 days of receipt shall be deemed approval of the plan. If the Commission disapproves a draft erosion and sedimentation control plan or a revised erosion and sedimentation control plan, it must state in writing the specific reasons that the plan was disapproved. Failure to approve, approve with modifications, or disapprove a revised erosion and sedimentation control plan within 15 days of receipt shall be deemed approval of the plan. The Commission may establish an expiration date for erosion and sedimentation control plans approved under this Article.

(a1)	If the applicant is not the owner of the land to be disturbed and the anticipated land-disturbing activity involves the construction of utility lines for the provision of water, sewer, gas, telecommunications, or electrical service, the draft erosion and sedimentation control plan may be submitted without the written consent of the owner of the land, so long as the owner of the land has been provided prior notice of the project.

(b)	If, following commencement of a land-disturbing activity pursuant to an approved erosion and sedimentation control plan, the Commission determines that the plan is inadequate to meet the requirements of this Article, the Commission may require any revision of the plan that is necessary to comply with this Article. Failure to approve, approve with modifications, or disapprove a revised erosion and sedimentation control plan within 15 days of receipt shall be deemed approval of the plan.

(c)	The Commission shall disapprove an erosion and sedimentation control plan if implementation of the plan would result in a violation of rules adopted by the Environmental Management Commission to protect riparian buffers along surface waters. The Director of the Division of Energy, Mineral, and Land Resources may disapprove an erosion and sedimentation control plan or disapprove a transfer of a plan under subsection (d1) of this section upon finding that an applicant or a parent, subsidiary, or other affiliate of the applicant:

(1)	Is conducting or has conducted land-disturbing activity without an approved plan, or has received notice of violation of a plan previously approved by the Commission or a local government pursuant to this Article and has not complied with the notice within the time specified in the notice;

(2) Has failed to pay a civil penalty assessed pursuant to this Article or a local ordinance adopted pursuant to this Article by the time the payment is due;

(3) Has been convicted of a misdemeanor pursuant to G.S. 113A-64(b) or any criminal provision of a local ordinance adopted pursuant to this Article; or

(4) Has failed to substantially comply with State rules or local ordinances and regulations adopted pursuant to this Article.

(d) In the event that an erosion and sedimentation control plan or a transfer of a plan is disapproved by the Director pursuant to subsection (c) of this section, the Director shall state in writing the specific reasons that the plan was disapproved. The applicant or the proposed transferee may appeal the Director's disapproval of the plan to the Commission. For purposes of this subsection and subsection (c) of this section, an applicant's record or a proposed transferee's record may be considered for only the two years prior to the application date.

(d1) The Department may transfer an erosion and sedimentation control plan approved pursuant to this section without the consent of the plan holder to a successor-owner of the property on which the permitted activity is occurring or will occur as provided in this subsection:

(1) The Department may transfer a plan if all of the following conditions are met:

a. The successor-owner of the property submits to the Department a written request for the transfer of the plan and an authorized statement of financial responsibility and ownership.

b. The Department finds all of the following:

1. The plan holder is one of the following:

I. A natural person who is deceased.

II. A partnership, limited liability corporation, corporation, or any other business association that has been dissolved.

III. A person who has been lawfully and finally divested of title to the property on which the permitted activity is occurring or will occur.

IV. A person who has sold the property on which the permitted activity is occurring or will occur.

2. The successor-owner holds title to the property on which the permitted activity is occurring or will occur.

3. The successor-owner is the sole claimant of the right to engage in the permitted activity.

4. There will be no substantial change in the permitted activity.

(2) The plan holder shall comply with all terms and conditions of the plan until such time as the plan is transferred.

(3) The successor-owner shall comply with all terms and conditions of the plan once the plan has been transferred.

(4) Notwithstanding changes to law made after the original issuance of the plan, the Department may not impose new or different terms and conditions in the plan without the prior express consent of the successor-owner. Nothing in this subsection shall prevent the Commission from requiring a revised plan pursuant to G.S. 113A-54.1(b).

(e) The landowner, the financially responsible party, or the landowner's or the financially responsible party's agent shall perform an inspection of the area covered by the plan after each phase of the plan has been completed and after establishment of temporary ground cover in accordance with G.S. 113A-57(2). The person who performs the inspection shall maintain and make available a record of the inspection at the site of the land-disturbing activity. The record shall set out any significant deviation from the approved erosion control plan, identify any measures that may be required to correct the deviation, and document the completion of those measures. The record shall be maintained until permanent ground cover has been established as required by the approved erosion and sedimentation control plan. The inspections required by this subsection shall be in addition to inspections required by G.S. 113A-61.1. (1989, c. 676, s. 2; 1993 (Reg. Sess., 1994), c. 776, s. 4; 1998-221, s. 1.11(a); 1999-379, s. 1; 2005-386, s. 7.1; 2006-250, s. 1; 2011-394, s. 3; 2012-143, s. 1(f); 2013-121, s. 3.)

§ 113A-54.2. Approval Fees.

(a) An application fee of sixty-five dollars ($65.00) per acre of disturbed land shown on an erosion and sedimentation control plan or of land actually disturbed during the life of the project shall be charged for the review of an erosion and sedimentation control plan under this Article.

(b) The Sedimentation Account is established as a nonreverting account within the Department. Fees collected under this section shall be credited to the Account and shall be applied to the costs of administering this Article.

(c) Repealed by Session Laws 1991 (Reg. Sess., 1992), c. 1039, s. 3.

(d) This section may not limit the existing authority of local programs approved pursuant to this Article to assess fees for the approval of erosion and sedimentation control plans. (1989 (Reg. Sess., 1990), c. 906, s. 1; 1991 (Reg. Sess., 1992), c. 1039, s. 3; 1993 (Reg. Sess., 1994), c. 776, s. 5; 1999-379, s. 5; 2002-165, s. 2.4; 2007-323, s. 30.1(a).)


§ 113A-55. Authority of the Secretary.

The sedimentation control program developed by the Commission shall be administered by the Secretary under the direction of the Commission. To this end the Secretary shall employ the necessary clerical, technical, and administrative personnel, and assign tasks to the various divisions of the Department for the purpose of implementing this Article. The Secretary may bring enforcement actions pursuant to G.S. 113A-64 and G.S. 113A-65. The Secretary shall make final agency decisions in contested cases that arise from civil penalty assessments pursuant to G.S. 113A-64. (1973, c. 392, s. 6, c. 1417, s. 3; 1993 (Reg. Sess., 1994), c. 776, s. 6.)


§ 113A-56. Jurisdiction of the Commission.

(a) The Commission shall have jurisdiction, to the exclusion of local governments, to adopt rules concerning land-disturbing activities that are:

(1) Conducted by the State.

(2) Conducted by the United States.

(3) Conducted by persons having the power of eminent domain other than a local government.

(4) Conducted by a local government.
(5) Funded in whole or in part by the State or the United States.

(b) The Commission may delegate the jurisdiction conferred by G.S. 113A-56(a), in whole or in part, to any other State agency that has submitted an erosion and sedimentation control program to be administered by it, if the program has been approved by the Commission as being in conformity with the general State program.

(c) The Commission shall have concurrent jurisdiction with local governments that administer a delegated erosion and sedimentation control program over all other land-disturbing activities. In addition to the authority granted to the Commission in G.S. 113A-60(c), the Commission has the following authority with respect to a delegated erosion and sedimentation control program:

(1) To review erosion and sedimentation control plan approvals made by a delegated erosion and sedimentation control program and to require a revised plan if the Commission determines that a plan does not comply with the requirements of this Article or the rules adopted pursuant to this Article.

(2) To review the compliance activities of a delegated erosion and sedimentation control program and to take appropriate compliance action if the Commission determines that the local government has failed to take appropriate compliance action. (1973, c. 392, s. 7; c. 1417, s. 4; 1987, c. 827, s. 130; 1987 (Reg. Sess., 1988), c. 1000, s. 4; 2002-165, s. 2.5; 2006-250, s. 2.)


§ 113A-57. Mandatory standards for land-disturbing activity.

No land-disturbing activity subject to this Article shall be undertaken except in accordance with the following mandatory requirements:

(1) No land-disturbing activity during periods of construction or improvement to land shall be permitted in proximity to a lake or natural watercourse unless a

buffer zone is provided along the margin of the watercourse of sufficient width to confine visible siltation within the twenty-five percent (25%) of the buffer zone nearest the land-disturbing activity. Waters that have been classified as trout waters by the Environmental Management Commission shall have an undisturbed buffer zone 25 feet wide or of sufficient width to confine visible siltation within the twenty-five percent (25%) of the buffer zone nearest the land-disturbing activity, whichever is greater. Provided, however, that the Sedimentation Control Commission may approve plans which include land-disturbing activity along trout waters when the duration of said disturbance would be temporary and the extent of said disturbance would be minimal. This subdivision shall not apply to a land-disturbing activity in connection with the construction of facilities to be located on, over, or under a lake or natural watercourse.

(2)     The angle for graded slopes and fills shall be no greater than the angle that can be retained by vegetative cover or other adequate erosion-control devices or structures. In any event, slopes left exposed will, within 21 calendar days of completion of any phase of grading, be planted or otherwise provided with temporary or permanent ground cover, devices, or structures sufficient to restrain erosion.

(3)     Whenever land-disturbing activity that will disturb more than one acre is undertaken on a tract, the person conducting the land-disturbing activity shall install erosion and sedimentation control devices and practices that are sufficient to retain the sediment generated by the land-disturbing activity within the boundaries of the tract during construction upon and development of the tract, and shall plant or otherwise provide a permanent ground cover sufficient to restrain erosion after completion of construction or development within a time period to be specified by rule of the Commission.

(4)     No person shall initiate any land-disturbing activity that will disturb more than one acre on a tract unless, 30 or more days prior to initiating the activity, an erosion and sedimentation control plan for the activity is filed with the agency having jurisdiction and approved by the agency. An erosion and sedimentation control plan may be filed less than 30 days prior to initiation of a land-disturbing activity if the plan is submitted under an approved express permit program, and the land-disturbing activity may be initiated and conducted in accordance with the plan once the plan has been approved. The agency having jurisdiction shall forward to the Director of the Division of Water Resources a copy of each erosion and sedimentation control plan for a land-disturbing activity that involves

the utilization of ditches for the purpose of de-watering or lowering the water table of the tract.

(5) The land-disturbing activity shall be conducted in accordance with the approved erosion and sedimentation control plan. (1973, c. 392, s. 8; c. 1417, s. 5; 1975, c. 647, s. 2; 1979, c. 564; 1983 (Reg. Sess., 1984), c. 1014, s. 3; 1987, c. 827, s. 131; 1989, c. 676, s. 3; 1991, c. 275, s. 2; 1998-99, s. 1; 1999-379, s. 2; 2002-165, s. 2.6; 2005-386, s. 7.2; 2005-443, s. 2; 2006-255, s. 2; 2006-264, s. 53(a); 2013-413, s. 57(f).)


§ 113A-58. Enforcement authority of the Commission.

In implementing the provisions of this Article the Commission is authorized and directed to:

(1) Inspect or cause to be inspected the sites of land-disturbing activities to determine whether applicable laws, regulations or erosion and sedimentation control plans are being complied with;

(2) Make requests, or delegate to the Secretary authority to make requests, of the Attorney General or solicitors for prosecutions of violations of this Article. (1973, c. 392, s. 9; 2002-165, s. 2.7.)


§ 113A-59. Educational activities.

The Commission in conjunction with the soil and water conservation districts, the North Carolina Agricultural Extension Service, and other appropriate State and federal agencies shall conduct educational programs in erosion and sedimentation control, such programs to be directed towards State and local governmental officials, persons engaged in land-disturbing activities, and interested citizen groups. (1973, c. 392, s. 10.)


§ 113A-60. Local erosion and sedimentation control programs.

(a) A local government may submit to the Commission for its approval an erosion and sedimentation control program for its jurisdiction, and to this end local governments are authorized to adopt ordinances and regulations necessary to establish and enforce erosion and sedimentation control programs. An ordinance adopted by a local government may establish a fee for the review of an erosion and sedimentation control plan and related activities. Local governments are authorized to create or designate agencies or subdivisions of local government to administer and enforce the programs. An ordinance adopted by a local government shall at least meet and may exceed the minimum requirements of this Article and the rules adopted pursuant to this Article. Two or more units of local government are authorized to establish a joint program and to enter into any agreements that are necessary for the proper administration and enforcement of the program. The resolutions establishing any joint program must be duly recorded in the minutes of the governing body of each unit of local government participating in the program, and a certified copy of each resolution must be filed with the Commission.

(b) The Commission shall review each program submitted and within 90 days of receipt thereof shall notify the local government submitting the program that it has been approved, approved with modifications, or disapproved. The Commission shall only approve a program upon determining that its standards equal or exceed those of this Article and rules adopted pursuant to this Article.

(c) If the Commission determines that any local government is failing to administer or enforce an approved erosion and sedimentation control program, it shall notify the local government in writing and shall specify the deficiencies of administration and enforcement. If the local government has not taken corrective action within 30 days of receipt of notification from the Commission, the Commission shall assume administration and enforcement of the program until such time as the local government indicates its willingness and ability to resume administration and enforcement of the program.

(d) A local government may submit to the Commission for its approval a limited erosion and sedimentation control program for its jurisdiction that grants the local government the responsibility only for the assessment and collection of fees and for the inspection of land-disturbing activities within the jurisdiction of the local government. The Commission shall be responsible for the administration and enforcement of all other components of the erosion and sedimentation control program and the requirements of this Article. The local government may adopt ordinances and regulations necessary to establish a limited erosion and sedimentation control program. An ordinance adopted by a local government that establishes a limited program shall conform to the minimum requirements regarding the inspection of land-disturbing activities of this Article and the rules adopted pursuant to this Article regarding the inspection of land-disturbing activities. The local government shall establish and collect a fee to be paid by each person who submits an erosion and sedimentation control plan to the local government. The amount of the fee shall be an amount equal to eighty percent (80%) of the amount established by the Commission pursuant to G.S. 113A-54.2(a) plus any amount that the local government requires to cover the cost of inspection and program administration activities by the local government. The total fee shall not exceed one hundred dollars ($100.00) per acre. A local government that administers a limited erosion and sedimentation control program shall pay to the Commission the portion of the fee that equals eighty percent (80%) of the fee established pursuant to G.S. 113A-54.2(a) to cover the cost to the Commission for the administration and enforcement of other components of the erosion and sedimentation control program. Fees paid to the Commission by a local government shall be deposited in the Sedimentation Account established by G.S. 113A-54.2(b). A local government that administers a limited erosion and sedimentation control program and that receives an erosion control plan and fee under this subsection shall immediately transmit the plan to the Commission for review. A local government may create or designate agencies or subdivisions of the local government to administer the limited program. Two or more units of local government may establish a joint limited program and enter into any agreements necessary for the proper administration of the limited program. The resolutions establishing any joint limited program must be duly recorded in the minutes of the governing body of each unit of local government participating in the limited program, and a certified copy of each resolution must be filed with the Commission. Subsections (b) and (c) of this section apply to the approval and oversight of limited programs.

(e)     Notwithstanding G.S. 113A-61.1, a local government with a limited erosion and sedimentation control program shall not issue a notice of violation if inspection indicates that the person engaged in land-disturbing activity has failed to comply with this Article, rules adopted pursuant to this Article, or an approved erosion and sedimentation control plan. The local government shall notify the Commission if any person has initiated land-disturbing activity for which an erosion and sedimentation control plan is required in the absence of an approved plan. If a local government with a limited program determines that a person engaged in a land-disturbing activity has failed to comply with an approved erosion and sedimentation control plan, the local government shall refer the matter to the Commission for inspection and enforcement pursuant to

G.S. 113A-61.1. (1973, c. 392, s. 11; 1993 (Reg. Sess., 1994), c. 776, s. 7; 2002-165, s. 2.8; 2006-250, s. 3.)

§ 113A-61. Local approval of erosion and sedimentation control plans.

(a) For those land-disturbing activities for which prior approval of an erosion and sedimentation control plan is required, the Commission may require that a local government that administers an erosion and sedimentation control program approved under G.S. 113A-60 require the applicant to submit a copy of the erosion and sedimentation control plan to the appropriate soil and water conservation district or districts at the same time the applicant submits the erosion and sedimentation control plan to the local government for approval. The soil and water conservation district or districts shall review the plan and submit any comments and recommendations to the local government within 20 days after the soil and water conservation district received the erosion and sedimentation control plan or within any shorter period of time as may be agreed upon by the soil and water conservation district and the local government. Failure of a soil and water conservation district to submit comments and recommendations within 20 days or within agreed upon shorter period of time shall not delay final action on the proposed plan by the local government.

(b) Local governments shall review each erosion and sedimentation control plan submitted to them and within 30 days of receipt thereof shall notify the person submitting the plan that it has been approved, approved with modifications, or disapproved. A local government shall only approve a plan upon determining that it complies with all applicable State and local regulations for erosion and sedimentation control.

(b1) A local government shall condition approval of a draft erosion and sedimentation control plan upon the applicant's compliance with federal and State water quality laws, regulations, and rules. A local government shall disapprove an erosion and sedimentation control plan if implementation of the plan would result in a violation of rules adopted by the Environmental Management Commission to protect riparian buffers along surface waters. A local government may disapprove an erosion and sedimentation control plan or disapprove a transfer of a plan under subsection (b3) of this section upon finding that an applicant or a parent, subsidiary, or other affiliate of the applicant:

(1) Is conducting or has conducted land-disturbing activity without an approved plan, or has received notice of violation of a plan previously approved by the Commission or a local government pursuant to this Article and has not complied with the notice within the time specified in the notice.

(2) Has failed to pay a civil penalty assessed pursuant to this Article or a local ordinance adopted pursuant to this Article by the time the payment is due.

(3) Has been convicted of a misdemeanor pursuant to G.S. 113A-64(b) or any criminal provision of a local ordinance adopted pursuant to this Article.

(4) Has failed to substantially comply with State rules or local ordinances and regulations adopted pursuant to this Article.

(b2) In the event that an erosion and sedimentation control plan or a transfer of a plan is disapproved by a local government pursuant to subsection (b1) of this section, the local government shall so notify the Director of the Division of Energy, Mineral, and Land Resources within 10 days of the disapproval. The local government shall advise the applicant or the proposed transferee and the Director in writing as to the specific reasons that the plan was disapproved. Notwithstanding the provisions of subsection (c) of this section, the applicant may appeal the local government's disapproval of the plan directly to the Commission. For purposes of this subsection and subsection (b1) of this section, an applicant's record or the proposed transferee's record may be considered for only the two years prior to the application date.

(b3) A local government administering an erosion and sedimentation control program may transfer an erosion and sedimentation control plan approved pursuant to this section without the consent of the plan holder to a successor-owner of the property on which the permitted activity is occurring or will occur as provided in this subsection:

(1) The local government may transfer a plan if all of the following conditions are met:

a. The successor-owner of the property submits to the local government a written request for the transfer of the plan and an authorized statement of financial responsibility and ownership.

b. The local government finds all of the following:

1. The plan holder is one of the following:

I. A natural person who is deceased.

II. A partnership, limited liability corporation, corporation, or any other business association that has been dissolved.

III. A person who has been lawfully and finally divested of title to the property on which the permitted activity is occurring or will occur.

IV. A person who has sold the property on which the permitted activity is occurring or will occur.

2. The successor-owner holds title to the property on which the permitted activity is occurring or will occur.

3. The successor-owner is the sole claimant of the right to engage in the permitted activity.

4. There will be no substantial change in the permitted activity.

(2) The plan holder shall comply with all terms and conditions of the plan until such time as the plan is transferred.

(3) The successor-owner shall comply with all terms and conditions of the plan once the plan has been transferred.

(4) Notwithstanding changes to law made after the original issuance of the plan, the local government may not impose new or different terms and conditions in the plan without the prior express consent of the successor-owner. Nothing in this subsection shall prevent the local government from requiring a revised plan pursuant to G.S. 113A-54.1(b).

(c) The disapproval or modification of any proposed erosion and sedimentation control plan by a local government shall entitle the person submitting the plan to a public hearing if the person submits written demand for a hearing within 15 days after receipt of written notice of the disapproval or modification. The hearings shall be conducted pursuant to procedures adopted by the local government. If the local government upholds the disapproval or modification of a proposed erosion and sedimentation control plan following the public hearing, the person submitting the erosion and sedimentation control plan is entitled to appeal the local government's action disapproving or modifying the plan to the Commission. The Commission, by regulation, shall direct the Secretary to appoint such employees of the Department as may be necessary to hear appeals from the disapproval or modification of erosion and sedimentation control plans by local governments. In addition to providing for the appeal of local government decisions disapproving or modifying erosion and sedimentation control plans to designated employees of the Department, the Commission shall designate an erosion and sedimentation control plan review committee consisting of three members of the Commission. The person submitting the erosion and sedimentation control plan may appeal the decision of an employee of the Department who has heard an appeal of a local government action disapproving or modifying an erosion and sedimentation control plan to the erosion and sedimentation control plan review committee of the Commission. Judicial review of the final action of the erosion and sedimentation control plan review committee of the Commission may be had in the superior court of the county in which the local government is situated.

(d) Repealed by Session Laws 1989, c. 676, s. 4. (1973, c. 392, s. 12; 1979, c. 922, s. 1; 1989, c. 676, s. 4; 1993 (Reg. Sess., 1994), c. 776, ss. 8, 9; 1998-221, s. 1.11(b); 1999-379, s. 3; 2002-165, s. 2.9; 2012-143, s. 1(f); 2013-121, s. 4.)


§ 113A-61.1. Inspection of land-disturbing activity; notice of violation.

(a) The Commission, a local government that administers an erosion and sedimentation control program approved under G.S. 113A-60, or other approving authority shall provide for inspection of land-disturbing activities to ensure compliance with this Article and to determine whether the measures required in an erosion and sedimentation control plan are effective in controlling erosion and sedimentation resulting from the land-disturbing activity. Notice of this right of inspection shall be included in the certificate of approval of each erosion and sedimentation control plan.

(b) No person shall willfully resist, delay, or obstruct an authorized representative of the Commission, an authorized representative of a local government, or an employee or an agent of the Department while the representative, employee, or agent is inspecting or attempting to inspect a land-disturbing activity under this section.

(c) If the Secretary, a local government that administers an erosion and sedimentation control program approved under G.S. 113A-60, or other approving authority determines that the person engaged in the land-disturbing activity has failed to comply with this Article, the Secretary, local government, or other approving authority shall immediately serve a notice of violation upon that person. The notice may be served by any means authorized under G.S. 1A-1, Rule 4. A notice of violation shall specify a date by which the person must comply with this Article and inform the person of the actions that need to be taken to comply with this Article. Any person who fails to comply within the time specified is subject to additional civil and criminal penalties for a continuing violation as provided in G.S. 113A-64. (1989, c. 676, s. 5; 1993 (Reg. Sess., 1994), c. 776, s. 10; 1999-379, s. 6; 2002-165, s. 2.10.)


§ 113A-62. Cooperation with the United States.

The Commission is authorized to cooperate and enter into agreements with any agency of the United States government in connection with plans for erosion and sedimentation control with respect to land-disturbing activities on lands that are under the jurisdiction of such agency. (1973, c. 392, s. 13; 2002-165, s. 2.11.)


§ 113A-63. Financial and other assistance.

The Commission and local governments are authorized to receive from federal, State, and other public and private sources financial, technical, and other assistance for use in accomplishing the purposes of this Article. (1973, c. 392, s. 14.)


§ 113A-64. Penalties.

(a) Civil Penalties. -

(1) Any person who violates any of the provisions of this Article or any ordinance, rule, or order adopted or issued pursuant to this Article by the Commission or by a local government, or who initiates or continues a land-

disturbing activity for which an erosion and sedimentation control plan is required except in accordance with the terms, conditions, and provisions of an approved plan, is subject to a civil penalty. The maximum civil penalty for a violation is five thousand dollars ($5,000). A civil penalty may be assessed from the date of the violation. Each day of a continuing violation shall constitute a separate violation.

(2) The Secretary or a local government that administers an erosion and sedimentation control program approved under G.S. 113A-60 shall determine the amount of the civil penalty and shall notify the person who is assessed the civil penalty of the amount of the penalty and the reason for assessing the penalty. The notice of assessment shall be served by any means authorized under G.S. 1A-1. A notice of assessment by the Secretary shall direct the violator to either pay the assessment or contest the assessment within 30 days by filing a petition for a contested case under Article 3 of Chapter 150B of the General Statutes. If a violator does not pay a civil penalty assessed by the Secretary within 30 days after it is due, the Department shall request the Attorney General to institute a civil action to recover the amount of the assessment. A notice of assessment by a local government shall direct the violator to either pay the assessment or contest the assessment within 30 days by filing a petition for hearing with the local government as directed by procedures within the local ordinances or regulations adopted to establish and enforce the erosion and sedimentation control program. If a violator does not pay a civil penalty assessed by a local government within 30 days after it is due, the local government may institute a civil action to recover the amount of the assessment. The civil action may be brought in the superior court of any county where the violation occurred or the violator's residence or principal place of business is located. A civil action must be filed within three years of the date the assessment was due. An assessment that is not contested is due when the violator is served with a notice of assessment. An assessment that is contested is due at the conclusion of the administrative and judicial review of the assessment.

(3) In determining the amount of the penalty, the Secretary or a local government shall consider the degree and extent of harm caused by the violation, the cost of rectifying the damage, the amount of money the violator saved by noncompliance, whether the violation was committed willfully and the prior record of the violator in complying or failing to comply with this Article, or any ordinance, rule, or order adopted or issued pursuant to this Article by the Commission or by a local government.

(4) Repealed by Session Laws 1993 (Reg. Sess., 1994), c. 776, s. 11.

(5) The clear proceeds of civil penalties collected by the Department or other State agency or a local government under this subsection shall be remitted to the Civil Penalty and Forfeiture Fund in accordance with G.S. 115C-457.2.

(b) Criminal Penalties. - Any person who knowingly or willfully violates any provision of this Article or any ordinance, rule, regulation, or order duly adopted or issued by the Commission or a local government, or who knowingly or willfully initiates or continues a land-disturbing activity for which an erosion and sedimentation control plan is required, except in accordance with the terms, conditions, and provisions of an approved plan, shall be guilty of a Class 2 misdemeanor that may include a fine not to exceed five thousand dollars ($5,000). (1973, c. 392, s. 15; 1977, c. 852; 1987, c. 246, s. 3; 1987 (Reg. Sess., 1988), c. 1000, s. 5; 1989, c. 676, s. 6; 1991, c. 412, s. 2; c. 725, s. 5; 1993, c. 539, s. 873; 1994, Ex. Sess., c. 24, s. 14(c); 1993 (Reg. Sess., 1994), c. 776, s. 11; 1998-215, s. 52; 1999-379, s. 4; 2002-165, s. 2.12; 2013-413, s. 33.)

§ 113A-64.1. Restoration of areas affected by failure to comply.

The Secretary or a local government that administers a local erosion and sedimentation control program approved under G.S. 113A-60 may require a person who engaged in a land-disturbing activity and failed to retain sediment generated by the activity, as required by G.S. 113A-57(3), to restore the waters and land affected by the failure so as to minimize the detrimental effects of the resulting pollution by sedimentation. This authority is in addition to any other civil or criminal penalty or injunctive relief authorized under this Article. (1993 (Reg. Sess., 1994), c. 776, s. 12; 2002-165, s. 2.13.)

§ 113A-65. Injunctive relief.

(a) Violation of State Program. - Whenever the Secretary has reasonable cause to believe that any person is violating or is threatening to violate the requirements of this Article he may, either before or after the institution of any other action or proceeding authorized by this Article, institute a civil action for injunctive relief to restrain the violation or threatened violation. The action shall be brought in the superior court of the county in which the violation or threatened violation is occurring or about to occur, and shall be in the name of the State upon the relation of the Secretary.

(b) Violation of Local Program. - Whenever the governing body of a local government having jurisdiction has reasonable cause to believe that any person is violating or is threatening to violate any ordinance, rule, regulation, or order adopted or issued by the local government pursuant to this Article, or any term, condition or provision of an erosion and sedimentation control plan over which it has jurisdiction, may, either before or after the institution of any other action or proceeding authorized by this Article, institute a civil action in the name of the local government for injunctive relief to restrain the violation or threatened violation. The action shall be brought in the superior court of the county in which the violation is occurring or is threatened.

(c) Abatement, etc., of Violation. - Upon determination by a court that an alleged violation is occurring or is threatened, the court shall enter any order or judgment that is necessary to abate the violation, to ensure that restoration is performed, or to prevent the threatened violation. The institution of an action for injunctive relief under subsections (a) or (b) of this section shall not relieve any party to the proceeding from any civil or criminal penalty prescribed for violations of this Article. (1973, c. 392, s. 16; 1993 (Reg. Sess., 1994), c. 776, s. 13; 2002-165, s. 2.14.)


§ 113A-65.1. Stop-work orders.

(a) The Secretary may issue a stop-work order if he finds that a land-disturbing activity is being conducted in violation of this Article or of any rule adopted or order issued pursuant to this Article, that the violation is knowing and willful, and that either:

(1) Off-site sedimentation has eliminated or severely degraded a use in a lake or natural watercourse or that such degradation is imminent.

(2) Off-site sedimentation has caused severe damage to adjacent land or that such damage is imminent.

(3)     The land-disturbing activity is being conducted without an approved plan.

(b)     The stop-work order shall be in writing and shall state what work is to be stopped and what measures are required to abate the violation. The order shall include a statement of the findings made by the Secretary pursuant to subsection (a) of this section, and shall list the conditions under which work that has been stopped by the order may be resumed. The delivery of equipment and materials which does not contribute to the violation may continue while the stop-work order is in effect. A copy of this section shall be attached to the order.

(c)     The stop-work order shall be served by the sheriff of the county in which the land-disturbing activity is being conducted or by some other person duly authorized by law to serve process as provided by G.S. 1A-1, Rule 4, and shall be served on the person at the site of the land-disturbing activity who is in operational control of the land-disturbing activity. The sheriff or other person duly authorized by law to serve process shall post a copy of the stop-work order in a conspicuous place at the site of the land-disturbing activity. The Department shall also deliver a copy of the stop-work order to any person that the Department has reason to believe may be responsible for the violation.

(d)     The directives of a stop-work order become effective upon service of the order. Thereafter, any person notified of the stop-work order who violates any of the directives set out in the order may be assessed a civil penalty as provided in G.S. 113A-64(a). A stop-work order issued pursuant to this section may be issued for a period not to exceed five days.

(e)     The Secretary shall designate an employee of the Department to monitor compliance with the stop-work order. The name of the employee so designated shall be included in the stop-work order. The employee so designated, or the Secretary, shall rescind the stop-work order if all the violations for which the stop-work order are issued are corrected, no other violations have occurred, and all measures necessary to abate the violations have been taken. The Secretary shall rescind a stop-work order that is issued in error.

(f)     The issuance of a stop-work order shall be a final agency decision subject to judicial review in the same manner as an order in a contested case pursuant to Article 4 of Chapter 150B of the General Statutes. The petition for judicial review shall be filed in the superior court of the county in which the land-disturbing activity is being conducted.

(g)	As used in this section, days are computed as provided in G.S. 1A-1, Rule 6. Except as otherwise provided, the Secretary may delegate any power or duty under this section to the Director of the Division of Energy, Mineral, and Land Resources of the Department or to any person who has supervisory authority over the Director. The Director may delegate any power or duty so delegated only to a person who is designated as acting Director.

(h)	The Attorney General shall file a cause of action to abate the violations which resulted in the issuance of a stop-work order within two business days of the service of the stop-work order. The cause of action shall include a motion for an ex parte temporary restraining order to abate the violation and to effect necessary remedial measures. The resident superior court judge, or any judge assigned to hear the motion for the temporary restraining order, shall hear and determine the motion within two days of the filing of the complaint. The clerk of superior court shall accept complaints filed pursuant to this section without the payment of filing fees. Filing fees shall be paid to the clerk of superior court within 30 days of the filing of the complaint. (1991, c. 412, s. 1; 1998-99, s. 2; 2005-386, s. 7.3; 2012-143, s. 1(f).)


§ 113A-66.  Civil relief.

(a)	Any person injured by a violation of this Article or any ordinance, rule, or order duly adopted by the Secretary or a local government, or by the initiation or continuation of a land-disturbing activity for which an erosion and sedimentation control plan is required other than in accordance with the terms, conditions, and provisions of an approved plan, may bring a civil action against the person alleged to be in violation (including the State and any local government). The action may seek any of the following:

(1)	Injunctive relief.

(2)	An order enforcing the law, rule, ordinance, order, or erosion and sedimentation control plan violated.

(3)	Damages caused by the violation.

(4)	Repealed by Session Laws 2002-165, s. 2.15, effective October 23, 2002.

If the amount of actual damages as found by the court or jury in suits brought under this subsection is five thousand dollars ($5,000) or less, the plaintiff shall be awarded costs of litigation including reasonable attorneys fees and expert witness fees.

(b) Civil actions under this section shall be brought in the superior court of the county in which the alleged violations occurred.

(c) The court, in issuing any final order in any action brought pursuant to this section may award costs of litigation (including reasonable attorney and expert-witness fees) to any party, whenever it determines that such an award is appropriate. The court may, if a temporary restraining order or preliminary injunction is sought, require, the filing of a bond or equivalent security, the amount of such bond or security to be determined by the court.

(d) Nothing in this section shall restrict any right which any person (or class of persons) may have under any statute or common law to seek injunctive or other relief. (1973, c. 392, s. 17; 1987 (Reg. Sess., 1988), c. 1000, s. 6; 2002-165, s. 2.15.)

§ 113A-67. Annual Report.

The Department shall report to the Environmental Review Commission on the implementation of this Article on or before 1 October of each year. The Department shall include in the report an analysis of how the implementation of the Sedimentation Pollution Control Act of 1973 is affecting activities that contribute to the sedimentation of streams, rivers, lakes, and other waters of the State. The report shall also include a review of the effectiveness of local erosion and sedimentation control programs. (2004-195, s. 2.1.)

§ 113A-68: Reserved for future codification purposes.

§ 113A-69: Reserved for future codification purposes.

Article 4A.

Vehicular Surface Areas.

§§ 113A-70, 113A-71: Repealed by Session Laws 2013-413, s. 54. For effective date of repeal, see editor's note.

Article 5.
North Carolina Appalachian Trails System Act.

§ 113A-72.  Short title.

This Article may be cited as the North Carolina Appalachian Trails System Act. (1973, c. 545, s. 1.)

§ 113A-73.  Policy and purpose.

(a) In order to provide for the ever-increasing outdoor recreation needs of an expanded population and in order to promote public access to, travel within, and enjoyment and appreciation of the open-air, outdoor areas of the State, the Appalachian Trail should be protected in North Carolina as a segment of the National Scenic Trails System.

(b) The purpose of this Article is to provide the means for attaining these objectives by instituting a North Carolina Appalachian Trail System, designating the Appalachian Trail lying or located in the North Carolina Counties of Avery, Mitchell, Yancey, Madison, Haywood, Swain, Graham, Macon, and Clay, as defined in the Federal Register of the National Trails Act as the basic component of that System, and by prescribing the methods by which, and standards according to which, additional connecting trails may be added to the System. (1973, c. 545, s. 2.)

§ 113A-74.  Appalachian Trails System; connecting or side trails; coordination with the National Trails System Act.

Connecting or side trails may be established, designated and marked as components of the Appalachian Trail System by the Department of Environment and Natural Resources in consultation with the federal agencies charged with the responsibility for the administration and management of the Appalachian Trail in North Carolina. Criteria and standards of establishment will coincide with those set forth in the National Trails System Act (PL 90-543). (1973, c. 545, s. 3; 1977, c. 771, s. 4; 1989, c. 727, s. 218(61); 1997-443, s. 11A.119(a).)

Article 5.

North Carolina Appalachian Trails System Act.

§ 113A-72. Short title.

This Article may be cited as the North Carolina Appalachian Trails System Act. (1973, c. 545, s. 1.)

§ 113A-73. Policy and purpose.

(a) In order to provide for the ever-increasing outdoor recreation needs of an expanded population and in order to promote public access to, travel within, and enjoyment and appreciation of the open-air, outdoor areas of the State, the Appalachian Trail should be protected in North Carolina as a segment of the National Scenic Trails System.

(b) The purpose of this Article is to provide the means for attaining these objectives by instituting a North Carolina Appalachian Trail System, designating the Appalachian Trail lying or located in the North Carolina Counties of Avery, Mitchell, Yancey, Madison, Haywood, Swain, Graham, Macon, and Clay, as defined in the Federal Register of the National Trails Act as the basic component of that System, and by prescribing the methods by which, and standards according to which, additional connecting trails may be added to the System. (1973, c. 545, s. 2.)

§ 113A-74. Appalachian Trails System; connecting or side trails; coordination with the National Trails System Act.

Connecting or side trails may be established, designated and marked as components of the Appalachian Trail System by the Department of Environment and Natural Resources in consultation with the federal agencies charged with the responsibility for the administration and management of the Appalachian Trail in North Carolina. Criteria and standards of establishment will coincide with those set forth in the National Trails System Act (PL 90-543). (1973, c. 545, s. 3; 1977, c. 771, s. 4; 1989, c. 727, s. 218(61); 1997-443, s. 11A.119(a).)

§ 113A-75. Assistance under this Article with the National Trails System Act (PL 90-543).

(a) The Department of Administration in cooperation with other appropriate State departments shall consult with the federal agencies charged with the administration of the Appalachian Trail in North Carolina and develop a mutually agreeable plan for the orderly and coordinated acquisition of Appalachian Trail right-of-way and the associated tracts, as needed, to provide a suitable environment for the Appalachian Trail in North Carolina.

(b) The Department of Environment and Natural Resources and the federal agencies charged with the responsibility of the administration of the Appalachian Trail in North Carolina shall give due consideration to the conservation of the environment of the Appalachian Trail and, in accordance with the National Trails System Act, may obtain advice and assistance from local governments, Carolina Mountain Club, Nantahala Hiking Club, Piedmont Appalachian Trail Hikers, Appalachian Trail Conference, other interested organizations and individuals, landowners and land users concerned.

(c) The Board of Transportation shall cooperate and assist in carrying out the purposes of this Article and the National Trails System Act where their highway projects cross or may be adjacent to any component of the Appalachian Trail System.

(d) Lands acquired by the State of North Carolina within the 200-feet right-of-way of the Appalachian Trail and within the exterior boundaries of the Pisgah or Nantahala National Forests, will be conveyed to the United States Forest Service as the federal agency charged with the responsibility for the administration and management of the Appalachian Trail within these specific areas.

(e) Lands acquired by the State of North Carolina outside of the boundaries of the Appalachian Trail right-of-way will be administered by the appropriate

State department in such a manner as to preserve and enhance the environment of the Appalachian Trail.

(f) In consultation with the Department of Environment and Natural Resources, the federal agency charged with the responsibility of the administration of the Appalachian Trail in North Carolina shall establish use regulations in accordance with the National Trails System Act.

(g) The use of motor vehicles on the trails of the North Carolina Appalachian Trail System may be authorized when such use is necessary to meet emergencies or to enable adjacent landowners to have reasonable access to their lands and timber rights provided that the granting of this access is in accordance with limitations and conditions of such use set forth in the National Trails System Act. (1973, c. 507, s. 5; c. 545, s. 4; 1977, c. 771, s. 4; 1989, c. 727, s. 218(62); 1997-443, s. 11A.119(a).)

§ 113A-76. Acquisition of rights-of-way and lands; manner of acquiring.

The State of North Carolina may use lands for trail purposes within the boundaries of areas under its administration that are included in the rights-of-way selected for the Appalachian Trail System. The Department of Administration may acquire lands or easements by donation or purchase with funds donated or appropriated for such purpose. (1973, c. 545, s. 5.)

§ 113A-77. Expenditures authorized.

The Department is authorized to spend any federal, State, local or private funds available for this purpose to the Department for acquisition and development of the Appalachian Trail System. (1973, c. 545, s. 6; 1977, c. 771, s. 4; 1989, c. 727, s. 125.)

§§ 113A-78 through 113A-82. Reserved for future codification purposes.

Article 6.

North Carolina Trails System.

§ 113A-83. Short title.

This Article shall be known and may be cited as the "North Carolina Trails System Act." (1973, c. 670, s. 1.)

§ 113A-84. Declaration of policy and purpose.

(a) In order to provide for the ever-increasing outdoor recreation needs of an expanded population and in order to promote public access to, travel within, and enjoyment and appreciation of the outdoor, natural and remote areas of the State, trails should be established in natural, scenic areas of the State, and in and near urban areas.

(b) The purpose of this Article is to provide the means for attaining these objectives by instituting a State system of scenic and recreation trails, coordinated with and complemented by existing and future local trail segments or systems, and by prescribing the methods by which, and standards according to which, components may be added to the State trails system. (1973, c. 670, s. 1; 1993, c. 184, s. 1.)

§ 113A-85. Definitions.

Except as otherwise required by context, the following terms when used in this Article shall be construed respectively to mean:

(1) "Department" means the North Carolina Department of Environment and Natural Resources.

(2) "Political subdivision" means any county, any incorporated city or town, or other political subdivision.

(3) "Scenic easement" means a perpetual easement in land which

a. Is held for the benefit of the people of North Carolina,

b. Is specifically enforceable by its holder or beneficiary, and

c. Limits or obligates the holder of the servient estate, his heirs, and assigns with respect to their use and management of land and activities conducted thereon, the object of such limitations and obligations being the maintenance or enhancement of the natural beauty of the land in question or of areas affected by it.

(4) "Secretary" means the Secretary of Environment and Natural Resources, except as otherwise specified in this Article.

(5) "State trails system" means the trails system established in this Article or pursuant to the State Parks Act, Article 2C of Chapter 113 of the General Statutes, and including all trails and trail segments, together with their rights-of-way, added by any of the procedures described in this Article or Article 2C of Chapter 113 of the General Statutes.

(6) "Trail" means:

a. Park trail. - A trail designated and managed as a unit of the North Carolina State Parks System under Article 2C of Chapter 113 of the General Statutes.

b. Designated trail. - A trail designated by the Secretary pursuant to this Article as a component of the State trails system and that is managed by another governmental agency or by a corporation listed with the Secretary of State.

c. A State scenic trail, State recreation trail, or State connecting trail under G.S. 113A-86 when the intended primary use of the trail is to serve as a park trail or designated trail.

d. Any other trail that is open to the public and that the owner, lessee, occupant, or person otherwise in control of the land on which the trail is located allows to be used as a trail without compensation, including a trail that is not designated by the Secretary as a component of the State trails system. (1973, c. 670, s. 1; 1977, c. 771, s. 4; 1989, c. 727, s. 218(63); 1989 (Reg. Sess., 1990), c. 1004, s. 19(b); 1993, c. 184, s. 2; 1997-443, s. 11A.119(a).)

§ 113A-86. Composition of State trails system.

The State trails system shall be composed of designated:

(1) State scenic trails, which are defined as extended trails so located as to provide maximum potential for the appreciation of natural areas and for the conservation and enjoyment of the significant scenic, historic, natural, ecological, geological or cultural qualities of the areas through which such trails may pass.

(2) State recreation trails, which are defined as trails planned principally for recreational value and may include trails for foot travel, horseback, nonmotorized bicycles, nonmotorized water vehicles, and two-wheel-and four-wheel-drive motorized vehicles. More than one of the aforesaid types of travel may be permitted on a single trail in the discretion of the Secretary.

(3) Connecting or side trails, which will provide additional points of public access to State recreation or State scenic trails or which will provide connections between such trails. (1973, c. 670, s. 1; 1993, c. 184, s. 3.)


§ 113A-87. Authority to designate trails.

The Department may establish and designate trails on:

(1) Lands administered by the Department,

(2) Lands under the jurisdiction of a State department, political subdivision, or federal agency, or

(3) Private lands provided, fee-simple title, lesser estates, scenic easements, easements of surface ingress and egress running with the land, leases, or other written agreements are obtained from landowners through which a State trail may pass. (1973, c. 670, s. 1; 1979, c. 6, s. 1; 1991, c. 115; 1993, c. 184, s. 4.)


§ 113A-87.1. Use of State land for bicycling; creation of trails by volunteers.

(a) Any land held in fee simple by this State, any agency of this State, or any land purchased or leased with funds provided by this State may be open and available for use by bicyclists upon establishment of a usage agreement. The usage agreement shall be established between the land manager and any local cycling group or organization intending to use the land and shall specify the terms and conditions for use of the land. The land manager shall designate a representative with knowledge of off-road bicycle trail building to negotiate the agreement. Upon establishment of the usage agreement, any bicyclist may use the land pursuant to the agreement.

The land manager shall not be required to create, maintain, or make available any special trails, paths, or other accommodations to any user of the land for cycling purposes. However, once a usage agreement has been established, any local cycling group or organization may create and maintain special trails for cycling purposes. Any trails created for the purpose of off-road cycling shall be created and maintained using commonly accepted best practices.

(b)     Notwithstanding the provisions of subsection (a) of this section, any land may be restricted or removed from use by bicyclists if it is determined by the State, an agency of the State, or the holder of land purchased or leased with State funds that the use would cause substantial harm to the land or the environment or that the use would violate another State or federal law. Before restricting or removing land from use by bicyclists, the State, the agency of the State, or the holder of the land purchased or leased with State funds must show why the lands should not be open for use by bicyclists. Local cycling groups or organizations shall be notified of the intent to restrict or remove the land from use by bicyclists and provided an opportunity to show why cycling should be allowed on the land. Notice of any land restricted or removed from use by bicyclists pursuant to this subsection shall be filed with the Division of Bicycle and Pedestrian Transportation of the Department of Transportation.

(c)     The Division of Bicycle and Pedestrian Transportation of the Department of Transportation shall keep a record of all lands made open and available for use by bicyclists pursuant to this section and shall make the information available to the public upon request.

(d)     Any land open and available for use by bicyclists, pursuant to subsection (a) of this section, shall also be available to members of the public for hiking and walking. Persons using the land pursuant to this subsection shall yield the right-of-way to bicyclists when hiking or walking on any trails created and maintained for the purpose of off-road cycling and so designated along that trail.

(e)     Notwithstanding any other provision of this section, any hiking, walking, or use of bicycles on game lands administered by the Wildlife Resources Commission shall be restricted to roads and trails designated for vehicular use.

Hiking, walking, or bicycle use by persons not hunting shall be restricted to days closed to hunting. The Wildlife Resources Commission may restrict the use of bicycles on game lands where necessary to protect sensitive wildlife habitat or species and shall file notice of any restrictions with the Division of Bicycle and Pedestrian Transportation of the Department of Transportation. (2007-449, s. 1.)

# Vision Books Order Form

| | |
|---|---|
| Fax Orders: | 1-980-299-5965 |
| Phone Orders: | 1-704-898-0770 |
| E-mail Orders: | www.visionbooks.org |
| Mail Orders: | Vision Books, LLC<br>P.O. Box 42406<br>Charlotte, NC 28215 |

**Shipp To:**
Name_____
Address_____
City_____State_____Zip_____
Phone_____Fax_____
Email_____@_____

**Bill To:** We can bill a third party on your behalf.
Name_____
Address_____
City_____State_____Zip_____
Phone___(_____)_____Fax_____
Email_____@_____

| Pamphlet Number<br>($15.00 Each) | Qty | Total Cost |
|---|---|---|
| _____ | _____ | _____ |
| _____ | _____ | _____ |
| _____ | _____ | _____ |
| _____ | _____ | _____ |
| _____ | _____ | _____ |
| _____ | _____ | _____ |
| _____ | _____ | _____ |
| _____ | _____ | _____ |
| <u>Full Volume Set 1-92</u> | <u>92 Pamphlets</u> | <u>1,380.00</u> |

Free Shipping Shipping & Handling on Full Volume Orders
Add $1.00 Shipping & Handling per pamphlet          $_____

Total Cost                                          $_____

Thank you for your support. Management!

DID YOU ENJOY THIS BOOK?

Vision Books, LLC would like to hear from you! If you or someone you know has been fasely imprisoned, we would like to hear your story. If the 'North Carolina Criminal Law and Procedure' has had an effect in your life or if you have suggestions, we would like to hear from you. Send your letters to:

Vision Books, LLC
Attn: Staff Writers
P.O. Box 42406
Charlotte, NC 28215
Email: staff@visionbooks.org

Order Additional Copies:

| | |
|---|---|
| Fax Orders: | 1-980-299-5965 |
| Phone Orders: | 1-704-898-0770 |
| E-mail Orders: | www.visionbooks.org |
| Mail Orders: | Vision Books, LLC<br>P.O. Box 42406<br>Charlotte, NC 28215 |

www.ingramcontent.com/pod-product-compliance
Lightning Source LLC
Chambersburg PA
CBHW051628170526
**45167CB00001B/108**